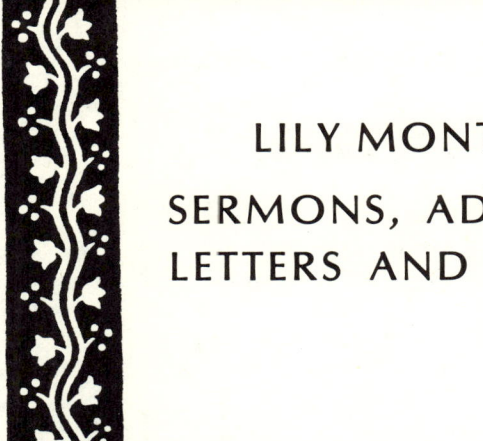

LILY MONTAGU
SERMONS, ADDRESSES, LETTERS AND PRAYERS

Edited by
ELLEN M. UMANSKY

Studies in Women and Religion
Volume 15

The Edwin Mellen Press
New York and Toronto

Library of Congress Cataloging in Publication Data

Montagu, Lilian Helen, 1873-1963.
  Lily Montagu : sermons, addresses, letters, and prayers.

  Supplement to: Lily Montagu and the advancement of liberal Judaism / Ellen M. Umansky.
  Includes index.
  1. Jewish sermons--Great Britain. 2. Sermons, English--Jewish authors. 3. Reform Judaism--Addresses, essays, lectures. I. Umansky, Ellen M. II. Umansky, Ellen M. Lily Montagu and the advancement of liberal Judaism. III. Title.
  BM740.2.M66 1985   296.4'2   85-3053
  ISBN 0-88946-534-7

Studies in Women and Religion
Series ISBN 0-88946-549-5

Copyright © 1985, Ellen M. Umansky

  All rights reserved. For more information contact:
            The Edwin Mellen Press
                P.O. Box 450
          Lewiston, New York 14092

Printed in the United States of America

For my parents, Abraham and Dorothy Umansky

TABLE OF CONTENTS

PREFACE ix

INTRODUCTION   1

UNIT ONE. RELIGIOUS VISION

CHAPTER I. THE NATURE OF TRUE RELIGION 21
    Introduction 21
    "Power of Religion"   24
    "Immortality in Literature"   31
    "Seen at the Tate Gallery"   40
    Club Letter No. 134   47
    Club Letter No. 3   51

CHAPTER II. CONCEPTS OF JUDAISM   55
    Introduction 55
    Club Letters No. 33-35 58
    Club Letter No. 6   73
    "The Sabbath"   76
    "A New Life Begins Today"   82
    Club Letter No. 133   88

CHAPTER III. JEWISH SELF-IDENTITY   93
    Introduction 93
    "Faith in God" 96
    "Why Do We Bother?" 103
    "Kinship With God"   111
    "Address Given at the Girls' Club"   120
    "Here Am I: Send Me" 128

                Club Letter No. 185 134
                Club Letter No. 139 139
                "Out of Zion Shall The Law Go Forth" 144

CHAPTER IV. THE ROLE OF WOMEN IN RELIGIOUS LIFE . . 155
                Introduction 155
                "Women's Contribution to the Spiritual Life of
                    Humanity" 158
                Address, Germany, 1930 167
                "The Spiritual Contribution of Women as Women" . 171
                "Religious Responsibility in Public Life" . . . 175
                "Jewish Women in the Rabbinate" 182

                    UNIT TWO.   RELIGIOUS VOCATION

CHAPTER V. LIBERAL JUDAISM AS THE JUDAISM OF THE
    FUTURE 187
                Introduction 187
                "Think, Thank and Do" 190
                "Can We Possibly Be Mistaken?" 200
                Club Letter No. 56 207
                Club Letter No. 165 212
                Presidential Address, U.L.P.S., 1958 219

CHAPTER VI. SOCIAL SERVICE 225
                Introduction 225
                "The Responsibility of Leisure" 229
                "A New Year's Talk to Girls" 241
                Addresses at Littlehampton, 1916 253
                Club Letter No. 26 268
                Club Letter No. 118 273
                Club Letter No. 154 278

CHAPTER VII. RELIGIOUS ORGANIZER 285
    Introduction 285
    Letter, March 24, 1899 289
    Letter, November, 1901 290
    Paper Read at First Meeting of J.R.U. 292
    "What I Owe to the Synagogue" 296
    "Unfinished Man" 307
    "Peace, Peace Where There Is No Peace" 314

CHAPTER VIII. RELIGIOUS LEADER 325
    Introduction 325
    "For Reform-Synagogue, Berlin" 327
    Service of Induction for Lay Ministers 335
    Service for the Blessing of a Baby 339
    Memorial Address 341
    Outline of a Wedding Ceremony 343
    Service of National Prayer 344
    Prayers by L.H.M. 350
    Club Letter No. 111 358
    "Strengthen the Things That Remain" 364

APPENDIX 371
    Introduction 371
    Letter to Louis Montagu, 1911 373
    Letter To Be Opened After Death, Sept., 1919 . . 376
    "Outline of What I Want Done With Regard to My
        Work," September 1, 1939 381
    Supplementary Letter, December, 1939 383
    Letter, June 15, 1940 388
    Outline, "Seeking and Finding" 397

ANNOTATED LIST OF PROPER NAMES 399

INDEX 407

PREFACE

This source book of approximately fifty of Lily Montagu's sermons, addresses, letters and prayers, is intended as a supplement to and corroboration of my earlier work, <u>Lily Montagu and the Advancement of Liberal Judaism: From Vision to Vocation</u> (Lewiston, N.Y.: The Edwin Mellen Press, 1983). In that work, I focused on Lily Montagu's assumption of religious leadership within the early twentieth century Anglo-Jewish community. I examined the religious and social climate that made it possible for her to achieve a position of public prominence. I further attempted to ascertain Montagu's own reasons for assuming roles for which she had few female models and no formal training and to which her father, to whom she felt a great emotional tie, was adamantly opposed.

In my earlier study, I relied heavily on Lily Montagu's eleven published books (including <u>Thoughts On Judaism</u>, <u>God Revealed</u>, and her autobiography, <u>The Faith of a Jewish Woman</u>), her numerous published articles, a good deal of personal correspondence, the Minute Books of the Jewish Religious Union and the Liberal Jewish Synagogue Council, and hundreds of unpublished sermons and addresses that were discovered in London, by me or through my instigation. These unpublished writings were discovered in a closet at the Liberal Jewish Synagogue, in the basement of what was once Lily Montagu's Girls' Club, and in the attic of her niece and nephew's home. In January of 1978, I returned to London, where I temporarily collected, arranged and had microfilmed many of my findings. The microfilm, which I later deposited at both the American Jewish Archives in Cincinnati and the Liberal Jewish

Synagogue in London, includes over one hundred sermons (most of which are in the form of typed or handwritten drafts); more than two hundred "Club Letters" (actually, sermonettes), written for members of the West Central Club which Lily Montagu founded; and letters clarifying Montagu's role in the founding of the Jewish Religious Union (the organization out of which the Liberal Jewish movement in England emerged) and the World Union for Progressive Judaism. Included too are personal letters revealing Lily Montagu's great emotional attachment to her sister, Marian; her father; Claude Montefiore; Israel Mattuck and others, outlines of special religious services that she created, and prayers that she wrote and incorporated into the worship services that she led.

While this microfilm collection is an important resource for those undertaking future research on Lily Montagu and more broadly, on Liberal Judaism in England, the microfilm itself is difficult to read. Montagu's handwriting is sometimes illegible, words are often crossed out or hastily written in the margins, and instead of spelling out the names of organizations and people, she frequently uses either abbreviations or initials. This volume thus seeks to make Lily Montagu's unpublished writings more accessible both to the scholar and to the general reader. It includes those works that are of greatest historical significance (e.g., the letter that led to the founding of the J.R.U., the first sermon Montagu delivered at the Liberal Jewish Synagogue, the sermon she delivered in 1928 at the World Union Conference in Berlin, and the address she gave when formally inducted as a lay minister) as well as those that clearly delineate the nature and content of her religious thought.

I have divided this book into two separate units. The first, entitled "Religious Vision," consists of four chapters, each of which contains sermons, letters and addresses that describe Lily Montagu's religious vision. The first chapter, on true religion, underscores the universal nature of that which Montagu understood to be spiritually real or true. The second describes her conception of Judaism as real religion while the third emphasizes the understanding of Jewish self-identity that emerged from this conception. Finally, the fourth chapter focuses on what Lily Montagu believed to be the role of women in religious life. Taken as a whole, these chapters reveal Montagu's understanding of Judaism as personal religion and her sense of spiritual mission as both a woman and a Jew.

The second unit, entitled "Religious Vocation," describes those roles that Montagu identified as vocations. Convinced that she had received a Divine call to spread God's teachings in ways that would be meaningful to present and future generations, she set as her life's goal the advancement of Liberal Judaism, believing that it alone was "the Judaism of the future" (Chapter V). Through endeavors in social service (Chapter VI), Lily Montagu sought to bring Liberal Judaism to Jewish girls of the working classes. The sermons, addresses, and letters contained in this chapter not only reveal the ways in which she attempted to do so, but also shed light on Montagu's conceptions of marriage, family and children. Chapter VII contains letters and addresses that clarify Lily Montagu's leading role in the creation of the Jewish Religious Union. Indeed, they establish her as the organization's founder and guiding (if not prodding) spirit. Last, Chapter VIII includes sermons and addresses that helped establish Lily Montagu's reputation as a religious leader as well as documents testifying to the variety of spiritual leadership functions that Lily Montagu assumed.

The documents in each chapter are arranged chronologically only when that seemed justified--e.g., when there seems to be a development of thought (as in Chapter IV) or, as in Chapter VII, an unfolding of historical events. On the whole, however, I have used content as my major criterion of selection, placing those documents that provide an overview of the chapter's theme at the beginning and those that focus on more specific questions (e.g., miracles, intermarriage, Jewish festivals, Zionism) at the end. All of the documents included here are reproduced in full. Given the fact, however, that most of the copies to which I had access were drafts and not printed texts, I have corrected spelling errors that are obviously typographical as well as names that are misspelled. I have also made additions, indicated in brackets, to texts containing missing words and/or incomplete sentences. Finally, I have indicated, through annotations, the many literary references on which Lily Montagu drew. In <u>Lily Montagu and the Advancement of Liberal Judaism</u>, I argued that Montagu's greatest sources of theology were the Bible, nineteenth century British poetry and contemporary liberal religious texts. This claim is substantiated through annotations identifying quotes and explicit literary references in many of Montagu's sermons and addresses. Individuals mentioned in these texts are described in a separate "Annotated List of Proper Names." The reader will note that few personal letters are included in this volume. This is because a) most only make sense in a larger context, i.e., they are part of an ongoing correspondence. Thus, in each letter, specific ideas are only alluded to and developed in part and b) those that might have been included were not made available to me for publication. Perhaps one day these too will be included in a published corpus of Lily Montagu's writings.

PREFACE

There are a number of people without whose assistance this volume might not have been completed. I am grateful to Malcolm Brown, archivist at the Liberal Jewish Synagogue, for sending me an inventory of the twenty-nine boxes of Lily Montagu's addresses and sermons that he discovered last summer in the Liberal Jewish Synagogue's basement. Their contents include final, typed copies of many of the sermons included in this volume. Added, however, are dates on which the sermons were delivered, some of which I had previously been unable to ascertain. I am also grateful to Eric Conrad for his enthusiastic support of this project and for his assistance in its final preparation. Equally enthusiastic was Herbert Richardson, whose willingness to publish Lily Montagu's sermons has encouraged me to believe that perhaps in the future, the achievements of great women may gain the recognition they deserve. I am indebted to Lynn Gordon for helping me to recognize Lily Montagu's contemporary significance and to Debra Blank, John Rayner, Lee Mitchell, Linda Zatlin, Jonathan Sarna, Mindy Agin, and Philip Miller and the library staff of Hebrew Union College - Institute of Religion in New York City for the assistance they provided. I am especially indebted to my colleague, David Blumenthal. More than anyone else, he has helped me to crystallize and develop my thoughts more clearly.

To Karen Parker, who typed much of this manuscript from dark, glossy and at times unintelligible sheets of paper, I offer my gratitude; to my family, who resigned themselves to not seeing me until this book was completed, my thanks; and to my husband, Alan Kannof, who has been my greatest source of personal and professional encouragement for the last thirteen years, my deepest love and appreciation.

Finally, I want to thank the following organizations for their financial assistance in the initial researching of this project: the National Foundation for Jewish Culture, the Memorial Foundation for Jewish Culture, the National Federation of Temple Sisterhoods, the World Union for Progressive Judaism, the Center for Israel and Jewish Studies at Columbia University and the American Jewish Archives in Cincinnati. I especially want to thank Emory University for providing me with the necessary release time to ensure this project's completion.

Ellen M. Umansky
Emory University

November, 1984

LILY MONTAGU
SERMONS, ADDRESSES, LETTERS AND PRAYERS

INTRODUCTION

Lily Montagu (1873-1963) stands out as one of the first Jewish women to have become a religious leader. Indeed, she may well deserve the title frequently, though mistakenly, bestowed upon her, of Judaism's first "Lady Rabbi." Though Montagu was never ordained, the roles that she assumed within the Anglo-Jewish community during the first half of the twentieth century were those of a modern Liberal rabbi, or minister. She served as a preacher and teacher; regularly led worship services; conducted weddings and funerals; created blessings for the birth of a baby; prepared proselytes for conversion; and functioned as socio-spiritual head of the West Central Liberal Jewish Congregation for over forty years.

Montagu, however, never aspired to this position. Her secular education was limited, her religious education minimal at best. By her own admission, she was shy and self-conscious. Thus, she often downplayed her achievements and modestly defined her ambitions. Yet her induction as a "lay minister" on November 14, 1944, was perhaps the greatest moment of Lily Montagu's life. It was what she would have called a "Red Letter Day," i.e., a memorable and exciting occasion, marking the formal validation of her leadership role within the Anglo-Jewish community.

As a lay minister, Montagu sought to bring others to an awareness of the eternal presence of God. It was this awareness that gave direction to her life, leading her to become a social worker, a religious organizer, and eventually, a religious leader. In assuming each of these roles, she attempted to express her vision of a loving, just and merciful God, Creator of the world and of all humanity. Expressing this vision through both her words and actions, she sought to make others aware of the importance, indeed the necessity, of "consciously let[ting] religion into life,"[1] and of recognizing, as she had, that spirituality was central to existence.

Lily Montagu came to this recognition after an early period of spiritual crisis. Finding the Orthodoxy of her father to be antithetical to that which she had come to define as real or true religion, she suffered, at the age of fifteen, what can at best be described as a serious nervous condition. Her recovery was largely facilitated by her discovery of the theological writings of Claude Montefiore, who not only shared her conception of true religion but also--in identifying this concept as "Liberal Judaism"--led Montagu to believe that it was possible to reconcile her father's faith with her own. By equating "Liberal Judaism" with "Judaism" itself, Montagu was able to arrive at a personally meaningful sense of Jewish self-identity. This identity held particular meaning for her as a woman since many of her childhood memories were of Orthodoxy's exclusion of women from full participation in the community's religious life.

Having come to this new understanding of Judaism, Lily Montagu began to feel and articulate religious sentiments of which she previously had been unaware. Before this religious awakening (detailed in Chapter Seven of my book, <u>Lily Montagu and the Advancement of Liberal Judaism</u>, Edwin Mellen, 1983), she had seen Judaism simply as an "external fact," that with which she identified externally though it possessed no inner meaning. Afterwards, as she never tired of saying, it became the moving force of her life. Basing her understanding of Jewish self-identity on the principles of Liberal Judaism, she came to believe that Judaism's core or essence lay in bearing witness to the reality of God. Included in this testimony were God's moral teachings, to be spread throughout the world through one's daily actions.

Those who knew Lily Montagu saw her as a religious, some said saintly, figure. They did not need to listen to her sermons to know that she lived each day in constant awareness of the Divine. Her inner faith illuminated her face, her dark brown eyes seemed to glow. According to Jessie Levy, her secretary of more than twenty-five years, after Lily Montagu spoke from the pulpit, she would close her eyes and one could feel her spiritual calmness.[2] This "spiritual aura"[3] led many--her admirers and her detractors--to maintain that she lived in two different worlds. While on the one hand, her immense organizational talents led people to think of her as practical and down-to-earth, her mind always seemed to be on God. That is, even her attention to ordinary detail never seemed to detract from what Lily Montagu and others recognized to be an essentially spiritual and moral outlook. Consequently, Montagu cared little about her appearance. She was often badly dressed, her clothing frequently out of style. The only vanity that she allowed herself was buying hats, occasionally commenting if a close acquaintance didn't notice that she was wearing a new one![4]

According to those who knew her, she frequently and often spontaneously engaged in prayer. She held a brief worship service in her home each morning before breakfast, primarily consisting of the _Shema_ (Deuteronomy 6:4-9) and either a Biblical selection or a poem, usually by Browning. Her entire household staff, non-Jews included, were invited to these devotions. Each evening at the West Central Jewish Girls' Club (a social, religious and educational club founded by Montagu in 1893), ended with a prayer led by Lily Montagu, and for most of her life, on Friday evenings, she led a brief Sabbath worship service at home.

During the day, Montagu would often pause and spontaneously thank God for His goodness. According to Sir Louis Gluckstein, former President of the Liberal Jewish Synagogue, it was this serenity and sureness of faith that made Lily Montagu unafraid of anything except possibly lack of support or failure.[5] Regularly working as much as fifteen hours a day (and continuing to work up until the end of her life), she never worried either about her health or about overworking. If, even in her eighties, Montagu could still be described as a dynamic figure, persistent in her efforts to enlist the help of others, it was because religion, and more particularly, Liberal Judaism, had become her life's passion. Spreading its teachings and bringing others to an awareness of God remained, to Lily Montagu, a sacred mission with which she had been entrusted. She therefore vowed to devote to it all of her energy and strength. This sense of mission not only helped shape Montagu's sense of vocation--as a social worker, religious organizer and religious leader--but also colored her views on everything, leading her to write articles, sermons and letters on such diverse topics as traditional observance and Orthodoxy, art and literature, assimilation and intermarriage, Zionism, feminism, socialism, the Holocaust, capital punishment and war.

In numerous sermons, some of which are included in this volume, Montagu maintained that traditional observance had no intrinsic merit. To be a good Jew, she believed, one only needed to be a good human being. Thus, traditional observances were valuable only in so far as they could serve as "vehicles towards holiness," bringing the individual closer to God (and hence, to His moral teachings). Out of deference to her father, Montagu attempted to portray Orthodoxy in a positive light, insisting that it was one of many paths through which the Jew might come to recognize his or her spiritual potential. Yet knowing that Orthodoxy had been unable to provide her with such a path and firmly believing that Liberal Judaism was the Judaism of the future, she frequently contrasted the "old" Judaism of Orthodoxy with the "new" or "living" Judaism to which she and Montefiore adhered.

Believing in God's eternal presence as continually revealed, Montagu maintained that God could be found everywhere--in nature, art and literature as a well as in prayer. Her universalistic view of God as Creator of the world and of humanity, led her to believe that God's beauty was revealed through (and potentially by) all of His creations. Consequently, she did not limit herself to Jewish artists, novelists and poets in searching for God through literature and art. Rather, believing that religious truth was universal and thus capable of being found anywhere, she simply turned to those artists and writers whose works she loved best.

Despite her universalism, however, Lily Montagu staunchly opposed both assimilation and intermarriage. While in part, she may have inherited this view from her father (since, as I argue in Lily Montagu and the Advancement of Liberal Judaism, her opposition was more vocal and more sustained than that of Liberal Judaism's other leaders), she understood her opposition to be religious in nature, based on her own understanding of her mission as a Jew. As she asserted in numerous sermons as well as in several short stories in What Can A Mother Do? (London: George Routledge and Sons, 1926), the purity of the message that she was entrusted to spread could only be preserved through marriage to another Jew who similarly felt bound by this mission. Hence, she included in her definition of intermarriage both marriage between a Jew and a Christian and marriage between a religious Jew (i.e., someone who recognized the importance of his or her spiritual mission) and a secularist. To her, being born of Jewish parents did not make one Jewish. Only those who acknowledged their membership in its "religious brotherhood," accepting its responsibilities and duties, could claim to be Jews.

Montagu's opposition to Zionism similarly rested on religious grounds. Since, for her, Jews were no longer members of a specific nation but of a religious brotherhood enjoined to spread God's teachings throughout the world, it was only in living among non-Jews, she believed, that these teachings could best be spread. She thus considered a return to Zion for reasons other than physical persecution to be a spiritual step backwards and a betrayal of the Jewish mission. Consequently, her opposition to Zionism continued even after the State of Israel had been established. While she was interested in ways in which the State might be influenced by Liberal Jewish teachings, this interest never became a major concern.[6] Fearing that the creation of the State of Israel might lead Jews to interest themselves only in Jewish affairs, Montagu continued to voice her opposition to Zionism (though not to the State itself), emphasizing, after 1948 as before, the contribution that Jews were to make to the "spiritual treasury" of humanity.

Though Lily Montagu insisted that the spiritual gifts of men and women were different from one another, her firm belief in the identical worth of these gifts led her to declare that men and women were equal. While admitting that she was not a "complete and thoroughgoing feminist" if feminism implied the desire to obliterate all differences between the sexes, she <u>was</u> a feminist, she maintained, in her commitment to women's gaining equal opportunity to develop their potential through equal access to every phase of religious and secular life. Similarly, in an essay published in 1896, she asserted that she supported efforts to transform England into a socialist state only if "under its rule the individual would receive a stronger stimulus and find greater scope to develop his personality than under existing conditions."[7]

Her opposition to both capital punishment and war rested on the religious convictions that: 1) Since God is the Creator of all life, only He can take life away; 2) Because all human beings are created in God's image, to kill another human being, even out of a sense of justice, in some way diminishes God; and 3) If the "Fatherhood of God" implies, as Lily Montagu believed, the "Brotherhood" of humanity, then we are obligated to transcend divisions of sex, race, and nationality and, as Lily Montagu entitled one of her sermons, to become our "Brother's Keeper." To Lily Montagu, this meant not only working to awaken a sense of spiritual devotion within others but also assuming responsibility for the perpetuation of evil in the world. Believing that one should show compassion even towards the guilty, she spoke out in favor of corrective detention as a more merciful form of punishment than execution.[8]

Montagu's belief in collective responsibility led her to speak with compassion, even about the German people during the Second World War. Though horrified by Nazi atrocities, she refused to lay sole blame on the Nazis, or on the German people as a whole. If there is evil in the world, she said, it is because we have been Godless. She thus admonished her adherents to frustrate the Nazi "spirit of hatred" by renewing the religious faith of others and infusing the world with love. While World War II put an end to Montagu's pacifism (she realized, she wrote, that Britain had no choice but to go to war), she continued to espouse peace as an ideal. Believing that evil would eventually be overcome, and harmony among nations established, she frequently asserted, quoting her favorite poet, Robert Browning, that "the best is yet to be."

MONTAGU AS ROLE MODEL

Though Lily Montagu's overwhelming sense of spirituality makes her, at the very least, an exceptional woman, she herself maintained that she was "ordinary." She insisted that her religious vision was accessible to everyone and her vocation no more special or unique than any other. Believing in the importance of role models in influencing one's self-development, she tried to serve as a model to those around her. Emphasizing the relationship between faith and conduct, she constantly reiterated her belief that self-realization was impossible without acknowledging and developing one's own spiritual potential.

To exemplify this claim, she pointed to her own life as having been energized and given direction by religious faith. She continually spoke about that which had exerted greatest influence over her--books, plays, people, nature etc., exhorting others to similarly discover within these everyday realities the power of "true religion." As Elisabeth Griffith notes in her recent study of Elizabeth Cady Stanton, a role model, as defined by the social scientist, is "someone whose 'role is modeled,' whose behavior is copied, or whose actions and attitudes can influence their own."[9] Given this definition, Lily Montagu's frequent and explicit identification of her own limitations and capabilities with those of her listeners or readers can be seen as a conscious attempt to serve as a model to them. "Though our thoughts and deeds are full of weakness and imperfection,"[10] she wrote, "I am going to suggest to you some of the ways by which in my view the work can be done, by ordinary people, by you and by me."[11] "We are not spiritual giants as was Isaiah." Yet "we can each in his small way feel the contact with God and His cleansing power operating over our human weaknesses and clearing them away."[12]

In order to illustrate her conviction that her spiritual capabilities were no greater than the spiritual capabilities of others, she published an anthology entitled God Revealed (1953). Edited by Montagu, it was intended to be a devotional work written by Jews "for themselves and their non-Jewish neighbors."[13] Divided into twelve sections, each focusing on a different month of the year, it contained a number of themes relating to Divine revelation, with one theme assigned to each section. Among them were God revealed in children, nature, human love, religious observance, suffering and friendship. While each section concluded with a prayer by Lily Montagu herself, the brief selections that made up each chapter included material from traditional Jewish texts (primarily the Bible), the writings of contemporary Jewish leaders, and the thoughts of Lily Montagu's colleagues, relatives and friends. Included in this latter category were Evelyn Peat, Lily Montagu's niece; Eric Conrad, her nephew; Ruth Nothmann, a secretary of the World Union for Progressive Judaism; Leila Levine, a member of the Liberal Jewish Synagogue; Marjorie Moos, a teacher at the LJS; Peggy Lang, its Organizing Secretary; Rosina Drayton, a housewife and member of the West Central Synagogue; Bruno Simon, an artist and German refugee; and Bruno Woyda, Treasurer of the World Union. The sections were written at Montagu's instigation. Her intent was to convince her contributors, especially those lacking self-confidence in their spiritual capabilities, that if they opened themselves to God, as she had, they too could discover--and articulate--the ways in which God was revealed.

While some revered her as a prophet and most, it seems, held her in awe, Lily Montagu succeeded in becoming an important role model for many within the West Central Club and the Liberal Jewish movement. Countless members of the West Central Club and Congregation consciously sought to model their lives after Lily Montagu's, seeking to fulfill their potential. Some who never married, lived with their sisters, as Montagu had, finding that "friendship between sisters is one of the most satisfying that life can afford."[14] Many of these single women followed Montagu's lead further in their total dedication to God. One such woman was Jessie Levy. Attending the West Central Club in her teens and in 1937 becoming Lily Montagu's secretary, she became completely imbued with "Miss Montagu's" ideals. Consequently, she became an active participant in the World Union for Progressive Judaism (initially serving, as Lily Montagu had, as its secretary) and in the West Central Liberal Jewish Congregation. While unlike Lily Montagu, Levy never became a lay minister, she did become President of Montagu's congregation, assuming, in this capacity, important organizational and religious functions.

Lacking the scholarly expertise of Claude Montefiore and Israel Mattuck--the movement's other driving forces-- Lily Montagu gained a closeness to others that Mattuck and especially Montefiore were not always able to achieve. As John Rayner, Senior Minister of the Liberal Jewish Synagogue, noted in a memorial address to her:

The most incredible thing about Lily Montagu. . . [was] that, incredible though it seems, we *could* be like her. We could, if we would, dedicate our lives wholly to the service to God.[15]

Thus, Lily Montagu was held in both awe and affection. Though that which others perceived to be her unique spiritual gifts inspired awe, as "Miss Lily"--founder and "mother" of the West Central Club, the Jewish Religious Union and the World Union for Progressive Judaism, she inspired great love, leading many to view her as a role model. Like Lily Montagu, they believed, they could become more religious, opening themselves up the Divine presence and dedicating their lives to the service of God. Yet convinced that they could never aspire to her greatness, most saw Montagu as only a partial role model, at best. Few felt that they could assume the kinds of leadership positions that Lily Montagu herself had achieved.

It is not surprising, then, that Montagu had no female successor to assume leadership of the West Central Congregation after she was gone. Like other early female religious leaders--including Ann Lee of the Shakers and Christian Science's Mary Baker Eddy--her talents were seen as so extraordinary that in an era in which female religious leadership was rare, no woman thought--or dared--to assume Lily Montagu's position. As Rabbi Bernard Hooker confided, undoubtedly echoing the sentiments of most of those who knew her: "There will never be anyone like Lily Montagu again."[16]

MONTAGU AS HERO

Perhaps the description that fits Lily Montagu best is not that of role model but of hero. A great admirer of Thomas Carlyle's On Heroes, Hero Worship and the Heroic in History (1840), she often pointed to the "wise, gifted, [and] noble-hearted"[17] men of Carlyle's study. The hero,

Montagu maintained, using Carlyle's definition, is one upon whom the spirit of God has descended, he who inspires within others the power of reverence and wonder.[18] As Carlyle wrote, the hero is an "original," an individual who speaks words that one feels no one else can utter. Though Carlyle later associated the hero with force (the concept of "might is right"), he postulated in his earlier work a concept of the hero which, despite his exclusive association of this concept with men, clearly can be ascribed to Lily Montagu.

According to Carlyle, the hero's primary characteristic is sincerity. He insists on "hold[ing] to the truth and fact" and is possessed by his ideas. Unambitious, the hero simply aspires to unfold himself, doing that which he feels to be his duty. Yet to others, he appears as a great man--a God, priest or prophet. He inspires those around him and leads them out of darkness and into light. To Carlyle, then, the hero is a "Hero-Teacher," a subduer of faith, possessor of valor, and worthy object of admiration.

Reminiscences of Lily Montagu similarly are filled with descriptions of her greatness. Even her private physician, Charles Lewsen, told me that at the hospital before she died, the nurses in attendance sensed that they were near a great woman.[19] To many who knew her, she was charismatic and saintly, seemingly touched by God. The hero, Carlyle maintained, has a certain "power of vision."[20] In a lengthy interview, Leslie Edgar, minister emeritus of the Liberal Jewish Synagogue, similarly referred to Lily Montagu as a "woman of vision," she who, rather than looking backwards, always looked with great optimism towards the future.[21] Lily Montagu may have preferred to identify herself as a "small hero," a label she equated with role model. Yet by occasionally defining

INTRODUCTION   13

the hero as one who influences others through the sheer strength of his or her personality, even she might have admitted to being a hero.

MODEL OR HERO? A CONTEMPORARY ASSESSMENT

As a woman of achievement, Lily Montagu may well serve as an important role model for women today. She acted out of her own sense of vocation, assuming roles that many thought improper, either for women in general (e.g., serving as a religious leader) or for women of her social and economic class (a good example is her early absorption in social work, leading her to neglect parties, dances and personal appearance). Having few models of female leadership to follow, she became a religious leader anyway. Wishing to lead services for adults, she organized her own. Hoping to be part of a movement that would help revitalize Anglo-Jewry's religious life, she founded the movement herself. In sum, she became a "feminist in action," using her vast organizational talents as well as her great sense of perseverance and courage to assume a religious role that no Jewish woman before her had achieved. Lily Montagu thus remains an important model of female ability, strength, and power. That she retained a sense of humor, even in the midst of her struggles, makes her especially valuable as a role model for contemporary women.

During the past seven years of research, I have found myself increasingly drawn to Lily Montagu. This attraction, however, does not lie with either her feminism or organizational ability. Unlike Lily Montagu, I am not content simply to be a feminist in action, leaving to others the formation of theoretical foundations on which these actions might rest. Moreover, while admiring her organizational skill, I myself have little interest in becoming a religious organizer, viewing my contributions to American Jewish life as scholarly rather than organizational in nature. Neither, I might add, do I share Lily Montagu's philosophical optimism. Indeed, I suspect that given the past horrors of the Holocaust and the possible spectre of a nuclear war, it is difficult if not impossible for anyone to say with confidence, as did Lily Montagu--and Robert Browning--that "the best is yet to be."

Yet as I have come to question the contemporary meaning of traditional liturgy and texts, I have found Lily Montagu to be an important model of personal religiosity. I have been inspired by her rejection of much of tradition for that which she intuitively felt was true. Her reliance on experience rather than on externally-imposed sources of authority has provided me, and may well provide others, with a new means of confronting the injustices of patriarchal religion. Indeed, like many feminist theologians, I have already come to rely on such experiences in beginning my own spiritual journey. Reading traditional texts with what Elizabeth Schüssler Fiorenza has labelled a "feminist hermeneutics of suspicion,"[22] I have begun to seek ways of incorporating these experiences into a new conception of Deity. In so doing, Lily Montagu's rebellion against her father and his understanding of Judaism has served as a significant model of religious protest. Though others could claim greater knowledge and authority than she, Montagu was convinced that she could not worship with her father's heart. For Judaism to be more than an inherited tradition to which she adhered simply out of family loyalty and commitment, she needed to transform Judaism into a "living religion."

My attraction to Lily Montagu, however, is rooted not only in what I perceive to be a shared spiritual need but also in beliefs emerging out of my religious background.

INTRODUCTION   15

   Having been raised as a Reform Jew, imbued with the principles of Liberal Judaism and the sense of mission to which
she was devoted, I speak the same religious language as
Lily Montagu. I too feel called to testify to God's
reality and to bring His moral teachings to others. I too
believe in the inherent connection between faith and
conduct and believe, as Lily Montagu did, that moral
behavior makes one a good Jew <u>and</u> a good human being.
Though I have greater confidence than Lily Montagu in the
ability of traditional symbols and observances to serve as
"vehicles towards holiness," I too reject the belief that
these observances and symbols possess intrinsic merit. In
short, I feel a certain spiritual affinity to Lily Montagu,
for like her, I feel the need to bear testimony to God's
reality through images and symbols that possess personal as
well as traditional meaning. In many ways, I wish that I
could be more like her. I wish that I could possess
Montagu's sureness of faith and <u>know</u>, with her sense of
confidence, that my experiences of the Divine are true.
   Yet the fact that Lily Montagu felt she had to choose
between love and work while also believing that her choice
of the latter consigned her to a "second best" existence,
diminishes, I think, Montagu's significance as a role
model. Indeed, these factors, combined with her spiritual
greatness, make her less of a role model to me than a hero.
Perhaps, in an age of few heroes, almost all of whom are
men, Lily Montagu's organizational and spiritual greatness
remains her most important legacy, not just to me but to
all women. To paraphrase Thomas Carlyle:

> We do not now call our great [wo]men God,
> nor admire without limit; ah, no, <u>with</u> limit
> enough! But if we have no great [wo]men, or do
> not admire at all, that were a still worse
> case.[23]

Female heroes, like Lily Montagu, provide broader visions of all that women can accomplish. Though for some, the hero may be inaccessible--an object of adulation--for others, including myself, she may serve as the inspiration out of which a "whole World of Heroes"[24] might be created.

In 1978, when I returned to London to have Montagu's letters, sermons, addresses, and prayers put on microfilm, I received a gift from Sheila and Eric Conrad, Lily Montagu's niece and nephew. The gift was a necklace of amber beads which they told me Lily Montagu regularly wore during the last twenty years of her life. They felt sure, they said, that their Aunt Lily would have wanted me to have it. Just as Lily Montagu believed that her father appeared to her after his death and handed her a document, symbolizing his "spiritual inheritance" to her, so these beads are my personal legacy from Lily Montagu, reminding me that while I may never achieve her spiritual greatness, I too have a contribution to make to that which Lily Montagu identified as the "spiritual treasury of the world."

NOTES TO INTRODUCTION

[1] Lily H. Montagu, *The Faith of a Jewish Woman* (Keighley, Yorkshire: Wadsworth & Co., 1943), p. 20.

[2] Interview with Jessie Levy, 21 July, 1977. West Central Liberal Jewish Congregation, London.

[3] Interview with Hannah Feldman, 25 July, 1977. West Central Club, London.

[4] Interview with Sir Louis Gluckstein, 25 July, 1977. Liberal Jewish Synagogue, London.

[5] Gluckstein interview.

[6] Interview with Rabbi Leslie Edgar, 27 July, 1977, at his home in London.

[7] Lily H. Montagu, "The Condition of the Individual in a Socialist State," *Westminster Review* 146 (October, 1896): 439.

[8] This view is expressed most clearly in an essay on "Capital Punishment and the Old Testament," printed by the National Council for the Abolition of the Death Penalty. (n.d., Liberal Jewish Archives, London).

[9] Elisabeth Griffith, *In Her Own Right: The Life of Elizabeth Cady Stanton* (New York: Oxford University Press, 1984), p. 221.

[10] Lily H. Montagu, Club Letter No. 6, see page 73.

[11] Lily H. Montagu, Club Letter No. 56, see page 207.

[12] Lily H. Montagu, "Here Am I: Send Me," see page 128.

[13] Lily H. Montagu, "Foreward," in Montagu, ed. *God Revealed* (Keighley, Yorkshire: John Wadsworth, 1953).

[14] Lily H. Montagu, Addresses at Littlehampton, 1916, see page 253.

[15] John D. Rayner, "The Next Chapter," Address, Liberal Jewish Synagogue, 2 February, 1963 (private possession of John D. Rayner, London).

[16] Interview with Rabbi Bernard Hooker, 15 August, 1977. North London Progressive Synagogue, London.

[17] Thomas Carlyle, *On Heroes, Hero-Worship and the Heroic in History* (1840; rpt. London: J. M. Dent & Sons, Ltd., 1908), p. 264.

[18] [Lily H. Montagu], "Hero Worship and Modernity," Sermon, 30 March, 1928. (Liberal Jewish Synagogue Archives, London).

[19] Interview with Dr. Charles Lewsen, 11 August, 1977, at his home in London.

[20] Carlyle, *On Heroes*, p. 325.

[21] Interview with Leslie Edgar.

[22] Elisabeth Schüssler Fiorenza, *In Memory of Her: A Feminist Theological Reconstruction of Christian Origins* (New York: Crossroad, 1983), p. 60.

[23] Carlyle, *On Heroes*, p. 266.

[24] Ibid., p. 358.

UNIT ONE

RELIGIOUS VISION

I. THE NATURE OF TRUE RELIGION

INTRODUCTION

To Lily Montagu, the core of true religion could not be found in outward observances or formally written creeds. It could only be found within the soul of the individual. To her, it was the attaching of oneself to God, the "bringing back of the soul to the God who gave it," that truly made one religious. Thus, for Lily Montagu, the "Power of Religion" was an emotional power. Its strength lay in its ability to awaken one's consciousness of the immanent and transcendent God, to stir the soul, and to make one aware that "eternity [has been placed] in our hearts." Equating true religion with personal religion, Montagu believed that such a religion was, by definition, universal. To find God, one need not study particular texts or observe particular precepts. One need only open oneself up to God's ever-abiding presence.

The sermons included in this chapter reveal some of the ways in which Lily Montagu felt that God might best be discovered. All, in other words, focus on what Lily Montagu perceived to be the nature of true--or real--religion. In "Immortality in Literature," she turns to the work of her three favorite authors: Thomas Carlyle, George Eliot and Robert Browning. Though she and the audience that she is addressing are Jewish, it is not surprising that the texts discussed here are not specifically Jewish texts. First, Lily Montagu's own knowledge of Jewish texts was, at best, minimal. Her formal religious education seems to have consisted almost entirely of semi-private

Bible lessons. Second, as I have shown in my book, <u>Lily Montagu and the Advancement of Liberal Judaism: From Vision to Vocation</u>, (Edwin Mellen, 1983), it was in reading the words of Carlyle, Eliot, Browning and other Victorian authors that Montagu first felt that which she came to identify as true religion. Growing up in an Orthodox household and forced to perform that which for her were "mechanical observances" possessing little if any meaning, religion was, for the young Lily Montagu, an "external fact" of her existence. It provided her with a sense of connection to her ancestors and her family, most particularly her father, but it seemed unable to stir her soul. When, in her early teens, Lily Montagu began to immerse herself in literature, she found ideas that she intuitively felt were correct. Taken as a whole, they identified religion as emotional, personal and universal, rooted in the discovery of one's spiritual power and one's essential kinship with God.

Thomas Carlyle clearly articulated that which she previously had been unable to express, namely, that one did not become religious through the observance of externally-imposed precepts but through the recognition of and response to a Divine Call. What was demanded, then, was not a specific code of behavior but rather a giving of oneself. Through George Eliot, Lily Montagu came to believe that such giving did not necessitate self-annihilation. Indeed, in Eliot's eyes, work afforded the individual a unique opportunity for self-actualization. For Eliot too, one could not claim to be religious without showing love and concern for others. This emphasis on feeling as well as on conduct appealed to Lily Montagu and again, echoed sentiments that she intuitively felt were right. Finally, in Robert Browning, Montagu found a kindred spirit who shared her sense of optimism, including her conviction, in Browning's words, that "the best is yet to be." In sum, Lily Montagu viewed these and other authors as sources of theology, first, because they were sources to which she had greatest access, and second, because their understanding of religion resonated with what she herself believed to be true.

Her purpose in building a Jewish sermon around the ideas of Carlyle, Eliot and Browning was to underscore the universality of religious truth. If, as I suspect, the sermon was delivered to members of the West Central Section of the J.R.U. (later, the West Central Liberal Jewish Congregation), her listeners were those with as little knowledge of (and/or access to) traditional Jewish texts as she. Her intent, then, was to show them that they did have access to real religion, if only they knew where to look.

In "Immortality in Literature," real religion is said to be found in great books of the day as well as in the Bible, probably the only Jewish source with which her listeners were familiar. In "Seen at the Tate Gallery," works of art become a means of finding God, with the true artist one who makes clear to us God's revelation in beauty. This revelation can also be seen in nature (Club Letter 134). Here, the sense of awe that accompanies one's recognition of God's creative genuis is identified by Lily Montagu as "the beginning of true religion."

Finally, in Club Letters 134 and 3, Lily Montagu begins to describe what a "right relationship" with God entails. As she makes clear in Club Letter 134, to serve God necessitates using all of one's knowledge in His service. It further necessitates a recognition of the responsibilities that accompany such knowledge. Club Letter 3, focusing on prayer, describes the importance of achieving "contact with the living God." It is only through prayer, Montagu writes, that one becomes a complete human being, for prayer, and in particular private prayer, awakens one's spiritual potential, empowering one to work with God in the removal of evil and in the establishment of His kingdom. To be religious, she maintains, is to live each day in conscious awareness of the Divine Presence. Yet along with this awareness is the conviction that what we do is as important as what we believe. True religion, in other words, is based on right belief <u>and</u> right conduct. As Lily Montagu frequently insisted, one cannot achieve a right relationship with God without also achieving a right relationship with others.

POWER OF RELIGION

North London June 2nd - West Central June 9th
1928

Some people think that religion has been a power for evil in the world because so much strife has been perpetrated in its name. Many of the wars of the middle ages - the persecutions of the Holy Inquisition, the Civil Wars in our own country were all identified with religion. In homes from remote history even to the present day, family life has been broken up in the name of religion. Indeed the sum total of human misery which can be laid at the door of religion makes up a terrible indictment. What can we say in defence? We say that all this misery, awful and hideous in its reality as it is, is due not to the influence of religion but to its absence.

You remember that child's story in which two people are quarrelling about religion and God's messenger comes to separate them. He asks what is the trouble - The answer from both is religion. "I shouldn't have thought it," says the angel.

THE NATURE OF TRUE RELIGION

Religion makes for peace, tolerance, love. The man who depends on his spiritual vision may see more clearly than the man who judges by appearances. We fight in the name of religion - but when we fight we forget its meaning and purpose. You can't hate a person for not loving God. You can pity him - you can try to bring him out of his misery - but if you do this by torturing or killing him you are not using the power of religion to accomplish your task. And you are certainly not making your religion acceptable to him. For what is religion? It is the bringing back of the soul to the God who gave it, by the conscious voluntary efforts of the soul to get into contact with the unseen, with the infinite, with the indefinable. A religion is best made known by the lives which express it. The Maccabeans did not love their persecutors; they were not impressed by the purity of thought which inspired the tortures from which they suffered. Do you remember Browning's Confessional? Here is the story of a girl who was anxious about the soul of her lover. She feared that he was wandering in unrighteous paths. So, under the holy seal of the Confessional, she asked advice of her priest. He probed the lover's secrets by urging the girl to talk freely, pretending all the while, that by doing so she was serving the interests of her beloved. Then the priest used the information to bring the young man to the scaffold. The girl, wild with impotent despair, saw her lover betrayed because of the action she had been induced to take in the name of religion. She does not find cause to love that religion or its representatives. She cries -

"No part in aught they hope or fear,"
"No heaven with them, no hell! and here,"
"No earth, not so much space as pens"
"My body in their worst of dens"

"But shall bear God and man my cry"
"Lies - Lies again and still they lie!"[1]
Do we wonder at her violence in the face of the priests - hateful perfidy!

But was the priest's action religious - was not he like the crusaders of old, like the Holy inquisitors working in the name of God but all the time defying it? God demands from us love, truth, justice, mercy - if we would bind ourselves to Him, if we would be religious. Treachery and Hate separate us from Him. I say to you my friends, that if we can consciously attach ourselves to God, our lives <u>must</u> become better - yes and happier - yes and more useful - altogether more worthwhile.

Now I want to develop that idea.

What difference will it make to the individual if he tries consciously in his life to attach himself to God? He will find authority for his moral life in the commands of God instead of in the conventions of Society. He will not dare to juggle with truth to advance his own petty purposes. Truth belongs to God. It is God who reveals it to man. Every now and then a lie would seem to be very useful; without religion a man sees no reason to turn away from it. Religion makes us responsible to God for the conduct of our lives - without religion we should be justified in eating and drinking and being merry for life would seem to be fleeting and it would not matter very much whether we used it well or ill. It would seem to be ours to do with as we like. But religion makes this attitude impossible. Man is a spiritual animal. If he pays no heed to the divine within himself, he loses the privileges of his manhood. There is no tangible reward for virtue:

"The wages of sin is death; if the wages of virtue
        be dust,"

"Would she have heart to endure for the life of
   the worm and the fly?
"She desires no isles of the blest, no quiet seats
   of the just,
"To rest in a golden grove, or to bask in a summer
   sky;"
"Give her the ways of going on and not to die!"[2]

The just reward lies in this that we can realise the possibilities of a complete life if we develop, instead of crushing the divine element which is in every human life. We ignore that divine element at our peril. I said that religion makes life better. If we believe in God, if we think that He has sent us into the world to work with Him and for Him to create goodness and joy, then surely life *does* become better. We dare not fail God. There are many things besides lying we *cannot* do. It is because we recognise our allegiance to God that we can love and go on loving even when we are disappointed and misunderstood. We can be just, even when our neighbour's weaknesses are apparent to us; we can be merciful even when we have the power to injure another life. We can put honour, social service, purity, before all else in the world and overcome our unworthy desires, control our passions, combat our selfish inclinations. We can do these things; indeed we must; for in no other way can we serve God. Then again when we are doing our best measuring it in the light of God, we shall know our insufficiency and our feebleness and feel eternity in our hearts and recognise that we can go on striving for ever.

I have said that religion has the power to make us happier. The element of faith in our lives helps us to adjust our minds to bearing the weight of insoluble problems which threaten their well-being. You can't understand why the innocent suffer, you can't explain the existence of unmerited wretchedness, of abject ignorance, of catastrophic disaster. Why? Why? you ask all the time - you go to science and get some kind of illumination. But the light which shows up human responsibility for some part of the evil and misery and pain, also makes plain the limitations of human understanding. Again you ask why? The new psychology reveals to you the subconscious mind in which good and evil inclinations find their resting place. At the same time it suggests the power of religion in dealing with these inclinations as soon as the desirability for so doing is recognised. Again it is religion alone, which gives good reason why man should become the master of his life and points out the way in which he should direct his conduct. Moreover it is religion which reconciles man to his own inability to understand the meaning of life. His inability instead of giving him cause for lamentation is really a cause for rejoicing. His humanity cannot contain the whole of God. Some of God's ways must be hidden, because they are perfect and therefore infinitely removed from man's ways. But human testimony, based on human experience and the results of man's communion all down the ages bears witness to the fact that the ways of God are good and righteous altogether. It is God, who through the power of religion wipes away tears from all faces, while revealing the eternity of love which destroys death for ever. Without this faith, human goodness and self sacrifice must be altogether unexplained. An atheist thinks he can explain the evil in the world - the explanation of goodness baffles him.

The power of religion makes the life of the individual better and happier. It also affects in the same direction, the life of Society. Again and again it would seem that the interests of Society clash with the law of right.

THE NATURE OF TRUE RELIGION 29

Progress is only possible if we insist on proving our allegiance to this higher law.

Why do you think good education has been held back from the masses of our people? Why are so many still badly paid, badly housed, badly nourished, intemperate and vicious and badly clothed? Is it not because Society is not yet religious? It does not want to spend on causes, which bring no visible profitable return. The policy of "laissez-faire", based as men thought on the survival of the fittest has still not entirely lost its influence. Leave men to settle their own affairs. Why should Society interfere? Let the employer get all he can out of his men, let the men give as little as they can to the employer. If men like to gamble away their homes, or drink themselves to death, let them do so. It is their own business. Why should men and women on Care and after Care Committees bother themselves about the welfare of other people's children? It is in these people's own interest to see the medical instructions should be carried out. If they don't understand or neglect the instructions given them, let them suffer for their stupidity. It is through the power of religion that reforms are affected. It is because, as the children of one Father, we admit the claim of our neighbour that disinterested fair dealing and even love of those, to whom we are able to be of service, is possible to us. Reforms seldom *pay* immediately in the utilitarian, commercial sense. It is not for us to count on their ultimate success, as paying propositions, although experience has shown that good social conditions are ultimately economically advantageous. The reformer sees that the life of Society must be harmonious with the life of God. So he takes risks and makes sacrifices and labours unstintingly, being influenced, always by the power of religion.

It is well, friends, that we should think of religion in this way - even as a stimulus to being adventurers in the cause of righteousness. Since we are trying under the influence of religion to attach ourselves to the God of life - we see that religion is not a sedative. It does not ask you to accept pain - it bids you conquer it, if it can be conquered and it bids you work on [it], in spite of it, if it is outside your sphere of control.

I have spoken of the power of religion and for us Jews - we mean by religion the power of Judaism. I say to you that it is Judaism which makes us better, happier and more useful citizens for it is Judaism, which by its teaching, brings us nearer to God.

Jewish observances are useful or useless in so far as they do or do not cause us to understand the way of life which shall further our progress towards the best. To the crowds of our people who neglect observances today, we would utter a word of caution. Are they sure that they have found another way to God? Is pleasure leading them? It is possible. But we need prayer to sanctify pleasure. Is success helping them? It is possible, but we need prayer to guide us in the search for success. It may be won at too great a cost. Sometimes we cry out with alarm at the daring, of the indifferent and self sufficient, who insist that they need no religion at all, that it is worthless and unavailing. What are we to do? I admit that the danger to our brotherhood, and indeed to the whole of Society is very real. Materialism is a disrupting force while Judaism makes for progress. But we can do nothing better, nothing more effective as far as I can see, to stem the tide, than to gather more closely together in our small groups, encourage one another and become ever more and more enthusiastic ourselves. Above all, we must show that in our own lives, the power of religion makes for righteousness and love. Then shall it be said to us "O people that dwellest in Zion at Jerusalem thou shalt weep no more. He will surely be gracious unto thee at the voice of thy cry; when He shall hear He will answer thee. They that sow in tears shall reap in joy".[3] We may even believe that our neighbours, seeing that faith brings confidence and hope, will before long follow us to the temple of our God.

Archives, Liberal
Jewish Synagogue, London

[1] From Browning's poem, "The Confessional."

[2] From Tennyson's poem, "Wages."

[3] Isaiah 30:19 and Psalm 126:5.

IMMORTALITY IN LITERATURE

February 16, 1924

<u>Isaiah</u>. Chapter 59, Verse 21. "My spirit that is upon thee, and my words which I have put in thy mouth, shall not depart out of thy mouth, or out of the mouth of thy seed, nor out of the mouth of thy seed's seed, saith the Lord, from henceforth and for ever. . ."

The first essential quality of an enduring book is the undying worth of its subject. We have to distinguish in literature as in life between the emotional and the rational, and between the rational and the aesthetic. Works that are purely intellectual may be forgotten or superseded. They partake of the finality of the mind which conceived them. Theories are refuted and discarded, and their author's influence is annihilated.

On the other hand, works may be immortal which app[eal] to the emotions, or to that side of the human faculty which is ever the same. These are the works which call into healthy exercise some emotion, whether exaltative or depressive, and which are centred about that highest of emotions - love; whether self-love, family love, state love, or cosmic love. So soon as literature becomes lacerative or morbid, it loses its chance of everlasting life.

Again, while rationalistic treatises on the philosophy of beauty perish and are forgotten, many works, being beautiful in themselves, live for ever. They are retained for their purely aesthetic power. As things of beauty their charm endures for ever. For example: certain poems of Tennyson may remain immortal for their sweet rhythm and polished form. There is also a class of immortal works which owe their position to the fact that they contain realistic descriptions of certain interesting times and places - in short, for their local colour. Thus we find in Chaucer's works an account of the manners and customs of early England. Froissart describes chivalric Europe with admirable skill and vividness. As the passion for tracing the evolution of thoughts and customs to their remote birth becomes stronger and more general, the consideration given to Chaucer and Froissart is augmented.

Equally important with the nature of the subject is the manner of treatment. The mind of the immortal must be capable of a vast breadth and range; it must be able to conceive a generalisation. A literary teacher who is to influence posterity must see beyond and above his generation. He must be able to withdraw himself from the conflicting maze of passing events, and must prove himself indifferent to contemporary prejudices. The calm understanding, which is pre-eminently part of his mental attitude, is only possible to him if he is untrammeled by the passing predilections and fleeting passions of his contemporaries.

We go to the Immortals for original life-giving thoughts - something we can take and assimilate and pass on. Hunger for ideas. Immortals never fail us - "That's true - That's beautiful - I shall not forget that."

I want to illustrate what I have said by reference to three different modern writers - who have been dead just long enough I think for us to estimate their worth, but I don't think you are very familiar with these three. - you know them a little only. Perhaps you will wonder how I dare to call them immortal in literature since so soon after their death you young people don't know them very well.

I believe you have absorbed their ideas - They have become alive in the world. You have taken them from other authors perhaps whom you have learned to love. They have entered into the current philosphy of the day - even of your friends and acquaintances and the writers of newspapers and magazines.

Take first Thomas Carlyle. John Morley has compared Carlyle to a spiritual volcano. May we say further that his action can never become extinct? Is it not probable that as the artificiality of life increases, the teaching of Carlyle, the lover of realities, will attain ever greaer value? For in these days of physical, mental, and moral exhaustion, the influence of Carlyle, with his devotion to the "Beneficent Whip" and "Masterful Mind," can only be stimulating. In the days of recuperation, which may follow with the turn of the pendulum, the world will listen with eager sympathy to Carlyle, as with ruthless severity he denounces those who tamper with fact, hiding themselves from life's sternness under a tissue of shams and lies.

Carlyle's immortality does not rest only upon his destructive criticism of life's vanities. We owe to him, in the second place, our appreciation of the rights of democracy. It was Carlyle who preached that a world is all out of joint unless the best men rule, and that class distinctions and conventional privileges should be of no real account to serious, honest thinkers. This is the note which he sounds in his Past and Present, and it echoes and re-echoes in all his works. With the progress of time, this teaching will win to itself even greater credit, and therefore, we may maintain that Carlyle's influence will permanently endure.

In the French Revolution, Carlyle showed that the upper classes are helpless, unless they keep up friendly connections with the people. Many of us believe that a period of anarchy can only be averted, in our present state of civilisation, by the blending of class with class in human sympathy, and in human honesty. If the contrasts between riches and poverty are to become ever more striking, the sight of unthinking idlers and of callous pleasure-seekers will inflame the minds of desperate men and women with ever greater effect. Then will men look to Carlyle for help and advice in postponing their doom.

Carlyle's third claim to immortality rests upon his gospel of work. He, better perhaps than any other writer, taught that work alone justifies existence and develops character. His invectives against the idle and luxurious have not been surpassed in fierceness by any modern socialist. In the fourth place we are indebted to Carlyle for forcing us to reverence that which is too grand for us to comprehend.

He drove puerile theorists and easy-going philosophers on to their knees while contemplating the "everlasting yes, and the everlasting no."[1] Whether he was writing history or biography, or musing on the enigmas of life, he loved to dwell upon the deep struggle which goes on continually between the nature of man and the problems and confusions with which he is surrounded. The idea of mist and gloom, penetrated her[e] and there by radiant light, controlled his life and thought. But Carlyle would not shut his eyes to the mist and gloom. He gropes his way about in it, all the time denouncing the more timid folk who try to lift a corner by artificial means, in order to lead a comfortable life.

Carlyle lives among us as the great preacher of action; he calls upon all generations to grapple with doubt, and to crush it or to die in the attempt. Like Dante and Browning he abhors the indifferent, colourless people, who move through life with "unlit lamps and ungirt loin."

George Eliot will, may we venture to say, be immortal for four distinct reasons.

Because of her truthfulness, since in none of her novels did she swerve from fact for the sake of effect. She was a writer of the realistic type and every page of her works contains some marvel of observation. As an example of George Eliot's faithful representation of human nature, I would remind you of Maggie Tulliver's love for Stephen Guest. George Eliot found in her own history an example of the way in which an intensely passionate, strong nature can devote itself to a superficial human weather-cock. We would have closed the <u>Mill on the Floss</u> with greater satisfaction if Maggie had not shown herself so pitiably weak. But George Eliot understood what Maggie was capable of, and in painting her life with a relentless pen, she familiarised the world with this phase of women's yearning for love.

George Eliot's delicacy and subtlety of mind afford the second explanation of her immortality. Perhaps she owed it to her scientific training that she could penetrate into the secrets of life and character. It was this power which made her find hidden beauties in characters, which to the ordinary observer would have been classed as commonplace. To our great psychologist, no human being is commonplace; in every character she can trac[ ] a peculiar idiosyncracy or peculiar tendency. Many of us would consider the Amos Barton of real life ordinary and dull. In the <u>Scenes of Clerical Life</u> we see him as a loveable soul, full of beautiful possibilities.

George Eliot owes her unique position, in the third place, to her extreme human sympathy. She felt the sadness of life, and grieved with the mourners; she recognised its happiness, and laughed with the joyful. When George Eliot once asked her husband what he thought of her works, he answered that he found them all terribly sad. The novelist was unconscious that her writing could have this effect. Her soul was imbued with the sorrows of the world, and it displayed its inmost depths in her novels. That is the secret of her sympathy. She did not only depict the troubles of others, she revealed her share in them.

But her homely humour is as sympathetic as her pathos. She painted work-a-day folk, "not too fine and good for human nature's daily food." She laughs at the Mrs. Poysers[2] of life with such delicious kindliness that we are infected and laugh also.

The fourth characteristic of George Eliot which makes for immortality, is her own consciousness of her mission. She felt that an artist who is true to fact, is in the van of political and social reformers. Novelists who can make their readers feel "that the whole world is kin," advance the cause of humanity more successfully than the most democratic statesmen, even though they succeed in bringing into law numbers of drastic measures of reform. Other tales besides <u>Uncle Tom's Cabin</u>, have become the mother of beneficent alteration and reform, and because their influence is less direct, it may be all the more powerful and lasting.

George Eliot's stern conception of right and duty, her spirituality and singleness of purpose, have dropped into her works the seeds of immortality.

Then let us consider Robert Browning as our third.

As the world grows more sceptical, men and women will turn with ever increasing eagerness to the arch-optimist, Robert Browning, for spiritual refreshment and consolation. It is for his intense, unswerving, unquestioning faith that he will always be valued. Browning was a poet of the individual, and his one study is human character. But, unlike George Eliot, he takes the exceptional character, places it in exceptional circumstances, and deals with it in an exceptional way. He introduces us to a great variety of characters, and perhaps this universality, which equals that of Shakespeare, and has been surpassed by no other poet, may be considered as his second claim to immortality. Above all, Robert Browning's doctrine of love deserves to be considered as a "pillar of light" to all ages, both for the grandeur of its conception and the depths of its significance. The poet taught that love and religion are interchangeable terms, for those who love intensely must, consciously or unconsciously, acknowledge that "God's in the heavens; all's well on earth."[3] Life is but a probation, a fight against evil circumstances, and there is a heaven for those who nobly fail. Because love is eternal, death can only be a turning-point in life; because love transcends and differs from all other emotions, it must be part of the Divine Spirit, which is revealed in every part of creation.

Browning feels no despair in contemplating brutal specimens of humanity. In the fact that Guido's mother loved him, he finds full justification for his creation, brute though he was, in the image of his Maker; because on the scaffold Guido cries to the wife he has wronged, Browning hopes for his possible perfectibility in another world.[4]

Thus Browning taught that we can reach God through love, and sees in His existence a perfect explanation of all doubts and perplexities.

We have called up from the dark past, the true and honest Carlyle, the brave and earnest George Eliot, and the faithful and loving Browning, and we hve tried to show that each one holds in his hands, a torch made of eternal fire. It may be that Carlyle, George Eliot, and Robert Browning are less read now than they were ten years ago. But, although the time may be past for them to be read by the many, it does not seem probably that the time will ever come when they will cease to be read by the few. The full weight is felt by the most cultured, and, by them, transmitted, to the masses. For this reason the style of the old masters hardly affects the question of their immortality, inasmuch as they are introduced to the general reader by men who have time and inclination to think before they try to understand. Carlyle, "with the deep no-meaning in his fiery heart," Browning, with his sturdy defiance of a lazy public, were often wantonly grotesque. They liked to clothe a rude thought in rough phraseology, and did not heed the protests of their critics. George Eliot's sentences sometimes [lacked] life, and often they are too involved to be impressive. But when once the mannerisms of the masters had been grappled with and their works had been found to possess the roots of life, they are passed on to posterity as an everlasting possession.

For the thoughts of great authors seem to live apart from the books in which they can be read; they are absorbed by humanity and so retained for ever.

Is it not this which has happened to the greatest of all books? People who never read the Bible - quote from it sometimes. Phrases are very familiar to them which they never suspect to come from the Bible. They may never have read those books of the Bible in which these familiar passages are to be found, but the world has seized these phrases and they belong to it for ever. The subject matter of the Bible is of eternal interest. In the Bible, described in fitting language, you find ideas about God and goodness, life and evil, joy and death, hope and peace, love and justice, all these ideas humanity needs for ever.

God says to the great men and women of the world, "My spirit that is upon thee, and my words which I have put in thy mouth, shall not depart out of thy mouth, nor out of the mouth of thy seed, nor out of the mouth of thy seed's seed, saith the [Lord] from henceforth and for ever." And these men and women make literature - not only the literature of the Bible but so-called secular literature which contains beautiful thoughts set in beautiful words - which indeed reveal God's eternal spirit through the art of man.

Your library can bring you near to these men and women. They become your friends ready to help you at all times - never weary - never moody - always reliable. On this Sabbath afternoon - in the name of Religion, I would appeal to you to seek real literature and not to waste time on books less good. Literature is not made up of serious books only - you can laugh with George Eliot and many other humourists and you find yourself laughing with the Immortals in literature. Their life-giving thoughts create joy - But young as you are you have not time for trash. Train yourselves <u>now</u> therefore to recognise trash and so be able to throw it away. Be able to take your authors measure - Learn to do this by communing with the highest - Seek God Himself - in prayer and in thought - then you will find all the things that are good, for these are part of God.

>Archives, Liberal Jewish
>Synagogue, London

[1] <u>Sartor Resartus</u>

[2] A reference to the sharp-tongued, shrewd, yet kindly, mistress of the Hall Farm in George Eliot's novel, <u>Adam Bede</u>.

[3] A paraphrase of the most famous lines in Browning's "Pippa Passes."

[4] From "The Ring and The Book."

SEEN AT THE TATE GALLERY

>February 7th, 1925

"And Moses called every wise hearted man in whose heart the Lord put wisdom and understanding, to know how to work all the work for the service of the sanctuary."[1]

Some chapters of Exodus are given up entirely to minute details about the building and decorating of the tabernacle. At first you are inclined to say "how dull" - then you gradually realise that behind all this dullness is real religion - the artist trying to put a message of God in the sanctuary to bind the worshippers to God, through beauty.

And we believers think of the world as a sanctuary because it bears on itself the impress of God. Beauty is one of the vehicles along which God passes into the hearts of man. This world becomes a sanctuary when we think of God in it. Quickly we clear away the ugly and the sordid and the evil which is under our control - so that the sanctuary, the world, may be more beautiful - more fitting for the Divine presence. From the earliest times we are told that men tried to produce with their brush ideas more beautiful than anything they saw. Then, gradually, if they are in touch with the Unseen they see in ordinary everyday objects, the impress of the Omnipresent Divine Spirit. So Browning says in [his poem] Fra Lippo Lippi:

    For, don't you mark? we're made so that we love
    First when we see them painted, things we have passed
    Perhaps a hundred times, nor cared to see;
    .... Art was given for that;
    God uses us to help each other so,
    Lending our minds out.

If you saw the Exhibition of drawings and paintings by Austrian children during the war you will have seen how this blending of the ideal with the real was carried out by untaught minds. By untaught I mean, that they found their own methods of reproducing what God gave them. Art is in this sense an expression of faith and can influence our outlook on life. George Eliot wrote to Burne Jones: "Your work makes life larger and more beautiful to me."

The great English landscape painter Constable said that landscape was one of the words which proceeded from God. It is then not inappropriate at a Sabbath Service to consider the meaning of a few pictures, probably known to you all, for they are to be seen at the Tate Gallery - a gallery you can visit whenever you have the time - for it is near and convenient. Our world, let me remind you again, is a sanctuary. We work there and feed there and dress there, and do all things which are, we say, on the material plane - but God is in the world with us all the time. That's why we dare to call it a sanctuary. When we aspire to a high standard in our every day activities we are engaged in a form of prayer. That prayer or aspiration is suitable for a sanctuary. The artist makes our sanctuary more beautiful and his work reminds us of the presence of God from Whom cometh wisdom and understanding.

First I would draw your attention to three pictures by George Morland who lived between 1763-1804. The first one is a very simple homely scene - a farm-house gate with a beautiful tree at the back and lovely sky effects behind the tree. The cowherd is leaning on the back of the cow - the milkmaid is coming out from the thatched farm building, her pail in her hand - she stops, holding the open door. It is so natural for her to look at the man - just as natural as it is for the cows and the pigs to seek food while they wait patiently the man's pleasure, poking their noses into the grass. The girl and the man look at one another and there is an arresting expression on his plain and rather dull face and a look of wonder in her eyes. We all know what is passing between them. The story has been the same since the beginning of life - the artist tells it to us in its purity and beauty. A few inches away Morland shows a wayside inn. Mother sits on the grass nursing her baby and two other children cuddle on to her lap. A little way off, two men - probably merchants, ride away, deep in conversation. The old inn suggesting rest and refreshment stands in its picturesque simplicity. It has supplied the meeting ground for all the different human groups - seeking fellowship - the need to exchange thought and friendliness - It is universal need - which we know so well - testifies does it not, to the common source of human life. Should we recognise our kinship if one God had not created us? Between these two pictures hangs the Fortune-Teller. A woman of the world sits at the table with a game of chance in front of her. A very sophisticated, self-righteous man of fashion has come to pay his court to a frightened girl who looks from the dice-board into his face, her expression full of anxious longing. She aches to know her future and feels that it depends on the whim of this magnificent superior being - in his foppish clothes with his supercilious smile. The fashionable mamma in her furs and satins sits complacently watching the game in which her own child is the central play-thing. Here we have the same dread of loneliness - of being left out in the passage of life, which the wayside inn satisfied so beautifully and simply in the other picture; here we have the story of the girl's expectancy which we saw in the dairy-maid but this picture is very different from the other pictures. Here life is represented in its artificiality - the divine phases of human life are smirched by contact with something mean and sordid. Here the men and women of the sanctuary are appraising their life values without reference to the Perfect standard, God, the author of Life. They are influenced by that which is petty and evanescent and ignore the essential and eternal.

Do you remember Gainsborough's Parish Clerk? You can't look at him without recognising a man who has lived. His face is marked by the passage of years, by sorrow. His hands hold the Bible open while his eyes wearing a rather pained, dissatisfied expression look up out of the Church window into the world outside. From that world light comes and touches his face and makes it beautiful. But there is a look about this Parish Clerk of pained protest. He is the sentinel standing by the book of Books. He has toiled all his life to make men obey the regulations of his Church - but the old eyes have seen much waywardness in that world outside, many signs of irregular living and rebellion. The world may want to cover his face with its light but the old servant defies it. He clings to the power of the spirit and will believe in it to the end, even though his faithfulness involves some pain, some bitterness, some disappointment. He will defy the onslaughts of time however much these may bruise.

I felt that Millais' "Vale of Rest" was wonderful in colour but the faces of the girls who were engaged in preparing the grave were anything but peaceful. There was a tensity in the pose of the figures - a look of agony in the eyes. These women knew that death has its terror - they knew it meant suffering and separation which cannot be ignored. They could dig the graves - they _must_ obey the law of life - rebellion was useless. Yet all the while they _did_ rebel. Their faces make this clear. Nevertheless God's earth is green and God's sky is glorious, and love is eternal and the sisters are working in the Vale of Rest - and the beyond is full of hope and joys for evermore. Yet they rebel.

Burne Jones' girls admiring their reflections in the beautiful lake have also curiously intense expressions. They are not influenced by mere personal vanity. They press forward to read in their own faces, revealed in the water, the secrets which the future holds for them.

We lose some of this emotional tensity in the room dedicated to Watts. This great master dresses great intellectual conceptions in beautiful forms. Hope surmounts the whole world - her eyes are blind as her path is lighted by the glow of faith, symboli [sed] by the one solitary star.

THE NATURE OF TRUE RELIGION 45

Love takes Life over the rocks; in vain love tries to push death away from the door of his home. Everywhere all round the room are thoughts clothed in man and woman idealised for the purpose, speaking first to the mind of man and then through sheer beauty entering his heart. Contrast these pictures with the homely reality of Luke Fildes' "Doctor". I remember well when this picture was first exhibited - the excitement it created - it was not because of its good painting - not because of any intrinsic beauty it contained but chiefly because everybody knew so much about it. We all knew the doctor - sitting watching the little suffered asleep on two chairs. He was watching - he had done all he could - he knew the limits of his skill - he had given it all but the child on the chairs was desperately ill. We knew what the Father was feeling as he stood up behind facing the hideous possibility, while he tried tenderly to comfort his wife, the child's Mother who had momentarily succumbed to grief. We knew how it was she was bowled over. The child slept, there was nothing more she could do. The uncertainty of her child's fate overwhelmed her we understood. And we found ourselves praying for that child, as is our wont; and the child made us feel our dependence on our God, as children always do.

Before we go, let us just pause for a moment before two more pictures. The one shows us a lovely green vale - beautiful trees on either side and a carter bringing home his last load, on his wagon. He and his horses are weary. They have had a heavy day but they have nearly done, and they are swinging along, full of the joy of achievement. A happy group of children run out to meet them and dance madly in front of them. This picture suggests joy - in its freshness and purity - joy which makes the blood in ones veins course more quickly. It is just the joy of life which physical exertion brings - the joy of harmony with the general scheme of things; the joy of human sympathy. These toilers <u>live</u> the truth inscribed in our prayer-books. They know that work sweetens rest and rest gives meaning to work.

Lastly we watch for a moment the young man and woman on an open boat, working in the teeth of fierce wind and rain and collecting their only harvest, a harvest of seaweed which they are snatching from the sea. We recognise the hardness of the life - and the courage of these young people. While we look we feel the dignity of the partnership and the triumph of their humanity. Surely these people are working with their God, who folds them in His eternal arms, and their God is the God of the elements, Who taketh up the world as a very little thing.

Friends, you and I have few opportunities to visit galleries and to stand in reverent wonder before works of art, but let us take these opportunities whenever possible, remembering that our God is the God of Beauty, Who is revealed through Beauty. The true artist who makes the revelation clear to us, is one of those wise-hearted men in whose heart the Lord has put wisdom and understanding to know how to work all the work for the service of the Sanctuary.

Archives, Liberal
Jewish Synagogue, London

[1] From Exodus 36:2.

THE NATURE OF TRUE RELIGION

CLUB LETTER NO. 134

May 1951

I am going to talk about the Garden of Eden in this month's letter. Why? you ask. It <u>was</u> planted so long ago. Is it of interest to us now? I don't think it was ever <u>planted</u> at all, but it has given the world a beautiful allegory which we can adapt to our present day life.

The Garden was full of the loveliest plants and Adam and Eve revelled in the beauty of the place. You, I am sure, love beauty for its own sake, and try to make your homes beautiful. So the thought of a perfect garden interests you. We have in modern times a school of painters satisfied with their works being original and individual, queer, but not primarily beautiful. For myself, I want loveliness all the time - I share with John Ruskin and William Wordsworth the desire to make common articles reveal beauty through their shape or colour; but you may prefer the modern art. Adam and Eve roamed in their beautiful garden in which God had planted every species of flowers and plants. Reading into the story, I don't think our primitive couple worshipped God. I don't fancy they loved Him. They were afraid of Him and His power and they were intimate with Him. They thought they shared the beauty of the Garden and God walked in it even as they did.

The beginning of true religion is generally traced to the feeling of awe, but Adam and Eve hardly felt that at all. When the serpent suggested that Eve should taste the forbidden fruit and know the difference between good and evil, the adventure of disobedience interested her, and probably she did not think she would be found out. We ask if we would consider any knowledge forbidden to us today. God as the God of Truth reveals Himself gradually to those who seek Him in sincerity. The search is generally fraught with painful efforts, but if a successful discovery is made, success is attended with satisfaction. Indeed, a new item of knowledge gives us joy but also inevitably a sense of new responsibility. According to the legend, Adam and Eve were not yet ready for more knowledge. They were quite undeveloped. They wandered about their beautiful garden, unaware of their nudity. They had no ugly thoughts about sex. To them sex must have seemed just beautiful and in harmony with the surrounding beauty of the Garden. They would surely have said that when ignorance is bliss it is folly to be wise.

Today we hold generally the exactly opposite view and encourage people to seek knowledge. Much vice originates, we think, in ignorance. Because parents have not taught their children the laws of life clearly and reverently, the young people associate lust with love and license with the highest enjoyment possible to human nature. The thought of a God who would be jealous of His children's acquisition of knowledge is repugnant as well as absurd. God lays the Book of Knowledge open before His children, and the more complete their knowledge, the greater their virility and in consequence their power to work with and for their God. Adam and Eve having the knowledge for which they were not prepared, were sent forth into the world to learn that they must work in order to attain, and that pain is part of the human inheritance to be borne with courage until, as often happens, pain is conquered through a better understanding of the laws of causation. Eve would suffer through ignorance, but gradually some new knowledge would bring her a measure of relief. Through pain she might obtain understanding, and acquire the power of sympathy. It might make her capable of greater self control and, indeed, of self knowledge. In the Garden of Eden both Adam and Eve were

THE NATURE OF TRUE RELIGION

provided with all their wants without any effort on their part. They might think the change to hard work a form of punishment for their disobedience. But in time they would know that "getting something for nothing" brings a curse to mankind. In the mistaken belief that gain without effort can prove a blessing instead of a curse, we find the beginning of the gambler's and the spiv's[1] philosophy. Once endowed with the power to distinguish between good and evil, Adam and Eve were free to make their own lives. But it must have been brought home to them that with their knowledge of good and evil they had acquired the responsibility for their own conduct.

About 3,000 years have elapsed since the story of Adam and Eve was written. Quite a long time! But we have still many of their lessons to learn. When you read the story, did you notice the eagerness with which Adam and Eve tried to pass off the responsibility for their disobedience to someone else? Eve had been beguiled by the serpent; Adam had been led astray by his wife. But out into the world they were no longer carried in safety by their God; they had chosen to have knowledge of life. Surely they could seek God's guidance, but the responsibility for their actions must rest henceforth on themselves.

Today people are lamenting the discovery of the Atom Bomb. If it was not known, they say, we should not today have to face the probability that civilisation is to be wiped out. No defence can really be adequate. But knowledge is good. The responsibility for using the Atom Bomb for good or evil purposes belongs to those in possession of it. Good comes from God and therefore must prevail. We dare no longer try, as did Adam and Eve, to shift the responsibility from one person or one national group to another. We have to find the way to use all knowledge in the service of God who gave it. Do you aspire to raise yourself above the masses in knowledge and experience and achieve your resolution? But make no mistake - God and man will expect more from you now that you have advanced to a higher plane. Let us work for the time when the power which is inherent in the Atom Bomb may be used for the happiness and prosperity of all men.

Once more we come back to consider the necessity to bring our experience before God and to seek His direction. Life is confusing. Adam and Eve, we may suppose, were thoroughly enjoying their idle lives surrounded with beauty which challenged all power of description. They were helpmeets for one another. The beautiful word helpmate emerges and suggests perfect companionship to our modern young people who are inclined to mould their lives on a big query. But Eve sinned. She took of the forbidden tree because, having enough in her own right, she wanted something more which she could not legitimately have. In the light of developed spiritual light it was no sin to seek greater knowledge. But Eve fully believed she was sinning and yielded to temptation and fell. It was because she so yielded, believing herself tempted and to be disobeying the command of God, that posterity has held her to have sinned. Insofar as Adam followed her and allowed himself also to be tempted, he too stands out for all time as a sinner.

I ask you to draw the tremendously important lesson from this legendary story of Adam and Eve. Our liturgy includes prayers which suggest that we should be guarded against temptation. We have to acquire knowledge, but we must not shirk the responsibility of having knowledge. Generation by generation we learn through our own efforts; maybe through the endurance of pain, certainly also through the experience of joy, the true values of life, i.e. that which is good and that which is evil. We have no right to think we can accept God's blessings and nothing more is

THE NATURE OF TRUE RELIGION   51

expected of us. God and humanity challenge us to choose
the good and reject the evil. Light will be thrown on our
paths if we seek to work for God. "Thus saith the Lord:
Stand ye in the ways and see and ask for the old paths,
where is the good way and walk therein, and ye shall find
rest for your souls." (Jeremiah, VI, verse 16.)

> Private Collection,
> Hannah Feldman, London

[1] A British colloquial expression used, by the 1890s, to refer to someone living by his wits, without working, especially by the "racing game." (E. Partridge, <u>A Dictionary of Slang and Unconventional English</u>, London, 1970, Vol. II, p. 1425.)

CLUB LETTER NO. 3

March 1939

"He every one that thirsteth, come ye to the waters."
This call, taken from Isaiah 55, is a call to prayer. Some
of you ask: "Why pray? What is the good of it?"

I think we need to pray. We are incomplete without
contact with the living God - and that is what prayer
means. We are beings created by the living Spirit of
Goodness, Truth, Love and Justice, who wish to return and
draw from our source renewed energy with which to carry on
our lives. We pray, then, for the increase of our
spiritual power. We need sustenance and exercise for our
spirits, quite as much as we need food and gymnastics for
our body. We meditate on God's law of righteousness, and
the desire to be better and to do better fills our hearts.
Why pray? <u>We pray in the first place that we may live more fully</u>.

We are all conscious of some wrong doing in our lives which separates us from God. We pray for the power to overcome evil in ourselves, and to become one with God. We are each of us directly responsible for the conduct of our lives. We have to destroy the wrong by our own efforts. The consciousness that God is real - that something of His spirit is in our hearts, even while, in its perfection, it is the supreme life force in the universe, this faith gives us the power to overcome sin, for it makes our will strong and directed towards good. <u>We pray, therefore in the second place for self advancement in righteousness.</u>

As we pray, we feel ourselves united with every aspiring human being; his life and well being are part of our own lives. We understand his needs, for we actually share them, and so <u>the third blessing which we discover in praying is the unity of mankind.</u>

But we would like to alter the world; we would wish to see some of the evils and misery, cruelty and injustice swept away. <u>So we pray for the removal of evil</u>, though it still persists and sometimes seems to grow in magnitude. What then is the good of praying?

The good lies in another direction. In prayer, we realise the value and power of human personality. We pray, and the possibility of achievement is unveiled before our eyes. We can choose good and reject evil. That is our human prerogative. The same privilege belongs to the men and women who are in positions of great power and responsibility. We would not surrender the freedom of human personality. <u>When we pray we show the connection between belief and conduct</u>.

Freedom is part of the human inheritance. Prayer has revealed the power of man to create the better world through obedience and loyalty to the laws of God. It is <u>for us</u> to help in establishing the kingdom. We must not ask

God to do it for us, and so surrender our human independence. He has offered us the power to work with Him. Arise, shine![1]

We love to pray for our dear ones, and sometimes we pray and the calamity we wish to avert comes just as if we had not prayed at all. Why then, we ask, does not God hear? I believe that God <u>does</u> hear, and it is well for us to think of our dear ones when we are considering the reality of God in prayer. Let us seek from His revelation ways to increase our wisdom and our power of loving. Perhaps we shall lose some of our selfishness and our ability to give pain. But when things don't do right, as we believe, for our beloved, we must remember the limitation of our vision and that what seems evil to us may in the end be good. <u>Through prayer we learn to trust in the supreme love of God, and that He acts only through love</u>.

Life is sweet for you all. In spite of its sad, gloomy passages, you have the power of learning and loving. You can see some beauty in the world, even if the glimpses are few and far between. You can sometimes see the wonders of nature and hear glorious music. Most of you have behind you the security of home life and the trust of those who love you. You, because you are young, can experience the pleasures of the body and the mind. You feel grateful for life. <u>In prayer you can give thanks</u>.

May I appeal to you to pray daily - to feel yourself consciously in the presence of God? If doubts assail you, face them and wrestle with them. In the end, they will, I believe, add strength to your faith. Don't give up prayer because it is difficult. Learn to create the right atmosphere for prayer, the atmosphere of reverence and humility. Clear your hearts before you pray from selfishness and insincerity, and your mind from impure thoughts. Then throw yourself into the "Everlasting arms"[2] of God, and in the depths of your heart you will hear Him speak. "Speak Lord, for thy servant heareth."[3] I beg of you not to delay praying until you are too faint and weak for want of spiritual nourishment to pray at all. <u>Pray now</u>! Tomorrow it may be too late.

Private Collection,
Hannah Feldman, London

[1]"Arise, Shine," a phrase Lily Montagu repeated in numerous sermons (and the title of an address delivered at the West Central Club on October 11, 1959) is from Isaiah 60:1.

[2]Another phrase frequently used by Lily Montagu, the image of God's "everlasting arms" is from Deuteronomy 33:27.

[3]1 Samuel 3:9.

II. CONCEPTS OF JUDAISM

INTRODUCTION

Lily Montagu believed that above all, Judaism was a religion. Its adherents were bound together not by blood or sense of nationality but by faith in the One Universal God. Moreover, as the sermons and letters included in this chapter reveal, Judaism, for her, was a <u>true</u> religion--personal in nature, universal in outlook, and based on religious faith as expressed in the conduct of one's daily life.

Club Letters 33-35, part of a series of five, focus on Lily Montagu's conception of Judaism. One finds here the equation of Judaism with ethical monotheism. In Club Letter 33, Montagu insists that Judaism "does not mean keeping laws. It means a way of life." This life, as she describes it, is a life of holiness, of acting righteously in imitation of God. In Letter 34, Lily Montagu makes a connection between faith in God and faith in the possibilities of the human personality. If God has created us, she maintains, we must be like Him in some way. That is, as children of God, we possess an innate spiritual power that can make "all good things possible." It enables us to develop our capabilities, act kindly and lovingly towards others, and work, again with others, towards making the world a safer and better place in which to live.

In formulating this conception of Judaism, Lily Montagu was deeply indebted to Claude Montefiore, whose scholarly writings convinced her that it was possible to equate Judaism with true religion. The Orthodoxy of her father seemed antithetical to real religion as she understood it. Yet unlike her father, Montefiore insisted that there were many equally valid interpretations of Judaism. His own interpretation, which he identified as Liberal Judaism, closely matched Lily Montagu's conception of true religion. Based on the moral teachings of the Biblical prophets, it emphasized the personal relationship between the individual and God, maintained that the "Fatherhood of God" implies the "Brotherhood" of all human beings, and stressed the intrinsic connection between faith and daily conduct.

Like Montefiore, then, Lily Montagu came to use the terms "Judaism" and "Liberal Judaism" interchangeably. For her, Liberal Judaism *was* Judaism, and Judaism (or Liberal Judaism) an example of true religion itself. These equations become clear in Club Letter 35. Maintaining that "we can no longer believe in a personal Messiah, for we cannot conceive of any human being with power to lead the world," she declares it to be a "principle of Judaism" that each individual become a "Messiah or messenger of God, working for righteousness and together bringing nearer the dawn of the perfect day." In other words, she takes the Liberal Jewish concept of a universal messianic age of peace in substitution for the traditional notion of a personal messiah and, like Montefiore, simply labels this concept as "Jewish." Her justification for making this substitution rests on the Liberal Jewish belief (or as she maintains, on the *Jewish* belief), in spiritual progress, here referring both to personal spiritual growth and to the collective growth of religious knowledge.

Club Letter 6, which gives expression to Lily Montagu's belief in immortality, stands out as a rare instance of her using rabbinic writings as a source of her theology. This reference, however, is vague and not

CONCEPTS OF JUDAISM   57

surprisingly, reveals no real knowledge of rabbinic texts. On the whole, as Club Letters 33-35 reveal, and as the other sermons in this chapter and elsewhere also show, the ancient Jewish sources to which Lily Montagu turned were almost exclusively Biblical in origin. What's more, with the notable exceptions of the Levitical injunction to be holy and the Deuteronomic "Shema" (Dt. 6:4 ff., declaring God's Unity and Israel's promise to love and obey Him), she seems to have gained greatest insight from the teachings of the Psalms and the Prophets.

In quoting from these texts, Lily Montagu consistently maintained that faith in God, which she identified as the "first principle of Judaism," did not depend on intellectual knowledge but rather on opening oneself up to the Divine Presence. It was the emotional rather than the intellectual component of Judaism, she believed, that brought one closer to God. Yet recognizing that communion with God did not always occur spontaneously, she placed great value on those traditional holidays and observances which were capable of stimulating inner piety. During her lifetime, Lily Montagu delivered tens if not hundreds of sermons on Jewish observances, festivals and holy days. Those included here are illustrative of such sermons. In "The Sabbath," Montagu describes synagogue worship as an important means of stimulating private devotion. It helps us, she writes, "feel the influence of the past" and stirs us to commune "with the living God." In "A New Year Begins Today," she labels the custom of placing a Mezuzah on the door of one's home an important "call to love" whose words are continual reminders of God's eternal presence, and in Club Letter 133, points to the seder (the Passover ritual meal) as that which helps consecrate the home by transforming it into a Divine Sanctuary.

The universal significance that Lily Montagu attached not only to ritual observances but also to Judaism's holidays is very much in keeping with her understanding of Judaism as real religion. She viewed the Sabbath principle as "one of the great gifts which Jews have given to the world" and the New Year and Passover festivals as opportunities for greater self-expression. She further noted the intrinsic connection between conduct and faith, insisting that the New Year's "new beginning" was one of a "stronger faith which will affect our lives," revealing the principles of Judaism through our actions. Similarly, she saw the freedom of Passover not simply as a "casting off of control" but as an assuming of responsibility and a developing of one's potential. In conclusion, Lily Montagu's reassessment of Judaism's traditional observances and holidays stands out as part of a larger effort to redefine Judaism itself. Equating Judaism with Liberal Judaism, she helped create a conception of her ancestral religion that, by her definition, was necessarily and eternally true.

CLUB LETTERS NO. 33-35

WHAT IS JUDAISM?

No. 33
January, 1942

I was present at a conference a short while ago when a young mother asked that a pamphlet should be produced in answer to this question as it affects the modern boy and girl. It occurred to me that our young people might care for me to deal with this question. I cannot promise to offer a reply in one letter, but perhaps I might use a series of letters in the new year to deal with so important a subject.

There will be an immediate reaction among some of our young people to my suggestion that the question has a particular application to themselves as representing the youth of the day. They will probably protest that Judaism is the same for all time, since the days of the giving of the commandments on Mount Sinai until the present day. Judaism must be the same religion to be upheld at all costs without any relation to the time factor, past, present and future.

From one point of view this reply may be true, from another, it is essentially false, and I am going to try and explain in this and subsequent letters why this is the case.

When I was young, Judaism meant observance. A man was a good Jew if he kept his religion, and keeping religion implied the loyal observance of ancient laws and ceremonies. It was believed that God Himself was the authority for the importance of observances, that His will was revealed in the Pentateuchal code through a series of laws and commandments.

This point of view is no longer upheld today by our young people, but there are some eternal truths which Jews must and will believe in for all time. It is no use your saying: "Oh yes, I do believe that Judaism is in no way changed. Its obligations are for us what they were for our ancestors, but I just can't obey them in this country at the present day." If you really believed after the manner of your father, and you persist in your mode of life, you are living in sin. But you do not so believe. You say to yourself: "I like the old laws and customs. They meant so much to my dad when he was young, but the Eternal God who knows our ways could not have meant the laws for all time and in all countries. He knows that I just can't keep them. I keep three days a year and do what I can, and nobody will say I am not a good Jew, as far as is possible."

Now I want you all to use your minds in connection with these problems because the argument used above, which I hear over and over again, is not at all satisfactory. If Judaism is to be what it should be, the central fact in your life, you must find its meaning in quite another direction.

Judaism does not mean keeping laws. It means a way of life. Judaism is based on the belief in God, and that belief is good for all time. A man who professes Judaism should lead a life which he should attempt to harmonise with the God idea. The first principle in Judaism is the unity of God, and it is upon this principle that I want to dwell in this letter.

If you believe in God, you believe that God, the spirit of perfect righteousness, love, justice, beauty and truth, is in the universe and above it, that He lives in man and above him. The world, we are told by the Psalmist, reveals the glory of God, the earth declares His majesty. We read in Genesis that man was created in the image of God, and in Deuteronomy that His word is very nigh to us, in our heart and in our mind that we may do it.

Because God is one, the knowledge of God should fill the whole world and all parts of life can be made holy. All peoples are His children; there should be no conflict or divisions. Don't you think that the message of Judaism to the world concerns the brotherhood of man, and if it were properly delivered - through the example of our lives - there would be peace and cooperation between all men?

As regards your personal life, is it not clear that if you believe in God, you must have a standard in your work life and recreational activity, in your thoughts and in your feelings? God is one and indivisible. You cannot switch Him off your life when His presence seems inconvenient. If all of us who profess Judaism were to become conscious of the presence of God in our lives, and in our power to make contact with Him, don't you think that we should become better men and women?

The Jewish teachers of the past told us to seek to imitate God. They said that we needed no intercessor; we were responsible to God for the conduct of our lives and that we should go direct to Him for guidance and assistance. They spoke from their own experience, and it is your privilege and duty, if you profess Judaism, to verify the truth of their statements by your own efforts in testing their method. "Seek the Lord at all times: call upon Him while He is near."[1]

If we try to imitate God, we seek to act righteously. Everybody is tempted to fall below the best he knows, and it is only with God's help that we can keep ourselves free from the domination of selfishness or passion or greed. But the God of the universe is in our hearts, and we must give heed to Him. The God of truth demands truth from us even in the inward parts. Subterfuges, deceits and swindling won't do, nor will a pretence at sincerity, for God is one, and we have in our weak imperfect way to accept the ideal of truth which is another name for God.

Our God is the God of love, and He is ever present. Just think how often we try to act as if love did not exist in the world. We are unkind and thoughtless and indifferent and <u>forget</u> all about love. Yet we say the Shema once or twice a day and believe that God asks us to give love with our entire being, so as to leave no room for ugly, jealous, sordid feeling. We can serve our God only with our best. The second best won't do.

If you profess Judaism, you must seek to be just to yourself by self discipline and self control and self development. You dare not spoil the good that is in you, for through being a Jew you dedicate that good to the service of God. You must use in God's cause your power of body, mind and soul. Then you must seek the good of other people, and see that they have the best opportunities for a good life, those indeed which you desire for yourself. The one God, being just, requires you to practise justice yourself, if you would imitate Him, not only for the people you love, but for those from whom you are distant by accident or by choice. There is room in God's world for every man and his right to be here is as good as yours.

God has made His world beautiful, and we have found it possible to spoil it. Through our wilful blindness, even the glory of nature may be wasted on us. Unless we train the eyes of children to see and their ears to hear, beauty makes little appeal to them.

We have all an artistic sense which can be cultivated because it is one of God's gifts which is universal. Let us seek beauty and reverence it, because it contains an element of the divine spirit.

I have spoken about the unity of God as the first principle of Judaism, and shown how it can affect our life as a community and as individuals. In my next letter, I will try to show more fully man's relation to God, and the possible effect of our loyalty to God in making the world progress towards goodness.

As I said at the beginning of my letter, in my view Judaism does not consist in keeping observances, though observances have an important place nevertheless in Jewish life. They will be put in their right place when we find the way of life which is Judaism. In conclusion I would only ask you to consider the difference between the way of life with God and the way of life without Him. Most of us <u>do</u> fear to be unworthy of the best we know. Some Jews today are trying to live in defiance of their Judaism. Nevertheless, Judaism is blamed for <u>their</u> shortcomings.

We would try to witness to our faith, to show that it is good to know that God is the Lord. Holding that faith we say: "The Lord is with us, we shall not fear."[2]

No. 34
February 1942

This is my second letter in the series: "What is Judaism?". In my first letter, I wrote of faith in God, and what it implies. In this letter, I want to write of our relations with one another. Perhaps it would be simpler to call this part of our discussion 'Faith in Man', for if we accept the suggestion that there is something divine in human personality, we must feel reverence for every man and trust that he is 'making for righteousness'. If, however, we can, as we want to do, consider <u>real</u> life, we claim that we cannot be expected to reverence our enemies when they have proved themselves cruel and treacherous, mean and crafty. As Jews, we can, I think, nevertheless, affirm that if we had, from the beginning, shown proper faith in man, the sadistic tendencies, which lead to moral degradation, and which we notice particularly in our enemies, would never have developed.

War is a large factor in creating the evils which we deplore most at the present time, but we cannot hold our enemies altogether responsible for the war conditions.

Before there was any idea or expectation of this present war, the moral and religious standard of life in every country, in every city, in every home, was far below that which belongs to those whose faith in God has led them to have faith in man. If we reverence the divine in man, we must again give him the 'large place' in which that divine element can grow. I recall with love and appreciation those words of the Psalmist: "God has set me in a large place."[3] This verse does not refer to good housing and open spaces, although we know that the child's satisfactory spiritual growth does require space and privacy, light and air; the words mean, I think, that every man requires freedom. He must not be bullied or oppressed; he must be given his opportunity to develop his personality; he must not be allowed to suffer through neglect from any curable form of ignorance or disease. He must be trained to show love and kindness to his fellow men, to seek truth, and to show mercy and justice to all with whom he comes in contact.

I say that none of us has been sufficiently alive to these obligations and war is one of the evils which has ensued. How often in our prayers, we ask for the power to distinguish between good and evil. We need God's light, in order that we may see light. Nevertheless, we allowed the economic misery of the Germans to become so intense, that they could find no true deliverance, and stumbled into hailing the advent of Hitler, and thought he was their saviour.

We must believe in the divine spark in every man, and yet with shame and anxiety we must say that it may be altogether hidden by human unkindness, if evil is allowed to increase without restraint. A magistrate told me the other day that an old man of 79 was brought before him for stealing a coat and put on probation. It was found on enquiry that the old man had been charged 55 times beginning when he was quite a young man and sent to prison for 6 weeks. When at long last, the man was told that the method of probation was to be tried, he looked surprised to the degree of bewilderment. Every week the probation officer lunched with him and was deeply interested in his account of himself, interested, you see, in <u>him</u> as a personality. Friends obtained for him the old age pension for which, till then, he had been considered ineligible, and his self respect rose wonderfully with the assurance of a reliable income. That man has made good because another man believed that in spite of his record there must be good in him, and that good must always be worth finding.

Will you consider for a few moments how your own life will be affected by faith in yourself as a being possessing something of God? The effect on yourself will be tremendous. Do you want to be something really worthwhile, a witness to the reality of God's existence, a <u>very</u> humble partner with God in creating righteousness and joy in a very small and very restricted corner of the world, that corner in which you have some small influence? You can achieve this high privilege, if you make yourself really fit in body, mind and soul. Sometimes, you say you are fed up, and it is no use your going on trying for the best; you are misunderstood, or circumstances are unfair and altogether hard. You feel you must give up trying. Judaism teaches that you have the power within you which makes all good things possible, and makes you feel ashamed to give up or even to fail. Take courage and remember that more than 2,000 years ago a religious genius wrote from experience: "The Lord is with me, I shall not fear." Take courage and test the power within you by formulating your faith in prayer, telling God about your hopes and difficulties, and asking for renewed faith in yourself. You will make good through your Judaism.

Faith in humanity makes a high standard of home life possible, for love between husband and wife, parents and children, sisters and brothers contains a great element of faith. As you are anxious for the well being of your beloved, you can easily believe that those who are bound to you by family ties reciprocate the same feeling. We are inclined to trust our home folk more than anyone else in the world, because through believing in the ideal of God's unity, we come to believe that the different elements in our home can be united by Him into one perfect whole. Our conception of friendship is based on faith. If any feeling of suspicion once gets into our hearts, our relation with our friend is spoiled. It is best to admit this fact and to let each go her own way. But if we have faith in man through faith in God, we do not suspect easily. We forgive readily, even as God does, although ours is the weak, imperfect way. We give opportunity for clearing up mistakes and misunderstandings in our human way through frank talk with one another, even as God invites us to lay our doubts and difficulties before Him in prayer.

We know that there is room in God's world for every type of man and woman, and they are our sisters and brothers, for we are all the children of God. We must not make life harder through our conduct for any individual we find in the world, for our faith in man which arises from our faith in God convinces us that his right to live is the same as our own. We all believe that we are working to build up a better world. That is our great hope and consolation in these days of suffering. The world can only be better when we can trust one another in our business life, our recreational life, and in our international life. It is, however, no good to try to live in a fool's paradise.

We <u>know</u> that there are crooks in business, men and women who have no appreciation of fairness in sport, governments which cannot be trusted. The time will certainly come when faith in man will be established, for God Himself, who created man in His image is a guarantee for the possibility that man can attain to trustworthiness, and if individuals can reach this stage in moral development, so assuredly must it be possible for nations.

It seems to me that the progress of the individual and of the nation depends in a large measure on man being able to complete satisfactorily a term of probation. As individuals, we must prove that we merit the confidence of God: "Ye shall be holy, for I the Lord Thy God am holy." In contact with God we can raise our standard of life, and this process leads to holiness. God will know if we ring true even to the inward parts. We cannot deceive Him. We must fit ourselves to become His servants and accept the fact that the process of probation will be hard and last a long time. If we deserve to be trusted by God to do His work, I believe we shall merit the confidence of man. In the world of the future, men will have the governments which reveal the stage of morality which they themselves have reached. In the past, some nations have been backward in intelligence, and had to struggle for ages before they could attain the standard of their generation. Some have been hopeless defectives and have been allowed to disappear. Perhaps the same thing must happen on the moral plane. Nations must prove their ability to reach the average standard of their time, and be willing with other nations to attain an infinitely higher stage of moral and spiritual progress. Our faith in man, based on faith in the Fatherhood of God, forbids us to despair of human progress.

Again and again, I say that you and I must begin our probation at once and seek God at all times, for Judaism teaches us that He is near and ready to assist us in our forward journey. In my next letter, I will write of the Jewish belief in progress both for the individual and for the community. So far we have seen that Judaism asks for faith in God and faith in man.

No. 35
March 1942

BELIEF IN SPIRITUAL PROGRESS

We think of Judaism as a spiritual influence binding us to the living God. Through Him our lives must progress. He has commanded us to be holy because He is holy. We have to establish our kinship with Him and to endeavor to imitate Him. God has put eternity into our lives, and so the time is limitless in which we can approach Him.

There is a recurrent note of optimism throughout the Hebrew Bible. Suffering must be overcome, if possible. It should never be considered as a desirable end in itself, to be sought as a condition pleasing to God. If we read the Psalms, we shall find the spirit of progress clearly expressed. Man is expected to go from "strength to strength," overcoming difficulties, and be prepared to serve his God through his happiness.

The Old Testament has no definite teaching on immortality. In a few Psalms there are phrases which, taken from their historical setting, seem to indicate a clear belief in an infinite future. Take for example the verse in Psalm 16. "In Thy presence is fullness of joy; at Thy right hand are pleasures for evermore." The general trend of the Old Testament is to ignore dogma on the theme of immortality. Perhaps abstractions did not greatly interest our child race. They were gathered to their fathers by their God, and their fate could surely be left to His wisdom and love. Nevertheless, we find a well-developed faith in immortality among the teachers and writers of the early post-biblical period. Let us consider the words in the Wisdom of Solomon, Chapter 3: "The souls of the righteous are in the hand of God, and there shall no torment touch them. In the sight of the unwise, they seemed to die, and their departure is taken for misery . . . but they are at peace." Such definite affirmations can easily be multiplied. The biblical characters show no fear or rebellion in the face of death. Even Moses denied the entry into the promised land asserts the triumph of the human soul when confronted with apparent defeat. The Jew's season of fasting is succeeded by his joyous festival of ingathering. Even though he walks through the valley of death, he fears no evil.

The Jews' mission in the world is the message of hope. "O Zion, that bringest good tidings . . . lift up thy voice with strength."[4] We are here to speak to the world of an ever present God of love and justice who will cause righteousness to triumph in the end. He will bring every deed to judgment, whether it be good or whether it be evil. Atonement is possible to every sinner, if he turns himself to God, resolved to live anew in His presence. There need not be finality even in sin. Because God is the ruler of the world, liberty and security must be achieved by human effort made in cooperation with God.

Do we come to find progress in the community as well as in the individual, and understand why our messianic age is ever before us? We can no longer believe in a personal Messiah, for we cannot conceive of any human being with power to lead the world, with its multitude of conflicting tendencies, to abiding peace and happiness. It is nevertheless a principle of Judaism that each individual can be a Messiah or messenger of God, working for righteousness and together bringing nearer the dawn of the perfect day when the highest human aspirations will be satisfied. The testimony of the Jews to the reality of the All-Father, and the standards of human conduct revealed by Him for the sake of His children of every race and creed - this testimony will be a factor in building up the Kingdom of God.

Judaism requires the whole of man in the service of God. "Thou shalt love the Lord thy God with all thy heart, with all thy soul and with all thy might." There is an intellectual, as well as an emotional element in our religion. God is the God of truth, and we must seek truth in order to find God. We are sometimes rather too ready to excuse ourselves from making opportunities for study. We hear people say that they are unable to concentrate their minds on problems in these difficult days. They have no time for reading, they have too little leisure, and are altogether too tired to study. Nobody blames us for making these "good" excuses. They are valid and proper, but unless we are very strict with ourselves, we may lost the best that is in the world. "Seek ye the Lord at all times. Call ye upon Him while He is near." (Isaiah 55, Verse 6)

Even more dangerous than want of study is want of thinking. People accept what their fathers give them in the way of religion and do not assimilate their possessions through the power of thought. Even the belief in God which may be considered as the first principle of Judaism cannot influence our lives unless we think about it. It is not a matter of lip service. We have to turn this thought over and over in our minds every day of our lives. It is a tremendous thought! Then there are the simpler questions which give evidence of progress or stagnation, active loyalty to our Brotherhood, or mechanical acceptance of tradition, in order that we may go on in our way with as little trouble as possible. Our community stands for certain great truths which have been handed down from the past, and must be rejected, or revitalised by our devotion. How far were our fathers justified in making their faith our faith, and giving us the responsibility of carrying on? Our ancestors forged a chain of testimony, binding them to God. They used the best material available to them, and for doing that work so well, we offer them our homage and our gratitude.

But supposing we honestly know that in the course of ages new and better material has been found to increase the human store of truth? Are we to make no use of these discoveries for the strengthening of our relations with God? How are we to tell if the new discovery is good? God has given us prophets and teachers to help us, and however small our minds are, they have been given to us to use in His service. I will illustrate this point of view in my letter on the relation of man to God, which I have delayed sending out, but I think the way is now prepared by my letters on faith in God, faith in man, and the present one on spiritual progress. Some of you may agree more readily that Judaism holds for us an element of emotional interest than that it has for us a strong intellectual appeal. So often in our religious experience, we are up against insoluble problems and inexplicable conditions. Our intellects will not help us to explain fully the existence of evil. We shall not penetrate the mystery of life or of death. We cannot define God by thought alone. Nevertheless, we are prepared to stake our lives that God is within us, and His spiritual influence can be felt in all parts of the universe; that we derive our spirits from Him, and because He is perfect in truth, beauty, love and righteousness, we are charged to imitate Him and progress towards Him, so far as our faulty human nature will allow. We find by experience that the more love we give to humanity, the more love we feel coming to us, and we believe God is the source of love, and that love increases the more it is made use of. I should like you particularly to take away this thought from this letter.

The Jewish Brotherhood is called to the service of God. Other religions are called to similar service, but we have our own method of service, our own history, our own divinely appointed purposes. There are many men and women who call themselves by the name of Jew, but degrade the faith because they are indifferent to the teaching of Judaism, and to their sacred charge. They prefer to live for material advancement, and neglect spiritual progress. They ignore their call to service, and therefore refuse to prepare themselves for their great destiny. You can belong to the better set; then you will be sure of your advance, and even if you have to endure some suffering and exert yourself in an extreme measure, you will all the time be glad of your high office and determine to make yourself as worthy as possible. Remember, we are called to be a kingdom of priests ministering to the well-being of humanity. We have a long way to go before we deserve to be recognised as useful priests, but we may get there if we begin at once. "Tell the children of Israel," says God to Moses, "that they go forward."[5]

[1] Isaiah 55:6

[2] Psalm 118:6

[3] Psalm 66:12

[4] Isaiah 40:9

[5] Exodus 14:15

CLUB LETTER NO. 6

June 1939

The summer speaks of life, life so intense and beautiful that it seems as if it must go on for ever. Winter is only the sleeping time of nature - life goes on for ever. Shall we consider the truth of nature's inspiring message as we apply it to human life?

I hope you feel with me that as life comes from God, as man was made in God's image, he partakes of the nature of God and shares His eternity. If God is the God of love (and if he is not, why should we seek Him or worship Him), He did not give us our big dreams and our strong affections to mock us. When we love, we give ourselves for ever. Love is eternal, and it is because we believe that, we can bear to see our beloved drawn from our sight, even while we suffer the acute pain of separation. They live, because God lives, and they come from God and must return to Him.

Similarly, our feeling of personal insufficiency is strong in us. We do some work which has infinite possibilities. We are called away before much is done. Our thoughts and deeds are full of weakness and imperfection, but we believe they can be made strong and very good. We must wait until we get beyond the veil. Life is so full of inequalities and injustices. We must combat these wrongs <u>here</u> and <u>now</u>, and not wait passively for another world for greater achievement and the realisation of our strong hopes. We <u>do</u> so believe because God is good and His existence is the guarantee for full and complete life. Because He lives, righteousness and justice and truth must ultimately prevail.

When a person dies, those about him see a change. Very often he is more beautiful than ever. In the act of leaving the body, the spirit has left its impress. But when the spirit has gone, the body is no longer the same. The self has gone, the personality. God, the Creator, would not waste His creation. The self must fulfil itself. We know not where or how, but we believe in God. It is because of that belief, which I have inherited from my Jewish ancestors, and <u>made my own</u>, that I don't feel it necessary to have recourse to spiritualism, or any of the occult sciences.[1] Our teachers were satisfied that since God is good, no human life can be annihilated. All must grow toward perfection. No details are given us. No fear of death is ever noticed. Our people were gathered to their fathers, and God is the Lord of all worlds. They were satisfied. I am satisfied also.

In the Psalms and the prophets, more definite expressions of faith can be traced here and there, and David says clearly in Kings of his dead child: "I shall go to him, but he shall not return to me." And the Psalmist tells us that in God's presence is fullness of joy, and the prophet that He has swallowed up death for ever.

But we have to wait for the Rabbinical writings for <u>much</u> expression of the general faith in immortality. Even the details are left to the individual to put in for himself. I like that way best.

When through death we seem to lose someone we love, we feel his nearness in an astonishing way. His love becomes nearer to God's love, and we experience his protecting influence. Of course, I don't pretend we don't want more. We _do_. We long to see and to know. It must be better for us so. If we knew all, we might be in too great a hurry to go and experience what we believe to be in store for us. We should not be sufficiently interested in life here to learn our earth lessons properly. These must be learned before we are ready to go elsewhere. Moreover, if as I believe, our progress here is assisted by our dear ones in the beyond, we must fit our personality here for the great tasks we may have to do some day. Let the contemplation of death help our sense of proportion. let us cultivate the things which are eternal in life - truth, love, beauty and peace, and not waste our time over the trifles of ephemeral value. God has put eternity in our hearts.

Winter keeps the vital sap of plants to reproduce them in the glorious summer. Let us too try to do the same, and with the help of God plant the seeds of lovingkindness which shall eventually bear fruit. Think of Browning's verse:

> The high that proved too high, the heroic for earth too hard,
> The passion that left the ground to lose itself in the sky,
> Are music sent up to God by the lover and the bard;
> Enough that He heard it once: we shall hear it by and by.[2]

Private Collection,
Hannah Feldman, London

¹Belief that the human personality continues to exist even after death and can communicate with the living through a medium or psychic. These views became popularized in the late nineteenth and early twentieth centuries by the Fox sisters of Massachusetts (identified with the term "spiritualism"), Madame Blavatsky (founder of the Theosophical Society), and others.

²From Browning's poem, "Abt Vogler."

THE SABBATH

[No Date]

Jews have given to the world. The world has accepted the fact that it is good for men and women to make one day different from the rest of the week, to make it a day of rest and a great contributory factor in the sanctification of life. To the Jew, life was from the beginning meant to be holy, for his people had been called to be a holy people, to prove their kinship with the holy God. "Ye shall be holy for I the Lord Thy God am holy." (Leviticus Ch. 19, v. 2.) To us Jews, holiness does not mean withdrawal from life, or a peculiar unworldly way of living. We think we are meant to live *in* the world, and be of the world, but always to be in contact through prayer and the standard of our conduct, with the supreme spirit of the Universe, with the infinite, never changing God.

Sabbath observance originated for Jews in the Fourth Commandment. We have two versions of the Commandment in the Old Testament. In Exodus, Ch. 20 we read "Remember the Sabbath Day to keep it holy. Six days shalt thou labour and do all thy work, but the Seventh day is the Sabbath of the Lord thy God. In it thou shalt not do any work, thou, nor thy son, nor thy daughter, thy manservant, nor thy maidservant, nor thy cattle, nor the stranger that is within thy gates. For in six days the Lord made heaven and earth, the sea, and all that in them is, and rested on the seventh day, wherefore the Lord blessed the seventh day and hallowed it." In Deuteronomy we read: "The seventh day is the Sabbath of the Lord thy God; in it thou shalt not do any work, thou, nor thy son, nor thy daughter, nor thy manservant, nor thy maidservant, nor thine ox, nor thine ass, nor any of thy cattle, nor thy stranger who is within thy gates, that thy manservant and thy maidservant may rest as well as thou. And remember that thou wast a stranger in the land of Egypt, and the Lord thy God brought thee out thence through a mighty hand and a stretched out arm, therefore the Lord thy God commanded thee to keep the Sabbath day."

These are the two versions of the commandment, and of these I prefer the second which is found in Deuteronomy. The first is perhaps symbolic because we know that the world was *not* made in seven days. It took millions of years to evolve. Also we know that God never rests. His creative spiritual power is always above and within the Universe, guiding it towards good. It is a fine thought that the Sabbath should benefit all living beings, and upon this idea our democratic ideal may well be based. Moreover both versions of the Commandment include reference to the stranger within our gates who is not to suffer from discrimination as being what we would term "a foreigner."

We Liberal Jews think that the Sabbath is of benefit to all mankind, and it is for this reason that it has been generally accepted. Through its intrinsic merits it makes its claim on universal acceptance.

Never mind that Christians observe the Sabbath on the first day of the week, and Mohammedans render the sixth day holy. Orthodox Jews who take a liberal view of the Bible, observe the Sabbath because they think they were commanded to do so by God Himself, and obviously a command - if believed to be divine - cannot be set aside by man.

Our methods of observing the Sabbath vary according to the religious outlook which we accept. Our ancient Rabbis, believing the Sabbath to be directly ordained by God, felt that it must be accepted for all time, and in order to prevent any laxity in observance, made a fence round the law. With the greatest care they framed their injunctions, and men were not only forbidden to work on the Sabbath, but to do anything which involved the labour of others, such as travelling or recreation. They were not allowed to risk any form of destruction; they must not play instrumental music lest they break their instrument, or open their letters, for this was a manner of work. Liberal Jews regard the Sabbath as valuable in festering their spiritual life. They, like their Orthodox co-religionists should attend public worship on the Sabbath for in this way Jewish fellowship is nurtured. They should abstain from work even if this abstention involves sacrifice so long as it is economically possible. If the choice is between Sabbath work and being a burden on the community, it is, we think, man's duty to work for his independent maintenance, and so long as his work is honourable, he can pass from his workshop or office to his Synagogue, and remain all the while in the house of God. But he must not think it unimportant to hallow, as far as possible, the Sabbath through worship. The regular habit of Synagogue worship should satisfy the normal hunger of the average man or woman. Man is a social animal. The effort of his neighbour to contact his God stimulates his own desire. Even during, or perhaps, particularly during silent periods, the sense of unity with our fellow worshipper helps to reveal the unity of God who has provided us, in varying degrees with similar cravings. Our ancestors understood human psychology so well when they instituted weekly Sabbath worship. Our spiritual hunger, as well as our physical hunger, must be dealt with at regular intervals, or these are unsatisfied, and may cause deterioration in our spiritual as well as our physical well-being. Our historic sense is stimulated through public worship on the Sabbath. It is of value to us to remember that this observance has been ordered all through the ages, generation by generation. <u>Of course</u> we can pray at home just as well as in Synagogue, but we <u>do</u> derive help and guidance from the addresses given by our Ministers and from the readings from the Bible. Throughout the ages the Sabbath has been a day for rejoicing and worship, and rest and instruction. If our Service is in harmony with our actual needs and completely understood by us all, we can through its help not only feel the influence of the past, but be stirred also to make our own contacts with the living God.

There is a tendency today to make the Sabbath just another day on which we lead a secular life, even if through the reorganisation of work, a five day week for business can be instituted. People do not seriously consider the Sabbath as a means for the sanctification of life. Our spiritual growth is impeded, and our portion of aesthetic and cultural education is diminished through neglect. The hours for rejoicing on the Sabbath Day must not be neglected even though the time for rest and worship and study is given its due recognition. We Liberals consider the authority for observance to rest in the trained conscience of the individual, who is guided by the teaching of great scholars, and also by his own communion with God, the loving guide of all men. The appeal is to every man who would use Jewish teaching for the sanctification of his life, in conformity with his highest conception, to ask himself how far certain forms of sociability, or recreation develops his cultural, aesthetic, and spiritual well-being, and how far they may impede it. In the light of these questions he tries to order his life.

There is one part of the Sabbath which Orthodox, Conservative, Reform and Liberal adherents hold to be of the greatest possible importance, and that is the Sabbath Eve. All Jewish holydays and festivals have their beginning in the evening. New birth is always shrouded in the mystery of darkness. We welcome the Sabbath Eve. It comes as a messenger from the past to sanctify family joy and to consecrate the home. The purity of family life has always been one of the glories of our community, and it owes much to the observance of the Sabbath Eve as holy. The symbols are beautiful and suggestive. The two candles are generally lighted by the mother who, through this symbol, asks that all small quarrels and jealousies be cleared away by the flame of the Lord, which at the same time is an emblem of purity. Joy is sanctified with the blessing of the wine in the Kiddush Cup. Thanksgiving for the gifts of the earth is spoken by means of the blessing on the two loaves. The cup of wine is passed round to express family unity. The work and distractions of the week have perhaps kept the members of the family separate, but on the Sabbath they come together, and laugh and eat together after family worship, and also talk over family affairs. The opportunity is given and appreciated by parents and children who have been accustomed to regard the Sabbath as an institution deserving of faithful, inflexible observance. It can only be of value if it can claim absolute loyalty. If the members of the family can only be counted upon to remain at home if no other engagement offers itself, it is of little or no value.

Our poets and teachers have likened the Sabbath to a bride who comes with joy in her heart, beautifully attired, full of expectation, and complete trust. She is received with love which shows itself in many ways, and with reverence which each one offers according to his capacity.

"Come my beloved to meet the bride..."[1]

We have sorrowfully to admit that on account of the secular method of living which prevails today the Sabbath Eve home celebrations are no longer in vogue among the majority of our co-religionists. In many homes the candles are lighted but their meaning is lost for the family is divided and goes off on different paths to follow their every day inclinations. Our ministers have instituted Synagogue Services with addresses which may appeal especially to young people, and in many Synagogues these Services are often conducted by young people themselves, so at any rate the Sabbath is distinguished in some measure. In some parts of the world whole families go to Synagogue together and so retain the home atmosphere. All these changes seem to me to create a "second best" expression of the best in Jewish life, but since they are conceived for the glory of God we must accept them with thankfulness and reverence.

Archives, Liberal
Jewish Synagogue, London

[1] The beginning lines of a popular Sabbath hymn

A NEW LIFE BEGINS TODAY

West Central: New Year October 1959

A new life is beginning for us today. At this solemn hour, when we come together to welcome the New Year, we have to ask ourselves an important question. Do we want a new life and why? If, as I think, we do need it, how can it be obtained?

Some of you may have planned a change in the conditions and circumstances of your life. You may be considering going over seas; you may be contemplating marriage; you may be concerned in a special personal way with motherhood or fatherhood. The new life must then obviously come. I would only remind you that whatever the circumstances, you will always be taking yourself with you. Therefore, a change in self-adaptation will be as necessary as spiritual transformation. Most of us do want a big change in ourselves, even though our outward circumstances may remain the same.

We want stronger faith which will affect our lives. Faith does change a man's way of life. It would make a great difference to each one of us if instead of only holding theoretical principles of Judaism, we actually brought them into daily conduct. We accept the principles of Judaism. You recite the Shema with fervour. Does it occur to you today that this Oneness of God which you proclaim should mean a great deal to you? If life is One and reveals God, there is no death. Eternity is a reality. Then the whole of life is eternal. Our entire life can be made holy. There is no division between the secular and the sacred, nor between this life and that part which will follow it. We can reveal our God when we work and when we play; when we are alone or when we are in relationship with others. There is no division of society into classes. The well-being of each is the well-being of all. Because God, our Creator, our Ruler, our Father is one, we His children are brothers and sisters; there is no first or last.

We are the people of the Shema, but a new life is needed if we are to love God with our whole being, for then surely there would be no room in our hearts or minds for unkind feelings or cruel thoughts. These must be ousted by love, beauty, righteousness, truth, justice and peace. We have no room for aught else but God. A new life is beginning for us today.

In the old life we tolerated the fact that many people tried to live and die without any knowledge of God. Now we must be up and doing. We must spread the knowledge of God who "neither slumbers nor sleeps."[1] He requires good from us and not evil, truth and not falsehood. On what authority can unbelievers do justly and love mercy and walk in true humility with the God they do not know. We know. Therefore, we dare not be silent any longer. A new life is beginning for us today.

We insist that Judaism must be practised not only in certain places as Synagogues, or even restricted to our homes. It must be practised also when we go out and when we come in. Our business places and our dance halls, our places of rest and our journeys in buses and trains, all must be affected by our faith. Indeed, we must start a new life.

How about the children? Here and there you have brought in some children who were not being taught any religion. You did not bother about the others. You did not imitate your Father and go out to look for the lambs who were likely to be lost. You heard your friends make absurd remarks about children choosing their own faith later on. You know that the parents dare not leave that choice, which may make or mar a person's life, to the unformed mind of a child. But you did not argue with your friend. Perhaps you just smiled and went on your way. To use a horrid modern phrase: You could not care less.

In The Shema which you recite very frequently, for it is the central prayer in our daily liturgy, and in the liturgy prepared for Sabbaths and festivals, you proclaim the necessity to write the words about God's unity and His love on your door posts and on your gates. Why? Judaism has always laid emphasis on the sanctity of the home. No substitute can serve to replace home influence. It is for this reason that the idea of God's love must ever inspire husbands and wives, parents and children, to accept it as the foundation of their lives. It must be known throughout the Jewish home, and to secure this, it must be recognised even on entrance. The old custom of placing a Mezuzah on the door of a home is full of poetry and religious inspiration, for it contains the call to love. A few people may think the custom out-modish and unnecessary, but surely the need for true all-embracing sincere love in the home has not been superseded. Indeed, it is perhaps more needed than ever before in our history, for broken homes seem to be terribly prevalent. With the new life which begins for us all today can be perhaps put a new and very strong emphasis on the ideals of home life?

This is also the festival of remembrance, and it is well, while we are making the foundations of our new life good and strong, to cast a few backward glances; in fact, to remember what happened to us in the old life. We recall that petty crime has increased, and strife and jealousy. Of course, we here had nothing to do with crime, but what about petty jealousy and the acceptance of small immoralities, which we say everybody permits, and so why should we be better than others? Obviously, we are not responsible for the big industrial crises which have inconvenienced us all so much, but is not self-interest, the difficulty of considering the good of society as a whole, because we care over much for our own little corner, attitudes which we must try and improve? Let us in our new life pray for a broader vision. Let us be strict with our standards and keep them in our minds. We are inclined to raise these standards very high indeed in our theoretical allegience to our God who framed them. Perhaps now and again, these heights are surrounded with mist and we lose sight of them. Let us be more realistic in the new life.

The difficulty of settling international quarrels is most depressing. We can never open a newspaper without reading of actual fighting, acts of cruelty or the threats of war. Of course, we here are not in the high political circles which are responsible for these sad signs of national deterioration, but is it not true that settlement depends on mutual trust, and cannot we not practise a greater measure of trust in our small lives? The cold war does, I think, emanate from the attitude of individuals towards one another. Don't let us say any more: What can you expect nowadays? You cannot fully trust anybody. You cannot be too careful. These repulsive views start the general attitude of suspicion which ultimately leads to quarrels. Let us start a new life today.

In order to start the new life we all long for, we need help, and this help to be effective must come from God. We need to pray. Most of us have inherited our religion. We want to make it live. This can be done by letting our minds, for a short time at least each day, be permeated by God's spirit. We would obtain from Him through prayer, new strength, new courage, new enlightenment. Reminders are wanted. We obtain these through fixed times for prayer and worship, whether in our homes or in our Synagogue. But even this is not enough. We don't make religion live by regular habits. We have to find our own way to our God and use it on every possible occasion. Then the discipline of regular effort is helpful indeed, but the actual spiritual approach of the individual soul is imperative. Please remember this as the basis of the new life.

In our own Congregation, we have a splendid nucleus of loyal sincere members who belong to us because Liberal Judaism offers the presentment of their ancestral faith which they believe to be in harmony with their conception of truth. But there are too many who remain on the fringe of our group. Many of these have made a great effort to come today. They will probably come again in ten days' time. But what then? They will perhaps never generously support the Synagogue's efforts to complete our Synagogue, or even understand that we are a constituent of the Union of Liberal and Progressive Synagogues and have a duty to help the Union in gaining the means to develop Liberal Judaism in Great Britain. By coming to the Holyday services, these friends believe that they have fulfilled their duty. Are we to wait for another whole year before these members, members, mind you, contribute to the living religion which together with ourselves they accept? Can it be considered a living religion, if it only receives nourishment once a year? Is this food not rather useless to them? Do let us, all of us, begin a new life today. We need every member to rise from their luke-warm interest and bring new strength and enlightenment into our very midst. Are you ready? If you kindle your faith today into life, it will serve you if you accept the obligation for prayer, for study, for fellowship as something to live by and something with which to infect your children, and all the members of your household for good.

I want to put before you an important hopeful thought. We Liberal Jews have rejected the ideal of a personal messiah. We believe in a messianic age, and we think that each one of us by living his religion can spread the knowledge of Judaism through direct effort to reach our own indifferentists, and the a-religious section of humanity whatever their race or the community into which they were born. This must be done indirectly by example, and directly by precept. Will you in your new life which begins today contribute something to our sacred mission, believing that it is for this purpose that the Jews have survived the dangers of their existence, and here have been kept alive until this day.

I have one final plea to make this morning. I have several times introduced into my talk the word "Eternal," which if used thoughtfully may correct our sense of proportion in choosing between the essential and the trivial. Our life on earth would indeed be renewed if we established it on the basis of our faith in the hereafter. Let us try during the coming year to do something of permanant value. It may only be for ourselves. It is possible that we may conquer some small personal failing, that we may make with a single life happier, that we decide not to repeat gossip or unkind remarks, that wherever we go we bring an atmosphere of peace and harmony. Then what about starting some work without worrying that we must be paid for it within perceptible time? How about doing something we always meant to do, but never got down to? We might develop our love for nature and for art. We were always conscious of that love, but somehow never had time to foster it. Just think of the books you meant to read, of the gaps in your knowledge you had no time to cover. You believe in meditation, but your life has been a constant rush. You could not do all the things I have enumerated because you just had no time. But you have forever. Let your new life which begins today be governed by that thought. "On the earth the broken arcs, in the heavens the perfect round."[2] You must begin to mend the arcs now, and you will have the joy of making them perfect in the endless future, for you realise now more fully than ever before, that you yourself are now in God's everlasting arms,[3] and you will remain there in the new life which begins today and will continue to all eternity.

> Archives, Liberal Jewish
> Synagogue, London

[1] Psalm 121:4

[2] From Browning's "Abt Vogler."

[3] Deuteronomy 33:27 (cf. with similar image in Club Letter 3).

CLUB LETTER NO. 133

April 1951

The festival of Passover brings home to us the responsibility of freedom. All of you who read this paper believe strongly in your right to freedom. Even parental control must not be enforced beyond the early years of adolescence. If parents attempt to control or even to seek to guide their grown up sons and daughters, they often create rebellion in their children's hearts. You have begun to have your own ideas and consider those of your parents old-fashioned, and you cannot brook interference with the way of life you have chosen. Of course, the love you have for your parents is as great as ever. It could not be greater, but you want to test life for yourselves.

You want to seek your own adventures and, if necessary, pay the price of your own mistakes.

This casting off of control must add to your sense of responsibility. You want unhampered self-expression and before you can attain this on a satisfying basis you must realise your own selves. It would seem to be necessary to develop your bodies, minds and spirits. God in His Oneness has made all these important in His sight.

Life is one and cannot be taken in sections. We try to be complete people and to bring our whole personality under the guidance of God who leads us nearer and nearer to Him.

I beg you then to use your freedom in the first place to develop what is good in yourselves. You must pay attention to the whole of yourselves and do not plead want of time as an excuse not to do justice to your physical life by exercise and sport, by the study of hygiene and the acceptance of its laws in order to make your bodies as clean and pure and healthy as possible. Then you must give heed to the necessity for education all the days of your lives. Seize the opportunity to learn from every person who is better endowed intellectually than yourselves. Use your thinking powers and know that self-education, undertaken in the reverent appreciation of the wisdom of others, may bring you to the highest good. Further, I ask you not to neglect your spiritual powers. These too need regular exercise in prayer. Give yourselves the time to share your spiritual possessions with others. Unlike any other possession, instead of exhausting your gifts through sharing, you will increase their power and validity.

Do you know what Judaism means, what it stands for, what it demands of its followers? We have noticed that in times of danger and persecution, men and women run to places of worship and expect help from these institutions which up to the time of their difficulty they had consistently ignored. Sometimes, they begin to question their faith and find it wanting in many particulars. They are disappointed and hurt and ask what is the use of religion. But you must not wait until the moment of distress has arrived. You are free to think and to pray and to learn and to understand. Go to the people you trust and seek enlightenment from them. Share your spirituality with those who like yourselves were born in Jewish homes. You all have the right to call yourselves Jews, but the name brings infinite responsibility. Prepare yourselves to take it. Then you can ask God for blessing on your lives.

I have said that Passover suggests freedom for self-realisation. Most particularly it stresses the power of serving God by serving one another. When you joined the [West Central] Club you found that it offered you self-realisation and service, or I might almost say "through" service. You help in the administration of the Club and more important still, you feel your responsibility in making your fellow members as happy as possible. The club as a whole, advances as one corporate body, and your strength pulls it up while your weakness lowers its strength. I think that if we regard the Club from this angle, it offers good training to its members for service in the great world outside. Since you are free to serve and feel it to be your responsibility as Jewish people to help in building up God's Kingdom, you must be ready to take part as citizens in any useful activity which presents itself and in which you feel you can give worthwhile service. Your ancestors belonged to the Jewish faith. You are members of the oldest aristocracy in the world, and you are free to degrade its position or still further to uplift it.

After the exodus from slavery which Passover celebrates, the Jews become a corporate entity. You are called to serve your brotherhood, but your service must not be limited since the call comes to you from the God of the universe with whom there is no great or small, for all people are His children. Stimulated by your sense of service derived from your conception of Judaism, inspired by your devotion to God, you are also free to serve all people whenever and wherever the opportunity arises.

The Seder service helps to consecrate our home life and to create the happiest home background in our lives. You help to create your happiness in your home, and to see that everybody has a fair deal. The home is the sanctuary. You carry from its altar burning coals of fire which will kindle enthusiasm. But the work is not an end in itself. You must be free to choose good and to reject evil. You must choose your absolute standards. Your life must reveal God, in spite of its weakness and imperfection.

Passover is the festival of freedom. You who read this letter are most of you enjoying the freedom of youth to make your own lives, and I pray that your adventure will be happy and altogether worthwhile. If I might advise you, I would say that much depends on the companions you choose. Our real friends are very precious to us, and we keep them as long as possible, having once been assured of their worth. You must be careful not to let them down by any want of consideration on your part. It is delightful to go through life with people who have the same outlook on life, even though there may be a great difference between their opinions and yours. The basic principles must be the same in friendship as in marriage. Have you realised that many of these principles are derived from the fact that in the widest sense, wherever you are and whatever you do, you are free to work well or badly, to do what you can just to make a good living or to fulfill through your work some of the highest purposes of human life? I beg you to restore to your daily work some of its lost dignity. Wage earning is of the greatest importance, especially in these expensive days, but let it not be your sole obligation. Your work takes up a great portion of your time. You meet in business hours all sorts of people; your conduct towards them may help to make or mar their lives. Be careful how you choose, since your responsibility is great even while you are only a junior and it increases as you grow older. The tone of your business place is in a degree affected by you even though you still occupy a subordinate position.

Then you have your leisure and here your responsibility is very great. Use it for real refreshment for body, mind and soul, for, as I have indicated, in this way lies full self-realisation.

Passover is the festival of spring. As you rejoice in the beauty of its manifestations I should like to remind you that this season, like all others, follows God's laws of nature. The trees and flowers have heard God's call to a reawakening and they obey. The lesson for us is obvious as we seek God through His Creation. I ask you to let the beauty of the spring enter into your souls and as you do, realise your own responsibility to obey God's law of progress. It is good that you can be in touch if you will with the great Lawgiver, and seek His help and be conscious of His love. "Be still and know that I am God."[1] Meditate on these words and possess the God idea. Then indeed will your freedom be blessed now and evermore.

Private Collection,
Hannah Feldman, London

[1] Psalm 46:10

III. JEWISH SELF-IDENTITY

INTRODUCTION

In keeping with her understanding of Judaism as a religion, Lily Montagu believed Jewish self-identity to be religious in nature. She flatly denied both racial and nationalistic associations, maintaining that by nationality she was English. It was only her faith, she said, that made her a Jew.

Yet this faith was the most important component of Lily Montagu's life. It helped create a religious vision that guided her thoughts and actions and eventually, led her to assume a religious leadership role within the Anglo-Jewish community. In her sermon, "Faith in God," delivered at the Liberal Jewish Synagogue, she sums up her understanding of Jewish self-identification. To be a Jew, she insists, is to "bear testimony to the Reality of God." This testimony, as she maintains in "Why Do We Bother?," needs to be based on an all-pervading sense of being God-conscious and on the recognition that such faith "implies that you are prepared to work for [God]."

Lily Montagu's "Kinship With God," delivered on June 15, 1918, merits attention as the first sermon given at the Liberal Jewish Synagogue by a woman. Its theme is Judaism as personal religion, with an understanding of Jewish self-identity based on the acknowledgement that one's kinship with God makes communion with Him both possible and essential. To be a Jew, she writes, is to belong to a particular religious brotherhood whose members are enjoined to surrender themselves to the highest conception of righteousness and truth. Though at times, Montagu speaks of the "God idea" rather than God, her intent here is not to reduce God to a mental concept but rather to describe one's idea or understanding of God as it "varies from generation to generation."

The notion of Jews as witnesses becomes the theme of Montagu's "Address Given at the Girls' Club" in November, 1911. Bearing witness to God's reality is described as the mission of each and every Jew, the driving force behind all thought and action. It is for this reason, she writes, that Jews have been chosen. Chosenness, then, is a claim not to special privilege but to special responsibility. In "Here Am I: Send Me," Montagu uses the words of the prophet Isaiah as an example of the directness and simplicity with which one should answer the Divine call. Though lacking in self-confidence and thinking himself "unworthy to speak the words of the Lord," Isaiah became overwhelmed by the Divine presence, experiencing a sense of exaltation and purification that awakened the spiritual power within him. Lily Montagu insists that while she and her listeners are not "spiritual giants, as was Isaiah," it is incumbent upon them to discover and develop their own spiritual power in the service of God. Yet she also maintains that to develop this power, one not only must witness the religious truth inherited from one's ancestors and handed down through the generations, but also, by breathing a renewed spirit into it, recognize the real and "abiding influence" of one's religion.

In a different but related direction, Club Letters 139 and 185 describe Lily Montagu's understanding of Jewish self-identity as it affects marriage and the home. Despite the general, universal thrust of her conception of Judaism, she returns to the mission idea as that which prohibits intermarriage. The Jew must ensure, she writes, that nothing serves to dilute the message that emerges out of witnessing the reality of God. Though the Jew who marries a non-Jew might still claim to be Jewish, the non-Jewish partner might well exert a religious influence that would lead the Jewish spouse to betray his or her spiritual mission. Lily Montagu is not using the mission idea to cover over what in reality here is a national, racial or even cultural abhorrence of intermarriage. Her objections are clearly religious. Thus, recognizing that a secular Jew, married to a religious Jew, might also work to dilute the spiritual testimony of his or her partner, Montagu maintains that "when one who has been devoted to Judaism weds a materialist who has led a secular life, there is perpetrated a form of intermarriage which, I think, is nearly as dangerous as any other."

Once again, in "Out of Zion Shall the Law Go Forth . . . ," a sermon delivered at the West Central Club in November 1917, Lily Montagu reiterates her belief that Jewish self-identity is religious in nature. Here, this belief leads her to oppose Zionism and the British Government's recently issued Balfour Declaration promising to "view with favour the establishment in Palestine of a [Jewish] national home." While acknowledging that she is Jewish by religion, she adamantly insists that as an Englishwoman, she neither wants nor needs "another national home." As this and later sermons make clear, Lily Montagu's hostility to Zionism and in particular to political Zionism, was rooted in its equation of Judaism with nationality, i.e., its understanding of Judaism in purely secular terms. Political Zionism, as she understood it, not only sought to dilute Judaism's religious message. It threatened to destroy it all together.

This concern stands in sharp contrast to that of her brother, Edwin, Secretary of State for India, who also opposed the Balfour Declaration but for political reasons. Cited in a number of historical studies as the Balfour Declaration's major opponent, he feared that labelling Palestine a Jewish national home would bring into question Jewish political loyalty, thus endangering his own effectiveness in India and, more generally, threatening the social and political position of Jews in emancipated nations throughout the world. Though tied to Judaism by family loyalty, Edwin Montagu had little use for its "spiritual possibilities." To his sister Lily, however, it was precisely these possibilities on which she based her identity as a Jew.

FAITH IN GOD

Liberal Jewish Synagogue,
May 1, 1943

There are a great many people, who regard their faith as a light thing which can be taken up at any moment. It is static, they think, and needs no attention. One man says: "Because I am a Jew, I believe in God." Another, "Yes, of course, I believe in God. One must believe in something outside oneself, but I don't think about religion much." Another: "I am a Jew. I was born a Jew, of Jewish parents, and that's all there is about it." Another: "Yes, I am Jew, always have been, and my parents before me, but nowadays one can't really <u>believe</u> in religion. That's a bit out of date."

Friends, on this Sabbath of Repentance, when all members of our brotherhood take stock of their lives and decide how they are going to live in the future, which old methods they should discard, and which new methods they should exploit; at this holy and important session, I would say to you solennly and seriously, that if your faith is not going to mean more to you than an accident of birth, Judaism can't go on, and it really would be better if we as a separate brotherhood should pass away.

We have existed through the ages to bear testimony to the Reality of God. If that reality is meaningless now - let us acknowledge our failure. We <u>can</u> be of no further value to the world.

But I would appeal to the members of our Congregation to pause and consider. Many of you have been in the habit of coming together week after week, and through united prayer and thought brought religion into your lives. Still a larger number have made the same effort individually for themselves. But we <u>all</u>, every one of us have to make a greater effort to make religion <u>live</u> in the New Year. We have to know what we believe about God, why we believe it, and what the affect of our belief should be on our lives. Not one of us dares to say today that he is sufficiently alive to his religious responsibility.

The history of the Jews is the history of a people who throughout the ages were God conscious. They believed that they were directly under the government and control of God, and collectively, as well as individually, they referred to Him for guidance in moments of uncertainty. They appealed to Him for protection in times of peril. They gave thanks to Him at seasons of joy. They thought they belonged to God in a peculiar and special way. There were many gods in existence, and each national group had its own patron God, and the achievements of these groups redounded to the credit and greatness of their God. In their glory, he was glorified. Gradually, the conception of the Universal God was given to the Hebrews by their prophets, and, at the same time, our people learned that the God of the Universe was the God of every individual who sought Him through devotion to truth, the search after righteousness, the experience of love.

The God of the Old Testament is often described as the God of terror and wrath. Passages are quoted which do tell of an angry God who is jealous and vengeful, and wins allegiance through exercising terror and offering rewards to the faithful. These elements of teaching do appear in our Bible, and show how our people were groping their way towards the perception of the living God who lives in the heart of every man and guides him towards righteousness. The child race could not realise God as we realise Him today. Yet that same Bible which contains the fierce denunciatory passaged contains also verses expressing the sublime spirituality of the writers, "Love thy neighbour as thyself." "God's word is very nigh unto thee, in thy heart and in thy mind, that thou mayest do it." "God is longsuffering and full of lovingkindness." "Thou shalt love the Lord, thy God, with all thy heart and soul and mind." I could multiply these examples a great many times. But the point I want to make today is that we Jews were called in the far off days as God's chosen people, to bear testimony to our conception of God. It was a changing, growing conception, but it was the truth which was written in the heart of the Jew, and he was called to express it. That expression was for the sake of humanity, and it might bring to the witness, as indeed it did, sacrifice, tribulation and suffering. He might for his pains be hated and despised by men, but he was God's servant, and must fulfil the task for which he was appointed. Now you and I have got to do the same task today in our way. We have to bear witness to God; we have to prove our faith. So we have come back to the question: What do we believe?

I cannot answer this question for you, because I think that every man has the responsibility of finding the answer for himself. I can only make a few suggestions.

Turn your eyes to the wonders of nature, its laws and variety. Whence issues its harmony and regularity? Is there not necessarily one creative and unifying force behind? Do we not see evidence of one Perfect Mind revealing itself?

    The heavens declare the glory of God;
    And the firmament showeth his handiwork.
    Day unto day uttereth speech,
    And night unto night showeth knowledge.[1]

If you study humanity, are you not impressed by the similarity of human nature even in its diversity? "Have we not all one Father? Hath not one God created us?" We must have the same origin, for we are so much alike, and believe that our origin is God, since we have each within himself an urge towards righteousness and a sense of remorse when we fall below our standard of goodness. "In the image of God created He man."

There must be a beginning of life. There must be a source of goodness, beauty, truth and justice. Every normal man can find evidence of God in his heart; he can apprehend the existence of something infinitely greater and better outside himself. Every man is aware of the law of righteousness in his heart and mind. Even as a little child, he knows the difference between right and wrong. This perception grows unless it is starved through want of attention, or lost to recognition because human evil has been imposed upon it. The something not ourselves but in ourselves which makes for righteousness is God.[2] The creator of natural law is God. The ideal standard of perfection is God. Because God lives, and by seeking we find Him, we discover that God has relations with humanity.

Looking through history, we find that there is a gradual movement towards good. Evil is very apparent. Again and again, after a period of comparative progress, there is a bad retrogression. Humanity turns to evil, and seems to lose all it has gained, and the setback is all the more lamentable as humanity has had time and opportunity to recognise spiritual good. But seen over a long period, good does ultimately prevail, and we know that it is God who triumphs over the forces of evil created by man.

If today our Jewish brotherhood would stop bothering about dogma and minute ceremonial regulations, and its own cleverness and its own worldly success, and recognise anew its religious purpose, and became once more aflame with God, then, indeed we might hope to lay the foundation on which to build up the Kingdom of God.

But supposing nothing on a grandiose scale can be achieved. There is just ourselves - the small, weak, imperfect Jew and Jewess who is passionately yearning towards God. What about it? <u>You</u> are here. You yourself mean to discover God. You may be alone with the Alone, but you have the power within yourself, and if this Sabbath is to be <u>real</u> to you, you can make the tremendous effort which will lead to your complete at-one-ment with God.

But there is perhaps a growing feeling in your heart that God to whom you prayed all the year, in whom you trusted, has let you down. So much evil has been perpetuated in this last year, as well as in all previous years; so many innocent people have suffered; so many people have missed the opportunities which should have been theirs, as part of their human birthright. Why? Why?

Friends, don't you think we are a little unreasonable in the blame we cast upon God. He, through His teachers, revealed to us thousands of years ago what would happen. He told us what would occur if we worshipped force and material success, instead of exalting the power of the spirit and seeking the paths of virtue and of love. He is renewing His word again and again to us now. Why blame Him when we went off on the track which must lead to disaster? Don't we hear Him now? Why not? Are we deafened by the shouts of savages, by the cries of lustful men, by the poisonous whispers of self indulgent women? Is it possible that we have been indifferent to the cause of righteousness, that we have ignored the claims of love and truth, of justice and mercy, so we were not properly keyed up to hear God? Let us try again. Let us speak to Him in the morning and speak to Him at night. We are so busy! We have no time for God. We are too absorbed in other things. The interference must be that other things are more important and so we come back again to the cause of the world's misery. We have been putting other values before the value of faith.

But I am assuming a great deal in suggesting that the power in your souls which guides you to righteousness is God, and that you should give yourself time, at whatever cost, morning and evening, to speak to Him when you are not doing anything else, and all through the day when you are engaged in work or in recreation, take seconds all day long, to think of God.

The experience of Jews throughout their history has brought me to this faith. They lived in the light of God. They consciously sought His guidance. They placed their lives before Him for His judgement. They themselves compared their standards with His standards and sought to make good. "Seek the Lord at all times. Call upon Him while He is near." Isaiah conceived that way of life, and found that it worked. "Ye shall be holy, for I, the Lord thy God, am holy." Here the old teachers conceived their kinship with God. You are the descendants of the God of whom they spoke. Are you not going to claim your kinship too?

I venture to suggest that this New Year gives you the opportunity to try this mode of life. Then you will be able to say: "I recognise the one spiritual force as the origin of law and goodness, beauty and truth, and that force I call God." I find by experience, not by reasoning, but by my own discovery that God is near me, and I can be near God at all times. I cannot explain it, but I am as sure of my experience as I am of the fact that I live and love. I cannot explain _how_ I have come to live and love, but I know I do. In the same way, I know I am in contact with God.

This conception will not suddenly transform any of us into the people we want to become, but I believe it will give us new incentive and new hope. Above all, it will provide us with the standards we need. We will, in consequence, be able to _know_ when we fall short and we will feel encouraged to make new and far greater efforts in the cause of righteousness, and we shall never be alone. Of course, we shall fail again and again; perhaps we shall fail right up to the end; but we shall through contact with our God see evidence of a world beyond the veil with new hope and new opportunities. Our belief in immortality does, it seems to me, hang inseparably on to our belief in the God of love. He did not mock us when He gave us the power to love. He did not deride us when He made it possible for us to yearn infinitely even while we achieved little. All our insufficiency gives us hope in immortality. He wants us to fulfil ourselves, and He made it possible for us to do so. He will show us when and how in His good time.

So, in conclusion, I would beg of you to regard the world and its laws; and the individual life and its aims

JEWISH SELF-IDENTITY

and possibilities. Then speak to God. Throw yourself upon His love and you will become more loving. Draw from His truth and righteousness, and you will become more truthful and more righteous. Arise! Shine!³

                                                                                          Amen.

                                        Private Collection,
                                    Eric Conrad, London

¹Psalm 19:1.

²A paraphrase of Matthew Arnold's description of God.

³From Isaiah 60:1 (compare with similar reference in Club Letter No. 3).

WHY DO WE BOTHER?

                                                        February 21, 1925

We have asked ourselves this question over and over again, and in our answer we express our faith in God, in ourselves, and in our fellowmen. When we have denied ourselves and got little thanks for doing so - when we have seen other people who don't _bother_ at all getting all the sweet-meats of life, when we have been disappointed in a friend's behaviour and wondered at our own stupidity in caring so much, when we have knocked ourselves violently and uselessly against the wall of adverse circumstance, when we have made strenuous efforts to attain something for ourselves or put ourselves out immensely to serve others and reaped only failure and misunderstanding, when an appeal has been made to us to make some great effort in a great cause and we have gone a few steps and then back again, because we simply hadn't got the pluck to push forward over the hard places and through the prickly obstacles, we have said, articulately or otherwise "why bother?"

We generally know <u>why</u> we bothered but in order to cover pain, we tried to delude ourselves by asking the question. Facts made us smart and we didn't want to recognise them; still more, we wanted to make others think us indifferent to the pain we were experiencing. We were disappointed, perhaps a little weary, certainly rather sorry for ourselves and this <u>nobody</u> should know and so we asked cheerily, "why bother?"

You may every now and then call yourself a fool for bothering but you would despise yourself a great deal more if you <u>didn't</u> bother. What is the reason of it? I think the reason is that, in the words of Matthew Arnold, "We are influenced by the Power, not ourselves, which makes for Righteousness."[1] As Jews, we believe in that Power. We need to have Him in our lives - we feel our dependence on Him. We cry to Him in our sorrows - we pray to Him; we dare not deny Him. When Lord Roseberry [sic] was unveiling a statue of King Alfred some years ago in Winchester he said "That was a <u>man</u> - since he aspired - God has placed within us something of Himself - that God within us struggles towards the God without. Supposing your neighbour spends his time in eating and drinking, or neglects his home and plays cards every night for big stakes - supposing he seems to have a good time while you get very little fun out of life, you don't <u>really envy him</u>. But supposing you see a girl, possibly a bright and charming girl, dancing through life, indifferent to anything but getting on well at work and play - never doing anybody any harm, but never putting herself out for anybody - quite popular, perhaps a lot more popular than yourself - liked at home - perhaps a little spoiled - never asked or expected to do anything – Nobody depends on her but she doesn't trouble about anyone excepting herself. It _is_ hard not to envy _this_ kind of girl _sometimes_. But your faith makes _you_ bother all the same. It costs you a lot not to let your brains go fallow. It means self-control and concentration; nobody sympathises much with your efforts at self-education but you can't give it up because you have faith in yourself. Then, in spite of your self-condemnation for bothering about your home and your friends you would feel out of tune if you didn't. You have accepted your part in life. God has shown you what is good. You _can't_ turn your back on it – you can't fight against your own nature – Religion, Judaism, has made it necessary for you to bother. Is Religion, Judaism, then such a hard thing? Would not people be happier without it since it makes them bother so much? No, a thousand times no. In spite of the pain and effort, we have _so_ much joy from faith. Those people who don't bother, have happiness of a kind but they are blind. They are sliding along a certain road but it leads to nowhere. They are not learning their earth lessons. They are missing all their opportunities. They don't know _real joy_. God has made us a little lower than the angels. He has given us eternity to get the _full_ tone in our life. We _must_ practise with our instruments, body, mind and soul at once – otherwise we shall waste our time. The others will _have_ to begin sooner or later – we want to start at once.

RABBI BEN ESRA BROWNING
Verses 4 and 5

Poor vaunt of life indeed,
Were man but forced to feed
On joy, to solely seek and find and feast:
Such feasting ended, then
As sure an end to men;

> Irks care the crop-full bird?
> Frets doubt the maw-crammed beast?
>
> ———
>
> Rejoice we are allied
> To that which doth provide
> And not partake, effect and not receive;
> A spark disturbs our clod;
> Nearer we hold of God
> Who gives, than of His tribes that take,
> I must believe.

I have told you why, in my opinion, we aspire, as individuals, to rise in the scale and live more completely.

Now _why_ do we bother about other people? When Enoch Arden[2] returned after so many years to see his wife married to someone else, he looked at her happiness and withdrew. He might have tried to snatch her back to himself. After all his terrible suffering he might have tried to realise the hope which had kept him alive during all those grievous years. But he didn't. He loved his wife sufficiently to leave her without disturbing the happiness she had reached. We might not have done the splendid thing ourselves. Perhaps we are not capable of the highest kind of Love. But do we not give whole-hearted admiration to the man who _could_ behave thus? Love is one of the ways in which God reveals Himself to man. He shares with us the power to love. If we would take our share we must be prepared to suffer for the sake of our beloved. Are we going to shirk this privilege?

Last week we heard in the Synagogue addresses from L.C.C. members of different shades of belief, something about the issues underlying the elections in March.[3] We were reminded of the scope of work undertaken by the L.C.C. especially of its responsibility for education, housing and public health. Whether we agree with the Labour, the

Conservative or the Progressive candidate we <u>do</u> all feel that we <u>must</u> take an interest in these huge questions, for if we are just indifferent we make life harder for our own generation and for those who come after us. After those L.C.C. addresses we attended a meeting in this very hall on trade organisation. Why bother? Why ask girls and women in comfortable positions themselves to vex their minds about the overworked and unemployed, the badly trained and the ill-paid workers? Once more I say to you that it is religion - Judaism that demands this. Can we pretend to be sincere people when we say the Shema and when we talk about God's Unity revealed in the oneness of man if we don't bother about the needs of our neighbours? If we read history we are grateful to the people who <u>did</u> bother. Indeed, besides the labeled heroes and heroines we are well aware that countless men and women who in the rank and file of great movements have been alert to the needs of their neighbours have made life worth living for us today. They worried about abuses - they did better! They would not tolerate the wrong! Better still they found means to abolish it. That's why children are no longer employed. They were quite profitable at one time but humanitarian considerations pushed them out of the labour market. That's why prisons are no longer run for profit and the juvenile offender is getting his chance and an equal standard of morality is being established between men and women. That's why trade boards were set up to secure a minimum wage - sufficient for decent existence. That's why factory laws exist and unemployment benefit has been given and death duties have been imposed. We don't want to be fussy busy-bodies but we want to remember that evil can only be eradicated if it is replaced by good. Its influences are far-reaching and it is difficult to limit them. Take for instance the question of capital punishment. Most people say that happily the number of murderers is so small that we should not bother excessively about their doom. But the people administering the capital punishment, live after the event and their lives are influenced by the deed they have done. Society as a whole is affected by the responsibility it has assumed. The hysterical section of the community, unfortunately rather large, takes morbid interest in the trials, sacrificing time and strength to attend them because a death sentence is involved. The potential criminal is excited on the sensational side of his character and his power of resistance is weakened by his morbid emotions. No friends; if we are to live the religion we profess we must try to fight evil with quiet determination whenever and wherever it appears and believe we are fighting with and for God. This subject is interesting from the subjective as well as from the objective point of view. Surely besides bothering about the suffering of others we are considerably affected in the conduct of our lives by the fact that other people are bothering about us. Surely it does sometimes happen to us all to feel left out from the interest of others. We are failures, useless - nothing matters - we don't care! Our fate is our own concern. If you have had these feelings, you know as well as I, how terribly difficult effort becomes at such times. On the other hand, the fact that a lapse on the part of one woman degrades her sex; the fact that the unchastity of one man brings untold misery on his children; the fact that intemperance of all kinds affect not only ourselves but society as a whole, even to the third and fourth generation of them who turn their backs on goodness. Surely these facts strengthen us immeasurably in our efforts after righteousness. Cannot we imagine a girl of good character given to self-decoration of an outré kind saying "It amuses me to do this and it hurts no one. It is _my_ concern. I do nobody any harm." And when she says this she knows she is lying; as far as outward appearance [   ] and society as a whole has little chance of penetrating beneath her outward appearance. She is swelling the band of women and girls who sell themselves for profit. She is not that sort but society cannot tell and society is degraded. A man may say "I take my own risks - if I choose to bet and gamble it is my affair. My wife has her money all right - my children are cared for, why bother?" Yet he lies, for society cannot be healthy while in every section there are men and women getting something for nothing, letting worldly excitement absorb their God-self so that it can no longer get in touch with the Infinite.

Friends, let me appeal to you to keep away from that specious argument that a certain line of conduct is unobjectionable because it involves no direct evil doing. I am not sure that the negative person is sometimes not more harmful than the sinner who is guilty of one black deed and after that struggles to cultivate a decent character. The negative person - be he saint or sinner - is wasting the material society needs - God Himself needs, to complete His scheme which will lead to the triumph of righteousness. If you are not alert, active in the pursuit of goodness and the removal of evil, society cannot compensate itself for your neglect of opportunity. The first effort after righteousness makes subsequent effort possible. The existence of God is the guarantee of the existence of righteousness - your professed faith in Him implies that you are prepared to work for Him.

All the suggestions I have made in reply to the question why bother are illustrated in our attitude towards Judaism. As Jews we believe in the obligation to go, as individuals from strength to strength. No soul, we think, is alienated for ever from goodness but it is through his own efforts that he can attain to it. You may be <u>born</u> Jews but Judaism has no influence over your lives until you assimilate its teaching and force yourselves to act in accordance with its ideals. The demand is a stern one, but the God you serve is the God of Love. As soon as, in accordance with Jewish teaching, your lives have been touched by aspiration, all your windows are thrown open and the light of infinite hope enters. Then the community as a whole demands your help and you dare not say why bother? It is the honour of the community which encourages you to lead as decent a life as you can. It is the needs of the community which require you to bring your tiny portion of spirituality to the Spiritual treasury. <u>Of course</u> you can pray at home, but we need you here - of course A. B. & C. who never show any interest in Judaism are not related to you but they are missing the best, and your religion impels you to enthusiasm and your enthusiasm must convert the indifferentists and drifters who are keeping our brotherhood out of its religious inheritance. Surely we <u>must</u> bother a very great deal while so many of our brotherhood are indifferent. How else can we speak to the generations of God and of God's goodness? Is not this what we <u>want</u> to do - what God asks us to do?

On this Sabbath afternoon let us consider well, in the light of religion what are the things worth bothering about. Perhaps we shall find ourselves bothering about mere trivialities - indulging in fears which have no foundation now and never will have any reality. Perhaps we are wasting our opportunities altogether or using them in a futile way. Let us pray for guidance, and as we pray let us remember that when all the rubbish is pushed on one side there are many things which we shall <u>have</u> to bother about, which concern us immensely because they concern the well-being of the community as a whole. Yes friends, it is wonderful that <u>we</u> in spite of our absurd inadequacy, in spite of all our weaknesses, affect by our lives, the life of humanity in its progress towards God. So we <u>must</u> bother? So we pray.

Archives, Liberal
Jewish Synagogue, London

¹From Arnold's <u>Literature and Dogma</u> (1873).

²The title character of a poem by Tennyson, published in 1864.

³Lily Montagu is here referring to the London County Council, a local organization formed in 1888 to encourage the building of houses for members of the working classes. It later initiated or helped finance large projects in a number of areas (as indicated by Montagu) for the benefit of the poor.

KINSHIP WITH GOD

15th June, 1918

Many of you will remember a book published in 1907, called <u>Father and Son</u>.¹ It is the record of a struggle between two temperaments, two consciences and almost two epochs. After years of pathetic endeavor to produce reconciliation, the father charged the son with evading the Inspiration of the Holy Scriptures and with explaining away any particular Oracle of God, which pressed upon him. He felt that the son was sailing down the rapid tide of time towards Eternity, without a single authoritative guide excepting what he might forge on his own anvil, excepting what he might <u>guess</u> in fact. The son rebelled against this description of his spiritual state. He refused to regard this world any longer merely as the uncomfortable antechamber to a Palace, which no one had explored. He was told that he must cease to think for himself; defiance was offered to the intelligence of a thoughtful and honest youth, with the normal impulses of his twenty-one years, and disruption followed. Religious independence had to be emphasised, and two beings who loved one another intensely had to separate outwardly even as, through the action of the time force, they had for many years separated inwardly.

I doubt whether such cases of spiritual conflict in their extreme form could be instances in our Jewish Brotherhood, even in the last century. The fathers in our midst did not consider themselves responsible to God for their sons' secret thoughts and most intimate convictions. It sufficed that outward conformity was maintained, that no schism was introduced into the Community as a whole. In some instances, indeed, much agonising sorrow could have been averted if the logical connection between religious thought and religious observance had been more quickly recognised. Obedience which, in the father's life, led to holiness, seemed to be a good thing in itself, which should be adopted by the child with loyalty and fidelity. It was the discovery of a very obvious inconsistency between thought and ceremonial, which gave impetus to the liberal movement in this country. The spirit of the age gave a new importance to the value of truth - sought after for its own sake. Conformity could no longer be tolerated, if it involved the sacrifice of truth. Our leaders guided us in the work of adaptation. The relation between Jewish principles and modern life was proved anew and congregational life became possible.

Today the perspective has shifted slightly and we stand, each one of us, more keenly conscious than ever before of our own "Soul hanging in immensity."[2] Together with the readiness, so nobly prevalent today, to sacrifice the individual for the sake of a cause, there comes an intense respect for personality. We know today, as we have never known before, that God has put eternity into our hearts; and we protest with all the sincerity which is derived from intuition, unexplained and inexplicable, that life is not cheap, but rather precious beyond measure. Today we are far less concerned with the emancipation of the brotherhood from the oppression of arid legalism, than with the emancipation of the individual soul from the torture of arid negation. As a Community our shackles have fallen and we are free to enter into our religious inheritance. Our form of service is in harmony with our sense of fitness; we are no longer worried by the claims of tradition when these clash with our conception of truth. We have boldly enunciated our belief in progressive revelation, and this faith has quickened our hope for the future and intensified our reverence for the past. The congregation of today is free, and if it is to seize the fruits of its own emancipation it must gather together the thoughts and aspiration, the character and will, even the doubts and perplexities of each individual member.

It appears to me that the ideal of congregational life can only be approached when each individual member becomes conscious of his religious life, or, in other words, of his "Kinship with God." Upon this consciousnss depends the realisation of our origin and destiny, our faculty for prayer, our impulse to surrender ourselves to the highest conception of truth and righteousness. "Ye shall be holy, for I the Lord Thy God am Holy."[3] In all the agony of unrest which we are today experiencing, we cling with intense longing to the idea of an Eternal God, with Whom we can have communion, because we share His life and His nature. Perhaps we have occasionally chafed at the formula reiterated in our ancient forms of public prayer, the formula: "Our God and the God of our Fathers." Today we understand better, and chafe less. <u>Our God Idea</u> varies from generation to generation; we believe that it expands and develops, but we need to feel sure today of the existence of God and of our kinship with Him. We want to know Him as the Unchanging Spirit of absolute Love and Truth and Righteousness. The appeals of our fathers echo for us across the ages; their sense of kinship with God encourages us today. The unity of <u>longing</u> among God's children is one of the evidences of His Fatherhood; our spiritual need, shared, as it is, by the whole of humanity, can only be explained by reference to our common origin. I suggest that the sense of our kinship with God, based primarily on intuition, is supported by the testimony of the past and the character of our ancient worship. But our conception is also assisted by the actual experiences of every day life.

The prophet appeals to us to be holy, <u>because</u> God is Holy. The appeal is based on the possibility of men to imitate God. The pure soul shall see God. It is holiness, it is purity, which creates the kinship. What then is the divine holiness? Where is the point of contact between human holiness and divine holiness?

I can only touch on the fringe of this vast problem. The holiness of God implies an absolute standard of love, truth and righteousness. May not man's holiness be attained in the effort he makes to approach this standard, disciplining himself to obedience, even at the cost of material self-advancement and convenience? Jewish teaching gives us a Holy God transcending, and immeasurably excelling the human ideal; but it also suggests kinship with that ideal. 'Be holy for the Lord your God is holy.' The power of direct communion constitutes one of the glories of our faith; but without the sense of kinship the language of prayer, whether articulate or unexpressed, would fail us and, what is more important, there would be little room for human aspiration. Indeed, much of the joy and hope in human life lies in the "infinite pain of finite hearts which yearn." This yearning is conditioned by faith in the kinship of God. In one of his sermons, Professor [Benjamin] Jowett explains that God's holiness means the Spirit which is altogether above the world and yet has an affinity with goodness and truth in the world. It implies separation as well as elevation, dignity as well as innocence.

Belief in our kinship with God explains some of the aspects of human life which rouse our greatest veneration. Indeed, it accounts for the unconquerable optimism which should belong to every normal believer. No evil should be tolerated as characteristic of human nature - for kinship with God implies the ultimate perfectibility of man. It justifies the Jewish doctrine of the possible annihilation of evil by the substitution of good.

The universality of God's love includes the sinner as well as the Saint. Human love in its finest aspects reflects the divine in its inclusiveness and power of forgiveness. "Be sure his Mother loved him," was said of an evil doer, of whom nothing else that was good could have been spoken.[4] Today a little child asks as he goes to rest, "Has God been happy with me today?" Generation after generation have willed that their children shall be saved for the highest. In our educational plans we affirm anew, with every child that is born, our faith in his kinship with God. It is this faith which impels us to grudge no sacrifice to secure for the child the glories of his inheritance. Again, it is belief in man's kinship with God which rouses our indignation when we see innocent lives crushed and thwarted by the degrading struggle against unfair social conditions. Bad economic conditions may rob man of his freedom, and freedom is part of human holiness, which is akin to the divine. The thought of our kinship with God should make us disregard all that is fleeting and ephemeral in our appreciation of that which is eternal. Our hope is in God, as we endeavour humbly to walk with Him, doing justice and loving mercy when we catch a Ray of His divine Light. It is upon His rod and His staff that we rest, for we feel that we share His life as we pass through the valley, which men call the valley of death.

So far we have dwelt on man's claims to kinship with God as a state which, if consciously experienced, brings joy and peace and hope, and impels us to the highest effort. But we must remember that God, according to the teaching of Jewish prophets and psalmists, in His infinite mercy reveals His kinship with His human children. Throughout the Old Testament God the Ruler is also God the Father. "As a father pitieth his children, so does the Lord pity them who fear Him." God's extreme tenderness is further expressed: "As one whom his Mother comforteth so will I comfort thee." In the psalmist's view, surely, were there no kinship between the divine and the human spirit there could be little sympathy. Would pity then be acceptable? Would comfort then be possible? Still bolder, perhaps, is Isaiah's conception: "In all their affliction He was afflicted and He bore them and carried them all the days of old."[5]

This view of a suffering God brings Him into close relationship with human life, and it is this sense of close relationship which, I venture to think, we are needing today. God in His freedom voluntarily suffers with His suffering children. Our belief in the Supreme Spirit, who rules by law, is by no means shaken. Through intuition, through the sense of our own insufficiency, which causes us to reach out to Perfection beyond ourselves, through the actual experiences of every day life, we have learned that it is possible to establish our sense of kinship with the Holy Spirit, Who makes for righteousness. The God with whom we claim kinship, in spite of our weakness and our imperfection, is a Living God, and our kinship with Him suggests the possibility of a complete life. Permanent alienation is impossible because of that kinship: the hardened sinner has within his soul the power of saintliness.

The realisation of our kinship with God banishes the feeling of loneliness, which so often creates despair. The world may look, as it does today, terrible and even horrible. We may witness every hour the denial of God and of Goodness; but within man himself, in the fact of his kinship with God, is the promise of the ultimate triumph of love. The Ideal of God's love is imitable, though unattainable, on earth; the conviction that we are allied to it impels us to labour and to hope. God works through righteousness alone, and it is only by the establishment of Good that we can cast out evil. "Be ye holy, for I the Lord Thy God am Holy." It is as if the Father gently and tenderly bids us throw away all unworthiness and become conscious of our alliance with Himself. He bids us renew our faith in all that is good and pure, just and holy, because our nature is capable of this faith. He bids us love without stint, because we can draw love from the sources of love. He bids us be truthful, even in our inward parts, because no discipline is too hard for us whose lives are linked with the divine. He gives us the freedom to attain - even while He sets before us the Ideal of Righteousness. "Be ye holy, for I the Lord Thy God am Holy."

It has been well said that "God does not inhabit one world and man another, the <u>creation</u>, of which he is a part, is the incarnation of the life of God. God's nature is not radically distinct from man's nature. God's life and his are not mutually exclusive; if the man's life is part of the life of creation and the life of creation is the incarnated Life of God, there must at any rate be the possibility of conscious relation between God and man. The great central fact in human life, in your life and in mine, is the coming into a conscious vital realisation of our Oneness with the Infinite Life, an the opening of ourselves fully to the divine inflow. In the degree that we open ourselves to the divine inflow are we changed from mere men into God-men." 6

I would plead with you today that this glorious self-consciousness, implying, as it does, a sense of kinship with God, is derived from the actual experience of prayer, and from the effort after righteousness; that it alone explains the slow and often painful, but nevertheless steady, upward trend of human life. As we become conscious of our relationship with God, we become less and less attracted by evil associations. Is not this that which is meant by the command: "Ye that love God, hate evil." The self-conciousness which we have been describing stimulates man to the highest effort after righteousness and the strongest belief in the potentiality of that effort, <u>inasmuch</u> as it can be linked with the divine. But we remind ourselves that this sense of human dignity is dependent on our faith in God as the <u>Universal</u> Father. <u>Because</u> we have the power to attain holiness we are kin to the High and Loft One "that inhabiteth eternity, whose name is holy," but this power is allied in us with the human power to sin. Our kinship with God is inevitable, but we share it with the blackest sinner in our midst. We cannot deny the glory of this sinner's humanity without denying our own, for the God who conditions that glory is the Universal God, who dwells in every human soul to redeem and to save it for good. The point of contact between man and God is holiness - with the increase of human holiness does the relationship between man and God become closer. Man is united to man in his weakness as well as in his strength, in his failure as well as in his moral excellence. Let him deny both forms of kinship at his peril. The consciousness of our kinship with God is no passive state. It comes with our effort after righteousness. We have only to formulate our ideal to realise our deplorable short-comings. Belief in our kinship with God - in our human possibilites - fills our hearts with a sense of utter unworthiness, even while it stimulates us to a fuller hope.

We pray for the day on which "the Lord shall be known as one and His name one."[7] That day will become perceptibly nearer when the unity of human life will be recognised through the recognition of divine unity in the individual soul. The call is clear to us today. Let us hear it and obey; let us be conscious of our kinship with God through our reverence for absolute truth, through our humbly associating ourselves with Him in His work of redemption and salvation, through our power of loving without end, through our faith in the continuity of human life, which is linked with the divine for the purpose of creating righteousness.

Archives, Liberal
Jewish Synagogue, London

[1] Written by the Russian author, Turgenev

[2] Isaiah 26:8

[3] Leviticus 19:2

⁴From Browning's "The Ring and the Book"

⁵Isaiah 63:9

⁶This view stands in contrast to that expressed by Claude Montefiore in his <u>Outlines of Liberal Judaism</u> (London, 1912). On page 87 Montefiore writes: "God is other than man. He is pure spirit. He is the source. He is perfect. Man is none of these. Immense, then, is the difference between them. Man is not God, or a part of God . . . There is no right love possible, which is not based upon the conviction that man is other than, and different from God. The best and wisest man is separated by a huge gulf from the perfection of the Divine."

⁷From the Jewish Daily Prayerbook.

ADDRESS GIVEN AT THE GIRL'S CLUB AT 8, DEAN STREET, SOHO

26th November, 1911

"Ye are my witnesses, saith the Lord, and my servants whom I have chosen."[1]

Last week I spoke of hope, as affecting the life of the individual. My text was: "My hope is in God." And we found how the hope in God can, and does banish baser hopes. Sometimes the higher hopes can only be realised by acts of renunciation, and we illustrated this thought by reference to the life of the great Tolstoi, who has since passed away.

Today we want briefly to consider the hope of our brotherhood and the way it can, and must affect our lives - our <u>everyday</u> lives. We want to show that there is a distinct mission for our people and ourselves today, and to ask what that mission demands of us - of you and of me.

In order to make you understand the nature of our mission, I will draw two pictures and ask you to consider them. In a Russian village, in a small house, in a quarter inhabited almost entirely by Jews, there is a kitchen made to look bright and clean and fresh; there is a dresser at one end, with burnished copper vessels. On the table is a snow-white cloth, and two candles are burning. An old man in a skull cap is standing quite close to the stove. He is following with nods the words of his son, who is leading the Friday night hymn: "Come my beloved to meet the bride." His daughter-in-law is holding the old man's hand to steady him. There is a strained expression in her eyes - they are filled with acute pain. Every now and then, as a distinct cry echoes through the room, she looks at her husband - at the wooden bassinet, and her lips form the words: "Come, my beloved, to meet the bride;" and she does not know that no sound escapes her lips. A boy of seven is edging up to the door. He stares from his mother to his father and then to his grandfather. Questions are bursting to his lips; his face is flushed; he hears people coming nearer; he hears the sound of cries getting louder and louder. His little sister, sitting stolidly by the table, stares at him. She hears too, but she is bound to wait till after prayers to go and look at the soldiers. Then the door bursts open. A Christian neighbour rushes in and speaks a few words of warning and seizes the baby from the cradle, pushes the boy in front of him out of the room and into a place of safety. The mother lifts the little girl from behind her chair and screens her behind her skirt. The father and grandfather continue the evening service. In another minute men rush in, with brutal faces; the home is pillaged - the slaughter begins. It begins just as the old man is murmuring the words of the hymn: "The law of truth the Lord gave unto His people by the hand of his prophet who was faithful in his house."

The second picture is drawn in London, in a small house in Highbury. It is Friday night again. The table has just been laid; the maid has gone out of the room. An old lady in silk, with a white lace cap, is sitting looking out of the window, waiting - waiting. A tiny boy at her feet is trying to stuff a large piece of candy into a very small mouth. At last there is a loud ring. The old lady gives a sigh of relief. The mistress of the house bustles in and throws her parcels down on the sideboard. "Good evening, Mother," she cries, "I am going up to dress, I am rather late." "Light the candles first, dear." "Oh, the candles - yes, Friday night. How quickly the weeks go by." Very quickly, very perfunctorily, she seizes the candles from the sideboard, forages for matches, lights the candles, presses a quick kiss on her mother's forehead and darts up to dress. "Rudolph is so late," sighs the old lady. "Oh, yes, he will be back soon - kept late at business." In a few minutes the door opens again and a girl in a pretty evening dress runs in and throws off her coat. "Look at my dress, Granny! Nice, isn't it?" "Where are you going?" "To the Palace. Frank is taking me." "But it is the Sabbath." "Oh, yes, I know, but he is only staying in London for two nights and we are going out to supper afterwards. There is no other day possible; good night, Granny - I hear Frank's knock - goodbye! What is the matter? Oh, you want to bless me - all right - coming Frank!" The girl rushes out. The old woman stares at the candle. The room is empty - oh, so empty!

"Ye are my witnesses, saith the Lord, and my servants whom I have chosen."

The pictures are painful because they are true. When contrasted thus, it seems clear that there is something peculiarly mean in deserting our brotherhood while we live in security; while others meet their death because of their loyalty. Is their sacrifice to be of no avail, because we have come to worship a different deity? Our goddess seems

JEWISH SELF-IDENTITY

to be pleasure or convenience, while their hope is in God, and as they pass out to meet Him we ask whether their death is worthwhile.

As I draw these two pictures, you recognise the sordidness, the self-indulgence of the second home - the want of unity, the absence of hallowed love. You are sorry, shocked, and perhaps even disgusted by the contrast, and you feel sure, at least for the moment that the beauty and refinement of religion are worth preserving in the teeth of suffering and death. But afterwards, when you yourselves have to choose, when you have to order your life, you forget about these people in Russia, you forget about the meanness of desertion, you feel only one set of emotions clearly, and these include your own desires. Now, unless we have formulated a definite hope for ourselves; unless we can believe in our mission, I do not think we shall ever be able to reconsecrate and rededicate our lives. I ask you to recognise this mission - which justifies our separateness as a community and which as we shall see, purifies our individual lives. This is my appeal to you today. It is a positive appeal. If you will reply to it, you must be prepared to make sacrifices; you must be prepared to think out a guiding principle for your lives; you must be prepared to dethrone from within your hearts the deities, self-indulgence, self-advancement, and instead, you must admit the truth: "Ye are my witnesses, saith the Lord, my servants whom I have chosen." We must ask ourselves for what we as Jews stand - and when we know, we must be sure that our mission is worthwhile. Ours is a historic religion and today I would remind you of its origin.

Moses stood up before a tyrant king and said: "Let my people go that they may serve Me!" They were to be free from tyranny in order that they might voluntarily put themselves in bondage to the God of wisdom, truth and beauty. You are called to enter this bondage today, are you willing? <u>For this and nothing else is your mission</u>. In order to give the bondage outward signs, a religious system was founded - special times and seasons were appointed on which the people should become conscious of their higher selves and their great possibilities. The festivals were consecrated as symbols illustrating ethical ideas which should make for the sanctification of life. Work days and rest days should be hallowed. Family and social life were to reflect the love of God. Upon this basis, our religious system was founded by our fathers and their descendants had to contribute something towards its truth and beauty, although here and there, a wilful generation detracted from its holiness, and produced symbols of its own barbarity.

And now today we have still to consider this religious system, hallowed by the devotion of the past, made interesting by association with antiquity, and still demanding sacrifices. But why is this system still valuable? Because it contains symbols which reflect the love of God and the duties of man, which consecrate freedom and wisdom. If as individuals, you could dispense with these symbols, you could not afford to do so as a community for you might forget the service to which you are called, the message you have to deliver to the world. In old days, we Jews thought differently about our relation to God. We considered ourselves a special race whose glory glorified our God. Other people's disasters, if they brought us triumphs, were God's triumphs, and our material prosperity was pleasing unto Him. Then the prophets arose and laid emphasis on a new doctrine. They insisted upon national purity, and showed how this could be produced by suffering. A new construction was put on the declaration: "Thee only have I chosen," and we were bidden to train ourselves so as to become a light to the nations - silent witnesses of the highest conception of righteousness and truth. We were set apart, not for lordship, but for service, not for material triumph, but for spiritual education. The thought of this mission gives dynamic force to our brotherhood. Since we feel called to service, we become conscious of the power within ourselves to obey the summons. If we are to proclaim the messge, we must live as a people near unto God. For it is through our lives alone that the message can be understood. Is not this work worthwhile? Will you break away from the bond of service? Is it too small a thing, now that you have heard the call, to become a light to the nations? Again, you ask, why cannot we achieve the same result without the symbols? But <u>dare</u> we even attempt this, seeing that even now, with all our "aids to holiness" we fail again and again, we are woefully untrue to our great calling. Surely we need the special times and seasons for meditation and self-consecration. The world puts forth its claims so persistently, and it is hard to resist them even though we give ourselves special opportunities for self-purification. Dare we lose even these chances? In isolation enthusiasm waxes cold. When we come together, we feel the stimulus of mutual encouragement. We are drawn together by the common need for Love, and are encouraged to pierce through the clouds of evil, of misery and doubt to the God who is waiting for us and calling us to His service. In our homes, if we are able to dispense with the symbols for ourselves, have we the right to leave our children without the poetry which these symbols suggest? May they not serve as anchors to fasten these children to God? Life becomes vulgar very soon, if every day is exactly the same as the last, and there are no Sabbaths and holy days on which children may be taught to reverence the beauty of that which is divine. So soon as you introduce into everyday life the idea of the eternal, the word perfectibility ceases to be vague and meaningless, and instead, gives us a definite and stimulating hope. It seems worthwhile to enter the service of love in spite of frequent failures, and we no longer fear to hold ourselves responsible for our lives to the God Who has given us eternity in which to render them perfect.

If we are to remain true to our brotherhood today, we must be prepared to ask ourselves why we have left off keeping certain observances. Is the reason worthy or unworthy? Are we guided by conviction or by self-indulgence - by necessity or convenience? Are we prepared to retain, at whatever cost, the residue of observances which we believe to be founded on truth? These observances help us to remain a separate brotherhood so that apart from other communities we may cherish our faith and add to it, until it brings us as a people nearer to our God. Then the separation will surely cease for other peoples recognising the effect of our faith will run unto us and feed our hope by sharing it. To one or two of you in this room, the high bondage has already meant the supreme sacrifice of much of your own happiness; you would not disobey the call of the past and crush the hope of the future by allying yourself with a man of alien faith, however excellent and lovable he seemed to be. These sacrifices become more frequent as we realise more and more the joys of complete emancipation, but as time goes on, through reverent study and through self-control, you come to understand better the claims of your service as God's witnesses, and you know the sacrifices to be worthwhile.

I admit you can only come to this conviction if you share the common hope and if you understand the oneness of man as taught by the oneness of God, and consequently your obligation to the men and women of all races and creeds. You do not want to desert the brotherhood for the sake of those who are suffering in its name. This is a negative reason for your loyalty. The positive reason is far stronger. You must take part in the glorious work of God's witnesses; you want to remain with the people who have to live near God.

I must leave further discussion of the _way_ to witness to another address. Perhaps I have suggested something to you today by reminding you that we have a common hope, the hope of serving God, the God of our fathers, Who is the living God of righteousness and of truth. By communion with that God, by the direct communion which Judaism teaches, we can get at one with Him and draw some of His love into our lives. When you go out of this room today into the world, having prayed that you may conquer yourselves, you will have new courage to fight evil in the name of the living God Whom you have sought and found. That was why we assembled together today, to sanctify the Sabbath. What ambassador, speaking in the name of his human master, could have so much power as you, who during this week will silently serve the supreme Master and morning and evening ask the God of your fathers to renew the link with your soul - the same link by which they were bound to His service, the service which sets you free. This service will force you to seek the true and the beautiful in life and renounce the degraded and the ugly. Our common hope, our common service, demands of you and me the sacrifice of some comfort, the possibility of some self-advancement, perhaps it may be, of some intense happiness. It demands prayer, it demands effort, but as we stand here and pray for strength and try ever to strengthen one another, the voice sounds across the ages: "Ye are my witnesses, the servants whom I have chosen." Yes, we can make the sacrifice - we will make the sacrifice, because the word is good, it has come from God. If we yield now, we betray our truth. Through the service we shall find peace.

Archives, Liberal
Jewish Synagogue, London

[1] Isaiah 43:10

HERE AM I: SEND ME

June 17, 1944

These noble words were spoken by Isaiah when he felt himself called by God to go out among the people and to do his work. Isaiah had seen a vision of God Himself, and he had been overwhelmed by the realisation of God's greatness and holiness. He believed himself to be called to work for God, but he did not think that he was qualified for the undertaking. He failed in courage to say distasteful things, even to pronounce doom on his fellow countrymen for the sins of which they were guilty. Moreover, he knew himself to be morally weak, a man of unclean lips, unworthy to speak the word of the Lord. Then suddenly he felt that he himself was in contact with the divine spirit. He experienced a feeling of exaltation and purification. In contact with God, his lips were purged by the living flame from God's altar. He responded: "Here am I: send me."[1] It was grand, a wonderful experience.

You and I are not spiritual giants, as was Isaiah. We cannot expect ever to do great work for God and with God, but I venture to suggest to you that we can each in his small way feel the contact with God and His cleansing power operating over our human weaknesses and clearing them away.

JEWISH SELF-IDENTITY

In these critical days, we must each enter into our Holy of Holies, and there in quietness and in faith work out our relation to the community and indeed to all mankind.

We must accept the fact that we are related to all the inhabitants of the world, and that we have obligations to them. No man can separate himself and stand detached, alone. His human personality requires a social setting if it is to fulfil itself.

We Jews stand as witnesses to the truth of the existence of God, to the truth which we have inherited from our ancestors and which has been handed down from generation to generation by an unbroken chain of men and women who have served God and man by giving the testimony by which humanity is sustained. Today, we have to breathe into our belief the spirit of life which is taken from God Himself, but which is ours, and which we have to use in order that our religion should fit into our own individual souls and be recognised as a reality and an abiding influence.

It is important that you and I, in our humble way, even as Isaiah did, in his great way, recognise that we have work to do through our affiliation with the community, and that work is part of God's charge to each of His children. Like Isaiah, we recognise our limitations and our weaknesses. Even as we dare to say the words: "Here am I: send me," we know ourselves to be unworthy of our glorious privileges. But this very knowledge, painful though it must be, is at the same time immensely stimulating and encouraging. At this moment we are what we are, but in contact with God, our Teacher and Friend, our Master and Leader, we can each become a true servant. We can feel our kinship with God, and let it raise us to new heights and infinite possibilities. "Ye shall be holy, for I the Lord Thy God am holy."

Mr. Singer once said in a sermon: "While some assert that there was once a perfect man, born nineteen centuries ago, one of our own race too, we are to proclaim our belief in a more comprehensive ideal, in a perfect humanity to be developed in God's own good time. We are to testify to our conviction that, in that divine scheme, transcendant in its majesty and universal in its scope, we Jews are called to fill a place and to perform a part. Without some such purpose, the Jew is an enigma, insoluable alike to others and to himself. Others, unable to explain him, have sometimes tried to explain him away. God forbid that we should do so. Ye are my witnesses, saith the Lord." [2]

In this address, I want to try to make some practical suggestions. If we are to carry out our work as God's witnesses and servants, we must clarify our ideas in reply to the question: "What would God have us do?" That question can only be properly answered by each one of you alone with the Alone. But perhaps I may be allowed to make a few general suggestions which I have found useful in my own life.

Human beings do work most effectively through groups, and the platform from which we bear our testimony is, of course, our Synagogue. I wonder how many people regard their Synagogue as a useful centre for the holding of public worship which we like to think goes on from week to work, much in the same way, and which we may attend when it is convenient for us to do so, when the weather is propitious and we feel on the whole inclined for it. It is also a place where our children can receive religious education and where marriage and burial ceremonies are performed when required. Is that not all which a number of us Jews ask of our Synagogue? When we attend, we criticise the sermons, favourably or unfavourably; we say whether we think the building is too hot or too cold; we express our views on the strength or weakness of the choir; but membership in a Liberal Synagogue should not be of this kind. By belonging to a Synagogue, we stand for a certain presentment of Judaism which affords us spiritual stimulus and guidance. The authority for our religious conceptions is no longer to be found in a perfect code, verbally true, but in the trained conscience of the individual who has reverently studied the past teaching and for himself sought enlightenment in prayer and meditation.

Our Synagogues form part of a Union which exists to spread and to perpetuate this particular form of Judaism, because we believe that it contains within itself a guidance to right living in harmony with the conditions under which we live, and the knowledge acquired by the human intelligence working from the beginning down to the present day.

What do you give to your Synagogue? Of course, I know you pay your subscription and are ready to contribute money to every special need which arises. But important though that material assistance is, we ask for an infinitely more worthwhile contribution. We ask for some of yourself, some of your thoughts and emotions, the expression of your beliefs and aspirations. The Synagogue is meant to influence life. It supplies us with a spiritual outlook on the affairs and opinions of every day, on the well-being of our city, our country, and in fact the whole world. Many activities of social value should emanate from the Synagogue. By that I do not mean that we should all be engaged in social service with a capital S. Some people are not fashioned that way, and their efforts would be unacceptable to those they desire to serve. They lack the particular form of imaginative sympathy necessary for such work, but they can, nevertheless, be socially minded and in their homes and in their business and in their recreation, they can offer a very high form of service. They can indeed love their neighbours as themselves, and they will recognise and appreciate that the religious motive is necessary for the conduct of life, if it is to be as fine as possible.

From the Synagogue indeed can be evolved a high standard of life which challenges the loyalty of every member, and if you cannot find the standard you think right to accept, if you cannot discover in the services the stimulus you need, I would ask you whether you seek to offer something better which can be assimilated into Synagogue life, and if you don't, whether you are not seriously at fault? We must not increase the religious apathy and indifference which we believe can benefit mankind spiritually. Are you shocked at this claim? Do you think we are arrogant in making it? Are you aggrieved because people of other faiths lead equally good or better lives, and must also have a claim to influence humanity in its spiritual growth. I believe in the Light of the Perfect Day, but I believe we can only reach it if each group trims its own wick, and is loyal and enthusiastic, understanding and loving. Just consider some of the things we Jews have already done. We have given the Bible to the world. The world has taken our Bible, but not away from us. They have asked to share it, and we the people of the book are not always alive to the value of our possessions. Does the Bible have an important place in the personal life, and in your home life? Unless we discipline our lives under the teaching of the Bible, it is possible that we shall not be able to convince the world for all time of its value. Our Bible gives us a fine code of morality, and tells us that a good Jew must live in accordance with its highest teaching. Do you find time to read or to study the Bible? A great deal can be done if you are prepared to set aside every day a few minutes for this all important work. We have told the world that religion is based on morality. We must give practical object lessons, and not only the book in which the fact is proclaimed. We have given the world the Sabbath principle, a day on which we rest and rejoice, pray, think and study. Do you use at least part of your Sabbath in that way. We have shown the world the supreme importance of social justice which establishes the right of every man to live and work in decency and to fulfil himself in peace. Are we always sufficiently aware as employers of labour, or as responsible citizens, that we do not sin against our own ideal? We have affirmed the sanctity of home life. Do we remember to consecrate it by family services, by chastity, by holy joy? We exalt the idea that the whole of man is holy to the Lord. Do we do all we can to develop physically, intellectually and spiritually? We appreciate the beauty of life. Do we do reverence to the beauty of nature as the creation of God; are we always careful not to prostitute art to gratify unworthy desires? We have affirmed the value of truth in the inwards parts of every man and woman, and in his relations to his neighbours. Do we always refrain from giving false witness, or from backbiting acquaintances in order to gain a certain degree of popularity for ourselves? We have given the world the conception of the One God who is Eternal, and who has created man in His image. Do we always express the Fatherhood of God in our devotion to the brotherhood of man, to peace and democracy and the removal of all obstructions to the healthy development of mankind? God has put eternity in our hearts and so has given us for ever in which to realise ourselves, and to cling to our beloved. Do we actually believe in an infinite future which overcomes death towards which we can go with invincible hope and faith, believing that since God is rightousness, truth and beauty and love, these realities must prevail?

Isaiah said: "Here am I: send me." Let us on this Sabbath day accept God's charge. Let us here and now begin to prepare ourselves for God's work. Let us go forward in His name.

> Archives, Liberal
> Jewish Synagogue, London

[1] "Here Am I: send me," a phrase often quoted by Lily Montagu in her sermons and addresses is from Isaiah 6:9.

[2] These and other ideas are clearly expressed by Singer in *The Literary Remains of the Rev. Simeon Singer*, 2 vols. ed. Israel Abrahams (London: George Routledge and Sons, 1908).

CLUB LETTER NO. 185

June, 1956

I am venturing to take "Marriage" as my subject this month. Your first reaction will be: What can an old woman who has never married know about the subject? I admit that the lack of personal experience greatly limits the value of my opinions, but, during my long connection with young people, I have received the confidence of hundreds of those on the verge of marriage and for very many years after they have entered into this "holy state."

On the whole, I venture to say that the percentage of happy marriages among our Club people is a high one. This high percentage has become even more noticeable in latter years, partly because we are now definitely a mixed Club and the opportunity is given for friendships between men and women of the same religious sexes is maintained. So if a friendship develops into marriage, the personality of the man and the woman is mutually respected, and their equal share in the responsibility of home making is taken for granted. As we read in Proverbs: "The heart of her husband does safely trust in her."[1]

Nevertheless, I do not think it out of place to suggest that the highest degree of happiness resulting from marriage can be most hopefully expected if the standard of preparation is as high as humanly possible. I feel with most of my readers that marriage can produce the greatest happiness possible to human beings. But that happiness cannot be obtained if it is made a direct objective. That means that young men and women lose dignity and self-respect if they set out to marry for the sake of marriage and run after a partner and seek success without regard to the compatibility of personality. A superficial sense of attraction does not suffice.

I have been a member of the Marriage Guidance Council ever since its inception, and would recommend all young people who are contemplating marriage to seek advice from wise and experienced counsellors. These men and women have no other motive in their work than the well being and happiness of the young people concerned. Through a knowledge of all sorts and conditions of lovers, they explain the physical, moral and spiritual conditions which are essential to happiness.

We are told that young people are indulging in pre-marital relation without any feeling that they are lowering the moral standard. Modern science makes this intercourse easy. Such a decline in self-discipline militates against the best kind of marriage, and is at the same time irreligious and unJewish. We Jews in loyalty to the God of the universe bring the God idea into every part of our lives. If self-indulgence is our goal, if we wish to ignore the standards of morality revealed to us, we are separating ourselves from our people and from the teaching we have inherited from the past. It is no use the young people trying to annihilate such views by calling them old-fashioned, and I know that this term is the deadliest weapon our youth can use if they wish to get rid of any arguments distasteful to them. I defy any man or woman who is seeking direct contact with God to justify physical self-gratification as a road to happiness. Human personality is a sacred trust, and we cannot use the opportunities which life affords us if we countenance at the outset self-degradation. Edward Carpenter wrote not many years ago:

> And him thou lovest or her thou lovest, if without confusion thou beholdest such a one fixed like a star in heaven, and ever in thy most clinging burning passion rememberest whom thou lovest, then art thou blessed beyond words and thy love is surely eternal, but if by confusion thou knowest not whom thou lovest, but seest only the receptable of desire which inhabits the world of change and suffering, then shalt thou be whirled and gulped in a sea of torment and shalt travel far and be many times lost upon that ocean before thou shalt know what is the true end of thy voyage.[2]

A true Jew and Jewess who decide to unite in marriage cannot wish to exalt the physical above the spiritual. If their future home is to have a Jewish atmosphere, the owners must know the joys of spiritual relations as controlling all others. They sacrifice this possibility if they exalt the animal passions as supreme. I have in the past been rather shocked by being told not infrequently by engaged couples: "Yes, we are very happy, and are sure we shall always be so. No, we did not talk about religion. He or she is Jewish, of course, but I don't really know whether our faith has any interest for my friend." When one who has been devoted to Judaism weds a materialist who has led a secular life, there is perpetrated a form of intermarriage which, I think, is nearly as dangerous as any other, for it shakes the stability of the Judaism of the future.

We learn from those who investigate the records of marriages that civil marriages are becoming more and more numerous as against marriages in a Synagogue or Church, and we are asked: What is the difference? The difference seems to me to be in the character of the marriage. Either it is only a civil contract, in accordance with the law of our country, or it is in addition the most important religious undertaking of your lives. In a civil marriage, you accept legal obligations. In a Synagogue marriage, you uphold your ancestral faith and declare that in your belief, the God of the universe consecrates the vows you make in His presence. God is also present in the registry office, but you are more conscious of His authority when you seek His guidance in prayer, supported by the prayers of your closest friends and nearest relatives. In the modern form of marriage service used in the Liberal Jewish Synagogue, you are united as 'beloved companions.' The beautiful word 'helpmate' is also introduced.

You are united by the trust you have in one another and by desiring to share the best you know. You give one another love which animates the highest companionship. You are helpmates in together seeking the greatest experiences that life can give. I always hope that couples realise that after they are wedded they have to progress in the search after truth. They must desire also to increase their power of service. Through their mutual love, they must be stimulated to help in overcoming the problems and in understanding the difficulties in the outside world. Of course, the husband will have to attend to his business, and the wife if she does not go out to work, will have much to do at home to create happiness through comfort. But this is not enough, even though it represents one of the highest mountains that married folk have to climb, if it is to reveal complete mutual trust. Remember that you must make your mountains of difficulty a way to God, and trust that love, the "flame of the Lord,"[3] will help you to overcome those difficulties.

As citizens you have national and international obligations secondary only to those of your home. If your union is real, your individual usefulness will be doubled. If you open your intellectual and spiritual windows and bring your human love and religious faith to bear on current affairs, you will add to your happiness by enriching your lives.

If, as we hope and expect, you will be allowed the privilege of parenthood, you will be able to give your children the supreme advantage of being brought up in a religious home. Contact with God in prayer will create a natural happy peaceful background in which their personalities will grow. As Maeterlinck says: "Look inwards! For you have a lasting fountain of happiness at home that will always bubble up, if you will but dig for it."[4]

Finally, I trust your children will say: Our home is a sanctified and delightful place. There we can be at our ease, because we are understood. The father-mother love fills home and causes the best in us to grow. There we aspire after the unattainable and our eyes seek the invisible, and the search is always joyous, for it is never undertaken alone. Our home people are always ready to show us sympathy and encouragement, either for our successes or our failures. Our home reveals the presence of God, for it takes account of the personality of each one of His children and unites them with the bonds of love and loyalty. We go forth courageously to spread a little of the joy and peace which our home has given us. As we go into the big world, we know that we can never lose the eternal love and peace which our parents have planted for us in our home.

Private Collection,
Hannah Feldman, London

[1] Proverbs 31:11

[2] From Carpenter's poem "Disentanglement" in his Towards Democracy (London 1905), p. 347.

[3] From the Biblical Song of Songs 8:6 quoted, in context, by Claude Montefiore following the title page of both volumes of his The Bible for Home Reading (London, 1896-99).

[4] From The Treasure of the Humble.

CLUB LETTER NO. 139

December 1951

If I were to suggest to you a self-imposed ghetto life, you would be very wroth with me and quite rightly so. We have read about ghetto life in many Jewish stories; the narrowness and absence of scope, its pettiness, its superstitions and fanaticism, the mediaeval ordering of its life. Certainly some authors like Israel Zangwill managed to reveal the underlying sweetness and nobility of the inner life belonging to men and women who even though living in a ghetto had received a spiritual inheritance which excelled in beauty and grandeur. Through his sense of humour he showed the kindness and fun understood so well by the people who never moved out of the ghetto. The Jews above all people know how to rise above their limitations and created romance and lustre in their human relations.

Nevertheless, to all people living in this century the ghetto life and all its implications would of course be abhorrent and they would scorn any connection even with those who emerged from the ghetto and they would only see the ghetto "bond" denoting servility and the narrow life of discipline to strange and useless laws and customs. I fully agree with this point of view, but nevertheless I see how emancipation has increased the danger to Jews of disloyalty through assimilation with their neighbours. This danger takes many forms, for emancipation is a complex condition and its excellence can only be based on self-discipine and the recognition of individual responsibility. Freedom is only an unmixed blessing if it is held as consecrated to the service of God. We are <u>free</u> to serve the highest, not to create an anarchic pattern of life satisfying only the aimless and self-indulgent folk; but I want in this letter only to deal with one aspect of emancipation.

We are glad indeed that our young people can mix freely in this country and share their many privileges and pleasures and opportunities for work and recreation. But the danger of intermarriage has certainly shown itself to be a real one in the present generation, and I ask you to consider with me how it can be prevented, and even perhaps whether intermarriage is altogether an evil to be avoided at all costs.

Every week more of our young people <u>do</u> intermarry. We see the names in the general press. Many belong to our oldest and most distinguished Jewish families who are in consequence fast disappearing from our community. The parents helped to make Anglo-Jewish history, but they themselves are seldom counted as Jews at all and this fact perhaps tends to increase their satisfaction. They will, they think, no longer be handicapped by outside so-called racial prejudice and, in consequence, success in life will be far more easily secured by their children. I am equally, perhaps even more, concerned about the average Jew and Jewess who having been brought up in Jewish homes find their partner outside their community and think "this cannot be helped." It may be a pity, they say, but happiness must be sought first, and they cannot see any threat to Judaism because they follow the dictates of their hearts. So unimportant does the decision often seem from the religious angle that these boys and girls tell me what they have told the non-Jewish partners, that they are Jews and no objection has been raised and they are sure they can remain Jews and bring up their children in their faith. The man or woman of their choice is so broad-minded!

Now it is easy to be broad-minded if one is indifferent, and I think the terrible threat to the continued existence of our brotherhood - and it is nothing less - comes from indifference. The Jewish boy and girl may be devoted to their parents, but they know they will be forgiven and neither mummy nor daddy will upset their happiness. Now I do not approve the course taken by the last generation who considered the child who married out of the faith as dead and sat Shiva[1] for him. The parents' hearts may have broken, but they knew, even as we do, that the children were voluntarily deserting the ranks of God's Jewish witnesses, that they disregarded the task which God Himself had set them, and this was a real sin. These parents knew, as we do, that the call of the majority is irresistible even though at the beginning an effort is made to combat it. Gradually the interest in Judaism _must_ decline for mummy goes one way and daddy another, and the children cannot recognise any Jewish significance in the way of life. No, the erring child must not be cut off; for the parents' attitude of total rejection may remove from the children faith in the God of forgiveness and in the eternal human love which has so far protected them. They must not be uprooted from the family life even though they have lost their right to profess interest in the religion which has justified the survival of the family as a branch of that tree which God planted in his vineyard for a particular purpose. But so serious is the danger of intermarriage that we of the West Central, though retaining our appreciation of personal freedom for individuals on personal grounds, cannot any longer accept their membership in a Club established to perpetuate a living Judaism. The happiness on which the great decision is based is, we know, often most illusory. I do not deny that in some cases the mixed marriages prove very happy, especially when the religion has no strong hold over either party, but I think it is fair to say that in most cases the close sympathy probably apparent at the beginning fades away. There is a feeling at first subconscious, but gradually more and more real of difference and estrangement. A home, if worthy of its name, must be founded on complete spiritual unity; man and wife can differ intellectually and be very happy, but real marriage is a spiritual at-onement and no complete merging is possible between a Christian and a Jew. Through the force of heredity as well as through family contacts the severance generally is inevitable. The man or woman who marries someone of a different faith denies the importance of his mission and by breaking the chain of witnesses does as much harm as is in the power of an individual human being to weaken the value of his ancestral faith.

In all this I do not claim any superiority as a Jewess over other faiths. I have Christian friends who are as dear to me as any Jewish people and their lives are not less admirable. Both communities have each its separate and different approach to God, and the difference is of infinite importance although the goal is the same.

By intermarriage I do not of course mean the marriage of a man or woman born of Jewish parents with one who has accepted the Jewish faith in adult life. Since the days of Ruth the Moabitess we have accepted proselytes and if they join us in all sincerity we often find them more faithful and zealous than those born among us. We Liberals insist on a course of study which shall produce a real understanding of our principles and observances. Of course we are sometimes mistaken and deceived. But the great majority of our proselytes are quite as devout and loyal as those born of Jewish parents. But the Jewish partner in an engagement must be really Jewish in faith and observance before he or she dares ask the non-Jew or non-Jewess to accept the Jewish faith. It must be a reality and not a shadow brought down from a hazy past and possessing a name. It must cover the whole of life and give a certain spiritual outlook to those possessing it so that they feel the obligation at any cost of personal sacrifice to make it the centre and guide and inspiration of their lives.

Why is intermarriage becoming an increasing danger in our community? I am afraid it is because the children brought up in a Jewish home are taught so little or so badly that they hardly value their possession. They _may_ see a few observances in their home, but the indifference to the value of such ceremonials is so great that the children do not recognise their meaning and how they can stimulate goodness and truth in people's hearts. Worse than all, the children have no knowledge of the mission of

Israel, how it is to give light to all mankind. We exist to spread the value of Judaism. The God of the Jews is the God of the Universe and we are called to work as a group, scattered as we are all over the world, in order that we may bring nearer the day when God's unity will be accepted and the whole of mankind will call on His name. Then indeed strife and wickedness will tend to disappear from the world and all God's children shall live in peace and harmony. But, alas, we know that here and there children brought up in this faith suppress it for the sake of their own personal happiness. Therefore I appeal to you, young men and women, to obtain a real understanding of Judaism and make its principles part of your daily life. Do not wait until Cupid comes along before you begin to think about your religion and to seek God through the Jewish portal. We value you and we need you as Jews and Jewesses. God asks your cooperation in spite of your weaknesses and imperfections. He needs your Jewish allegiance. How then can we human beings disregard the supreme importance of Jewish fidelity and fail to see that intermarriage destroys it and therefore is hardly less than an act of betrayal.

Private Collection,
Hannah Feldman, London

[1] The traditional period of mourning.

"OUT OF ZION SHALL THE LAW GO FORTH AND THE WORD OF THE LORD FROM JERUSALEM"

West Central Club,
November, 1917

I am going to speak to you this afternoon on a controversial subject and I very seldom do this at our Services.

Some of you disagree with me altogether, for some of you are strong Zionists and I am not, and it is rather riling to hear views enunciated from this place, and not to be able to reply. But we must have some discussions on other occasions, such as Bible Classes and meeting, when you will have your chance. I believe that you want to know what I think about the recent important Government declaration about Palestine.[1] To many of you Zionism is part of Judaism, and although I have spoken to you so much about religion, many of you seem to think that for me also a return to Palestine forms part of my religious hopes, and I want to explain to you that this is <u>not</u> the case.

Let me first read to you the Government Declaration:

> His Majesty's Government view with favour the establishment in Palestine of a national home for the Jewish people, and will use their best endeavours to facilitate the achievement of this object, it being clearly understood that nothing shall be done which may prejudice the civil and religious rights of existing non-Jewish communities in Palestine, or the rights and political status enjoyed by Jews in any other country.

You have these facts - the Cabinet, a few individuals, without reference to Parliament, have promised to do their best to let Jews possess <u>Palestine</u>, and have there a <u>national</u> home. Note the word <u>national</u>. Now, as an English woman, my nationality is <u>English</u>, my religion is Jewish. I don't want another national home. I couldn't use it if it were given to me, because I am part of the English nation, and have never considered myself anything else. Some people misunderstand what devotion to England means. If one is born in a country, and brought up to share a country's ideals, if one's home is run on English lines, and one's friends are English, one absorbs the influences of England's past, and becomes anxious humbly to serve England, and through England to serve the world. This does not mean hostility to other nations. This does not mean approval of all that an English Government does or says. It means rather, that one recognises that the English nation has to play its distinct part, a part which is within its own powers and the expression of its own genius in the political development of mankind.

We all advance in groups and the English people is my group. I want to see every human being free to develop physically, mentally and morally, all that is best in himself. That is the aim of all nationalities, and England HAS her own WAY of achieving that object. She has a message, and I want to help her in my tiny way to carry that message. The Germans, the French, the Russians have very much the same aim, but different means of bringing it about, and so the German, French and Russian Jews differ from one another. They have the same religion, but their ideals concerning the work of the State, their political ideals are different. If a political State were established in Palestine, I should not be able to belong to that State. I feel I belong to England. The Government have promised to try not to cause prejudice to the political status of Jews all over the world. Now I want you to see if that is possible. Unless the Palestinians CALLED themselves by some other name than Jew, just think what a difficult situation would be created. Imagine, for example, a boy wanting to enter the Civil Service, or a man wanting to vote or enter the L.C.C.[2] or Parliament, he would be regarded as a foreigner. Nobody would understand that there were two sets of Jews, the Palestinian Jews who regarded Palestine as their country, and the others who had other countries. As soon as Jews had a national home of their own, they would no longer be considered as an integral part of other nations. In the eyes of other nations they would ALL be aliens. As Mr. Mattuck said last week, boys and girls who were brought up in England or America would deny they were Jews, if Judaism meant allegiance to another COUNTRY. They would want another name for their religion. Think of our religious brotherhood breaking up in this way, think of the tragedy; for if there were no unity how could we live and work so that through us all the families of the earth would be blessed?

In the Government declaration, we are told that the civil and religious rights of non-Jewish communities in Palestine would not be interfered with. Just think of the difficulties here. Christians and Mahommedans alike regard Palestine as closely connected with religion. As soon as a Jewish state was established, they would want to form part of that State. "Jews" would then no longer form a religious brotherhood, but a political community. We could not in these days apply a religious test to people who form part of a State, so, if we kept the name Jew for the Palestinian, we should have Jews of the Christian religion and Jews of the Mahommedan religion. See what a new set of difficulties would be created.

I cannot leave the analysis of the Declaration alone without telling you that, as an English woman, I protest against the right of our Government to make a Declaration of this kind, so important to the destinies of the world, without consulting Parliament, the people's representatives. I think, moreover, it is contrary to her pledges to take a country and dispose of it. She has said again and again, and I believe that many of her sons have gone willingly to their death because she said it, that we are not out to extend our dominions in any way. The British

Government does NOT say that England will take Palestine for herself, but it DOES say that it will help to give Palestine away, and make a national home there for a set of people who have no national home at present. The British Government has no power to say this, while Palestine is not in its gift. When England has completely conquered the present owners, would she even so have the right to give the country away? What would be her relation to the new nation of Palestinians?

I have criticised the Government Declaration on political grounds, now I want to deal with it on religious grounds. As far as POLITICAL GROUNDS are concerned, you may say to me: "It's all very well for you, as an English Jewess, to claim English nationality, but in certain countries Jews are regarded as a separate nation. They have no rights, except the right of martyrdom. Do these Jews not need a national home in Palestine, because they have NO NATIONAL HOME ELSEWHERE?" This rejoinder is, at present, tragically true in certain countries, but you will agree that it is a passing state. Till it has passed, we fully admit that our co-religionists suffer protracted agony, and we do NOT regard their sufferings with equanimity. But we look for the end of the suffering in the liberation from tyranny of the countries where the suffering now occurs. We see the freedom of the Jews as an integral part of the democratisation of the whole world. The Russian Jew will become free when his country is free--he is assisting now in the liberation of his country. If his RELIGION persists, he will help in the great work of emancipation, for he owes to his RELIGION his great ideals of freedom. He must apply them to the task of liberation to which his country has applied itself.

I have been reading a clever exposition of Zionism by Leon Simon,[3] and as I read I felt great sympathy with HIS presentment. In the past, some of the great Zionist leaders have openly stated that the Jewish religion, as such, makes no appeal to them, and they have rallied their followers through <u>race</u> allegiance, and nothing more inspiring than that. We have seen men and women, who are utterly indifferent to Judaism or any other articulate religion, call themselves Zionists. Their motives are openly political, not religious, and we consider their propaganda a menace to the highest interests of our brotherhood. We have felt that these people have not come into their inheritance, that they know nothing of their own treasures, which are spiritual treasures. We were bold enough to hope that we might gather some of these men and women to ourselves, when as Liberals, we were able to show them a living Judaism in harmony with progressive ideals of life. But <u>most</u> of these racial Zionists were deaf to our appeal.

But besides these people whom (for want of a better name) I have called racial Zionists, and to whom the most distinguished leaders seem to have belonged, there are masses of men and women, sincere Zionists, who are also sincere adherents of the Jewish faith, and although, for the reasons I have enumerated, I do not share their point of view, I sympathise with it.

Mr. Leon Simon feels that a national home is needed for the intensification of Jewish thought and feeling if our religion is to live. I am also of opinion that we need intensification, but this work can be carried on in every country through the faithful service of all Jewish Believers. At the present a wastage is occurring through the drifting of some individuals to other spiritual organisations because they fail to realise the claims of Judaism. The evil can only be met by greater religious fidelity.

Mr. Simon writes sympathetically, and with the deepest respect, of our point of view as expounded by Mr. Montefiore, which is briefly this. As a brotherhood we have to understand the teaching of our faith, we have to apply it to the life around us with which we are familiar, we have to express it in our own lives, and make it acceptable to the world <u>because</u> its transfiguring effect on our lives and characters proves its desirability. Mr. Simon thinks that our universalistic aspirations involve assimilation with the religions around us. We deny this statement with all the strength of our convictions. We are told that our religion, deprived of its tribal characteristics, is a Christianised religion. Again we deny this statement with intense feeling. We believe that the essentials of Judaism are meant to persist through all time and in all places. Our prophetic writings are full of universalistic teachings. We retain our interest in our ceremonials and observances, not because of their antiquity, although we appreciate the long history of devotion which has led to their survival, but because they lead men and women to holiness. We find the home for the expression of our Jewish faith in our very midst, because we fashion this home ourselves. The gift of a <u>political</u> home will not make <u>Judaism</u> live. The grouping together of believers all over the world, through a <u>voluntary</u> union in each country for the <u>purpose</u> of formulating a living faith; this is the way, as we think, to cause Judaism to live. The service is from within; it is here and now. Of course we are susceptible to the religious influences of our countrymen, as they are susceptible to ours. It is true that certain features in their faith have strengthened our development. Take, for example, the status of women in Jewish religious organisations! Some of us think that the Jewish point of view is still not quite satisfactory, but in Western countries, at least, we are on the <u>road</u> to the belief that religion makes equal demands on men and women. Our grandparents hardly thought so. Sometimes some of them even desired the exclusion of women from Synagogue at certain times. We have gone forward, and the progress has been assisted by Western ideals. I could, if there were time, show you how our religious progress has been similarly assisted in other directions, but surely this does not mean that we have been Christianised. Are we to be so hide-bound that we must not recognise a ray of light because it was generated outside our community? We believe that Judaism has certain <u>real</u>, definite, distinct teaching of its own, we believe that this teaching is its peculiar and distinct treasure, that it embodies truths which are eternal, and which therefore <u>cannot</u> be affected by other religious doctrines. Of what, then, are we afraid? Have we so little faith in our own doctrines? We believe that there is one God to whom every individual can speak, and from whom every individual can gather strength, without the help of an intercessor of any kind; that each human soul is responsible to this God for the conduct of his life, and that righteousness leads to God; that human life comes from God, and shares the immortality of the divine life; that love of God, based on the justice which implies respect for every form of life, expresses itself in love of man; that allegiance to God involves the consecration of body, mind and soul in the service of God. Have we so little faith in the truth of these doctrines as to think they must perish, if the religion which embodies them comes in close contact with other religions? We are often harassed by the intolerance of men of a different faith. Much of this intolerance is due to their ignorance and jealousy. We despise it because we recognise the <u>reason</u> for its existence. But some of this intolerance is <u>our</u> fault. We have not <u>lived</u> the Jewish life, and so the value of our doctrine has not been discovered. We have made small response to the demands which Judaism makes upon us. Some of our people have <u>even</u> degraded themselves by denying its value, and slurring over the distinctions, which separate it from other faiths. We have been ostentatious, we have cared for self-advancement, we have been greedy and uncontrolled. Yes, we Jews <u>have</u> been at fault, but not Judaism. Judaism has still the highest conceivable power for inspiring the best of which human life is capable.

A league is just being formed of British Jews.[4] I hope similar leagues will be formed in other countries, so that the movement may be international. Every British subject can join, on payment of a minimum subscription of 1/[ ] provided he professes the Jewish <u>religion</u>. Note this immense advance on the Constitution of other Jewish organisations. The accident of birth will not qualify us. It is <u>religion</u> and religion alone which can do this. I hope many of you will join this League. It will lead, I trust, to the intensification in each country of Jewish <u>teaching</u>. One of its objects is to assist the <u>settlement</u> in Palestine of Jews who want to make Palestine their home. Yes, those Jews who want to live in Palestine, who feel that Palestine can best give them the background they need for the development of their faith, should have every facility to make a settlement there. There would be all the difference in the world between such a settlement and a <u>Jewish State</u> run, as countries have to be run, on the usual political machinery. I should not be surprised if this settlement, attracting to itself men and women from many countries, would work out a wonderful destiny. Here people would flee from tyranny in order to serve their God. I can imagine Jewish art and philosophy flourishing here, and the genius for religion and social service developing well in

Palestine, with all its historical associations, and we should say "God Speed" to such a settlement, and might well draw some of our inspiration from its schools and universities, its pulpits and concert halls. But this settlement would not be our only source of inspiration. Once more let me implore you to strengthen the brotherhood in the country where you are living. Study your religion here and now. Live your religion in this English city, in English schools and workshops and offices, in English places of amusement, in English streets and meeting places. I desire an intensification of the Jewish faith through the lives of Jewish brotherhoods scattered over the world, but united by a common religion. I foresee that ultimately the Jewish ideals will prevail throughout the world. But we must work <u>together</u> to this end as a spiritual brotherhood, kept alive by the religious message which we are carrying to the world. Is it not a magnificent thought, this thought of a brotherhood scattered for this purpose and this purpose only: that of spreading the message of religious truth. This form of service involves sacrifice, for we have to keep together and separate ourselves in certain ways from the rest of the community, who have a different faith, if our message is to be preserved. We have to place ourselves under the discipline of the highest. But I ask you if you mind the pain and the sacrifice, seeing what are to be your glorious privileges of service? Are you afraid of suspicion and misunderstanding? Of these surely we must not be afraid. We may be afraid of our own inadequacy, of our own weaknesses and unworthiness, and being afraid, we must strengthen ourselves and equip ourselves better for our task. "Out of Zion shall the Law go forth and the word of the Lord from Jerusalem."[5] Yes, we must study our law, Zion's law, which is ours, and the spirit of Zion must enthral the world. The <u>Jewish</u> ideals, the ideals of peace and unity and love and righteousness are for all time and places. We are to express them to the world. That is our life's task. Will you join?

Archives, Liberal
Jewish Synagogue, London

[1] The Balfour Declaration, issued in the form of a letter from Lord Balfour, as Foreign Secretary, to Lord Rothschild, representing the Anglo-Jewish community, on November 2, 1917.

[2] The London County Council, see page 111.

[3] Presumably, Lily Montagu is here referring to Leon Simon's <u>The Case of the Anti Zionists: A Reply</u>, published in 1917.

[4] The League of British Jews, an Anglo-Jewish anti-Zionist organization, founded in 1917 to denounce the identification of Judaism with nationalism and to reaffirm the British patriotism of its members.

[5] Isaiah 2:3

CHAPTER IV. THE ROLE OF WOMEN IN RELIGIOUS LIFE

INTRODUCTION

The sense of mission that Lily Montagu felt as a Jew was intensified by her own understanding of what it meant to be a Jewish woman. While she consistently maintained that men and women were equal, she also believed that they were different. She thus felt that women had a distinct contribution to make both to religion in general and to Judaism in particular. In a great many sermons, five of which are included here, she attempted to outline precisely what that contribution should be.

It was Lily Montagu's contention that Jewish women, like their male counterparts, were to serve as witnesses to the reality of God, bringing His teachings to humanity. Yet women, she felt, had their own way of bearing witness. More emotional, creative and practical than men, they took greater risks, made steeper jumps in arriving at a position of faith. In "Women's Contribution to the Spiritual Life of Humanity," Montagu describes the mountain of God which men and women ascend together. While men insist on analyzing, sifting and reasoning as they climb each step of the mountain, women spring from ledge to ledge, viewing their ascent as an adventure. They may reach the top simultaneously, but have taken separate paths.

In this and other sermons, Lily Montagu views women's spiritual path as more easily communicable to children. Men, she writes, try to __explain__ religious beliefs to their children, while women teach by example. Thus, a mother, seeking to convey to her child the importance of prayer, might recall a walk that they had taken and, referring to the trees and flowers that they had seen, suggest that they thank God for His creations. Unlike the father, the mother does not present a particular interpretation or set of rules which the child then has to follow. Indeed, her concern lies not with the content of the child's prayer but with awakening, within her child, the spirit of devotion.

Though on the surface, Lily Montagu did not place value judgments on these different methods of teaching, given her understanding of religion as essentially emotional and based on inner piety, she inevitably portrayed women as those best able to revitalize the spirit of religion. As a result, she saw women as those who bore responsibility for its increase or degradation in their homes, their communities, and in the world at large. Her point, then, was not that women were more spiritual than men (as many in the late nineteenth and early twentieth century believed), but rather that the kind of spirituality that women possessed was of special value to humanity. Consequently, she insisted, women's religious influence could not, and must not, end within the home.

Yet in order to exert as great an influence as possible, women, she believed, needed to participate fully in every aspect of religious life. Recalling childhood memories of exclusion within the Orthodox congregation to which her parents belonged, she enjoined women to come down from their "synagogue galleries to enter into the life of the synagogue." Initially believing that feminism implied the obliteration of all differences between the sexes, Lily Montagu maintained that she was not a "complete and thorough-going feminist" (Address, Germany, 1930). Later, however, she dropped these qualifications, maintaining that she *was* a feminist in her commitment to women's equality ("The Spiritual Contribution of Women as Women," 1948).

THE ROLE OF WOMEN IN RELIGIOUS LIFE

In the early days of the Jewish Religious Union, Montagu apparently believed that the differences between the sexes precluded women from assuming certain roles. Thus, for example, both she and her sister, Henrietta, stood in opposition to a suggestion made in 1906 that women be allowed to preach at the J.R.U.'s Saturday afternoon services. By 1913, however, she became unofficial minister of the West Central Section of the J.R.U., a section emerging out of the worship services that Lily Montagu herself conducted at her West Central Girls' Club. By 1918, she began to preach at the Liberal Jewish Synagogue and soon after, in congregations throughout Great Britain and the United States. Lily Montagu never abandoned her belief that men and women were different by nature. Yet as she got older, this difference was reduced primarily to one of interest and style.

In later sermons, including "Religious Responsibility in Public Life," delivered at an interfaith meeting in 1950, Lily Montagu continued to insist that women's endowments were not identical to those of men. The thrust of these sermons, however, moves away from that which differentiates women and men, towards that which brings them together. "We women," she writes in "Religious Responsibility," "must be unafraid to enter public life by whatever door we think fit." In a 1956 sermon on "Jewish Women in the Rabbinate," she includes rabbinic ordination as that to which women should have access. Though recognizing that few congregations would be willing to "accept the spiritual leadership of a woman if a man were available," she confidently maintains that such prejudice will be removed in the future. Believing that some women, like some men, are called by God to be leaders, she answers those who would deny women ordination with a simple: why not?

This isn't to say, however, that Lily Montagu's view of women underwent great development. Her attitude towards "lady preachers" may have changed, but in all probability this shift in attitude was politically rather than religiously motivated, reflecting the changing goals of the J.R.U. itself. Through her own experience, Lily Montagu increasingly recognized the importance of equal opportunity and access. Thus, as she got older, she began to call herself a feminist without having to qualify the label, and focused more clearly on communal leadership roles for women. Again, however, these developments did not represent a great shift in attitude. They simply represented the growing conviction that unless women were free to act on their own sense of vocation, they could not stand before God and say, as did Isaiah: "Here am I: send me."

WOMEN'S CONTRIBUTION TO THE SPIRITUAL LIFE OF HUMANITY

[No date]

In trying to estimate the form and extent of women's contribution to the spiritual treasury of humanity, I should like to state my belief that although women should cooperate with men in all life's activities, if they feel themselves capable of doing so, they are not a mere replica of men. They are by nature different in character and attainments; therefore, their contribution to religion is distinctive; and humanity is enriched by the diversity between the sexes.

Even though there should be complete equality between men and women in the social, political and religious contacts, women must, like men, develop their personalities as completely as they can in order that they may serve their God as adequately as their qualities will allow. The more a woman excels in the power of loving and learning, in reverence for beauty and devotion to justice and truth, the better witness she becomes to the reality of God. It is probable that in fulfilling this responsibility, men and women cooperate most usefully.

Because woman's creative faculty is great, she must serve in the vanguard of humanity in the creation of peace. I think she must lift the problem of international relations from the realm of politics into that of religion, or, better still, she must bring a strong religious faith to bear upon political issues. The probability of war is created by jealousy and greed. Material advancement may be held to be of supreme importance. Consideration of the needs of others cannot stop the desire for aggression. It is only God's law of mutual responsibility which can restrain passion and covetousness. "Have we not all one Father? Hath not one God created us?"[1]

Men and women, of course, know equally well the misery and futility of war, and the demoralisation which is part of its aftermath. But women probably realise better the effect of war on home life. Today they have to overcome the sense of defeatism and frustration which is tragically depressing the human race. Men can think of war only in a realistic sense. They must strengthen their defences and increase the horror of their weapons. They must frighten people into maintaining peace by appealing to their desire for survival. On the other hand, woman with her quicker sensitiveness and imaginative power can appeal to the desire to redeem, which is latent in the heart of every one created in the image of God Who Himself can redeem the universe from destruction and invites us to work with Him in the building up of His Kingdom. Why should men slaughter one another instead of creating a fuller and richer life for which God supplies the material? Men's vision is blocked by the existence of the most terrible bombs and by the fear of totalitarianism. They have given much to the cause of liberty and they see it threatened by the worst expressions of tyranny. They are weary, but resolved not to show weakness. War preparations alone can secure peace.

Women, however, ask gently but insistently: "Is God's arm waxed short?" Surely His presence should convince us that the reign of peace and righteousness must triumph in the world. Mothers give birth to children in order that they may live and fulfil themselves. In the name of motherhood, women can denounce war and find other ways of settling international differences in order that their children should be saved. If they fail, home life perishes; the centre of civilisation is doomed to fall as a victim to war. Women can, if they exert their influence from the plane of religion, restore man's faith in man and in human responsibility by creating life and helping it to develop.

Outside the actual arena of fighting, it is easier to get a better perspective on the higher possibilities of life. Physical force, unrestrained, or perhaps misdirected, is not the source of man's highest influence. He exists surely to preserve and to stimulate his resources as a spiritual being in whom God has breathed eternity.

We are told that women's most effective work is in the sphere of home education. Here the progress of our faith is secured. Many of our fellow Jews say that a man is a Jew by birth and can never lose his birthright. I suggest that the Jew is characterised by the faith by which he lives and that faith is a product of the home and the responsibility of imparting it rests primarily with the mother who has her children almost entirely to herself at the most impressionable period of their existence, which is before they reach the age of 6. The father tries to explain externalities to his child; the Seder night symbols, for example. The mother seeks to share with her child her experience of prayer. Perhaps she asks him to give thanks for the trees and flowers they have seen together on their walk. "Johnny" says the mother, "do you remember our walk today and that fungus we saw, and the lovely streaks of colour, the red and yellow bits, and the little bits of green and brown, and how we wished we could have found a mushroom, but then, as we said, it would not have been half as pretty. Shall we thank God for making that fungus?" "Yes, lets, Mummy." "Thank you God for making that lovely fungus with red and yellow bits and the bits of brown and green, and next time please make it into a mushroom so that we can eat it." "Amen" says mummy. Perhaps together mother and child make a list of those they love and ask God to bless these friends. The tiny children sense in their baby way that mother is seeking to commune with the Unseen God. Gradually they imitate her in the way which suits them and fit the God idea into their souls as these grow in spiritual capacity. A man analyses and sifts and reasons while with the woman by his side he climbs the mountain of God. She springs from ledge to ledge and her spirit influences her children who are out to seek adventure and to take risks.

Today women are conscious that their sons and daughters are slipping away from institutional religion. They are less concerned than men about loyalty to tradition. Their great desire is to attract their children to the Synagogue by making the services understood and alive. Judaism is based on reason and emotion. Women being more emotional than men must help in rendering that element strong and pure. Liberal Judaism is criticised by those who do not enter deeply into our fellowship because it is said to be cold. Women must increase the warmth of life. In our women's societies women are so often satisfied to contribute to the upkeep of the religion school without desiring as adults to improve their own education and to clarify their own understanding of the history, principles and practices of Judaism. They provide beautifully for the social events of the Synagogue, but are unconcerned in improving the aesthetic influence of public worship and bringing their own experiences in depth and sincerity to the united prayers of their fellow congregants. Yet they care so much for beauty; they are so easily moved by contact with the divine; in their own lives they have found the connection between morality and religion and the power of prayer which should make this union a reality. The time has surely come when they must extend and increase their influence in Synagogue life.

It is the women who today can do much to arrest the deterioration of home life. A rottenness has set in which threatens the very foundation of those sanctities which have an essentially Jewish value. The social conscience is apparently little disturbed today by infidelity between husband and wife. A careless shrug or a flippant word is often all the interest shown in the fact that a home has been broken up. The position of the children of broken marriages is, it is agreed, unfortunate and often painful, but the best must be made of it. The moral code has fallen from its exalted place. Not only is the relation between men and women deteriorating generally, but there is also a looseness with regard to loyalty in word and deed. Women who understand the disastrous results of this decadence must examine their own faith and seek to strengthen it. They must then seek with all the power at their command to prove that Judaism is not a verbal creed. As our ancestors taught us, it inspires a righteous way of life and depends for its existence on our effort after righteousness and truth. After all Liberal Jews are not expected to receive their religion from the past and to remember its importance when it is convenient for them to do so. They must not use the observances their ancestors used when these are pleasing to them and cast others away without examination. These observances must only be discarded if they have no ethical or religious value, if perhaps they have been shown by scholars to be based on myth or superstition. It is not enough to disregard observance because it entails sacrifice or because it is considered by the members of one's social set or even by members of one's family as out of date or old fashioned. Sacrifice helps to purify the soul; independent thinking is essential to the men or women who wish to serve their God. Moreover, each generation is meant to add a contribution to the truth which their predecessors have discovered, and women as well as men have to respond to this challenge, to this trust.

I have tried to put forward my view that women's contribution to religion is in the field of religious education, in the creation of permanent peace, and in the quickening of the moral sense in her own life and in the lives of those whom she can influence. I have emphasised some of the positive ways in which she is called upon to fulfil her obligations. There is also a negative aspect to these important considerations.

Women can increase or degrade the influence of the religion school. It is not enough for them to join women's societies in providing splendid equipment for the school and the library. Every woman must also know what the child is taught and refrain even at the time of examinations from placing the requirements of the so-called secular school first, or in disparaging the religion school teachers by contrasting their skill with those of the secular school teachers. A mother must not weaken the background of the religion school by lightly saying: "We don't do that any more. I have no interest in the subject. I have forgotten all my Hebrew and am all right without it, as I never go to the Synagogue," when the child comes home full of enthusiasm about the lesson he has had and the meaning of the home observances, so interesting and colourful, which he never sees in his own home.

Again, we shall never attain international peace if we do not ourselves believe in it, if we are cynical about its realisation, if we glorify the trappings of war. Also there is a direct and important connection between the creation of the military spirit and the festering of our own petty hatreds and jealousies, our personal unkindnesses. Before we can be sure of the advent of permanent peace in the world, we must secure it in our hearts and homes and in our relations with those whom we serve or who would serve us.

Again, I have heard people through carelessness in conversation defy the moral code in which as Jews they profess to believe. Women occasionally like to spend large sums in self-indulgence and then by some small sharp practice win a few [_____] at the expense of somebody else. They tell others, perhaps even their children, how they got the better of some shop-keeper or some customs official. They give the impression that there is no absolute standard for integrity. It is absurd to expect truth in our own inward parts, if we can give an immoral or unchaste action a place of interest or even fascination in the life of society. It is mainly women who hold that a play based on wide interests is unacceptable. They miss the spice of sexual wickedness when it is absent. Yet they are capable of loving the good and rejecting the evil. It is only that sometimes they allow their moral sense to be buried and also it soon loses its alertness altogether.

I think woman's contribution cannot be very effective if she lacks the courage to be articulate. It is difficult not to swim along on the accepted conventions of your group, and to make a stand against the drift to religious indifference, immorality and the exaltation of war. It is far easier if you offer social service to undenominational organizations to suppress the fact of your religious affiliation. Of course, there is no need to refer to your religious faith at inappropriate moments, but I think you may increase the respect for Judaism among your colleagues if when occasion arises you are unafraid to make its principles known. Our Christian neighbours must not be allowed to think that they have a monopoly in conscientious scruples, or indeed in religion itself.

The contribution of women to universal religion must not be only an expression of impulse or instinct. We must cultivate and enlarge our possession of knowledge. We in our women's societies must not stop at organising social service in the best possible way; we must actually share with those whom we seek to serve our cultural and spiritual interests. By exchange of thought we increase the reality of our religion and can actually bring or receive light to illumine the dark places in our souls.

If organisation is our goal, we may work hard and achieve wonders, but we shall not do all which should be expected of us unless we consider the human contacts which are of supreme importance in God's Kingdom. We may raise through organisation the status of millions in politics or industry or in the domestic sphere, but are we sufficiently concerned with the weakness and suffering and spiritual loneliness of A. B. and C. who are only numbers to us, nothing more.

In our Women's Societies there is a tendency for the members to organise themselves as money-getters and to feel no responsibility for the gambling methods used to accomplish their end or even for the spending of the gifts that they accumulate. They are doing most useful work, but if they stop there, their contribution as shown in this paper loses much of its significance. Our women must also gain knowledge and use it in the best possible way. They must use their gifts of heart as well as of mind; they must show how to express religion in life; they must prove that these two are coextensive. Judaism must be studied and understood before it can be lived. It can only be lived when it is loved. Women in the Reform Movement have happily come down from the Synagogue galleries and entered into the Congregational lives of their Synagogues. They must show how their thought and actions are purified and illuminated by faith. They must raise the standard of citizenship for their own children and then for the general community by preparing their young people to face civic and industrial problems. If there is corruption in a city, mothers must help directly and indirectly in banishing it. If a girl or boy questions why no interest is taken in a civic election, it is no reply to say "I can't take an interest, the corruption is as iniquitous." You use the cities' supply of light and heat. Women have to create purity, wisdom and zeal in all kinds of social reform. As Mazzini the great Italian patriot said: To sanctify the Family more and more and to bring it ever closer to the country; this is your mission. Sanctify the Family in the unity of love. Make it a temple in which you may sacrifice together to the country. I do not know if you will be happy, but I do know that if you do this there will come to you even in the midst of adversity a sense of serene peace, the repose of a tranquil conscience, which will give you strength in every trial and will keep an azure space open before your eyes in every tempest.[2]

In the days of our grandparents women were expected to keep a Jewish home by observing all the dietary laws. Even today a potential proselyte told me she thought she had a good knowledge of Judaism as she lived next door to a kosher butcher. That was the religious stimulus given to her by the parents of her fiance.

A woman may also light the candles on the Sabbath Eve. But may I tell my readers that they must do infinitely more. Their candles must stand as symbols of truth and purity and love. These great divine attributes must be given to the nation to which they belong, and because they believe in the rule of God, they must know that He expects from them the most zealous cooperation in achieving this great purpose, for so they will be helping in their small imperfect way to build God's Kingdom.

Archives, Liberal
Jewish Synagogue, London

[1] Malachi 2:10.

[2] From Mazzini's <u>Duties of Man</u> (see <u>The Duties of Man and other Essays By Joseph Mazzini</u>, ed. Ernest Rhys. London, 1920).

ADDRESS

Germany, January 1930

Friends -

I have been asked to speak to you on one of our pressing needs, and I have chosen as my subject Women and Liberal Judaism.[1]

I think there is a pressing need for women to come down from your synagogue galleries to enter into the life of the synagogue. In England and America this reform has been achieved. From the very beginning of our movement in England, women had equal rights with men in synagogue management and responsibility. Since 1915 women have been allowed to read the service, and preach from the pulpit of the Liberal Synagogue.² Your hesitation here except in the case of the Reform Synagogue, shows, I venture to suggest, that you have not <u>completely</u> realised the necessity of making your religion harmonise with the experience of everyday life.

There is no country in the world in which women have achieved more than in Germany, in the field of learning and social service. Why not use this highly developed womanhood for the furtherance of synagogue life?

I am not a complete and thorough-going feminist. I do not hold that the powers and interests of men and women are identical. It is because they are, in my opinion, different - I give, you see, no estimate as to the quality or degree of their respective attainments - that I think we need for our spiritual treasury a contribution both from men and women.

When parents and children sit together at public worship they testify to their belief in the consecration of home life. Women have a message to give you not only on home life, but on the affairs of the city and the state, viewed from the religious angle. In your country they are completely emancipated as citizens. They are responsible with men for the education and care of the children of the State. They are responsible with men for the health and happiness of the next generation. It is right that they should testify that their thought and their actions are purified and illuminated by this faith in Judaism.

It is true that the position of the woman in the Jewish home is always upheld, but today the home is regarded as the nursery of citizens, and the Jewish woman must bring religious influence to bear in preparing her children to face all civic and industrial problems.

If, further you dare to consider Judaism not only as an influence on life, but also as a definite experience of the human soul and intellect, surely you cannot deny that woman's capacity for joy and suffering, her idealism and her intellectual penetration, renders her religious testimony valuable. As a mother too, she is mainly responsible for the religious education of her children, in the home which serves as the background for the teaching in the school. She can render this teaching effective by her influence, or perfunctory and worthless.

We are trying to interest our young people in public worship and synagogue life as a whole; we are trying to strengthen their social life by bringing it under synagogue influence. Surely women must help in this work. You need young women as well as young men to be affected, if you expect any success whatever.

I should like to emphasise my belief that the intellectual, as well as the emotional side of life is needed in the synagogue. The more completely trained the individual, the better the service he or she, can render. I would not label our emotional or intellectual contributions with a sex label, but I would say that the cooperation of the sexes will tend to make the synagogue life effective and harmonious, and I cannot admit that there is any phase of this life which should be outside woman's jurisdiction. The old conception of physical unfitness among women has retarded the progress of Judaism as a Universalistic religion.

Liberal Judaism has in theory removed these degrading disabilities and the time has come when your leaders must give practical expression to your belief in the emancipation of women. By doing so they will, I think, strengthen the Jewish religious life in this country and help to remove some of the disabilities oppressing women most heavily in the countries of Central Europe and the East, and tending to degradation and immorality.

The idea of sex inferiority in the synagogue tends to a moral confusion which is deplorable, and must be finally removed.

During our World Union Conference in July we hope to have a session to consider Women's problems. I trust that by that time a great step forward will have been made in securing reforms here, so that in this as in so many other spheres of thought, we may look to our German contingent for leadership.

Archives, Liberal
Jewish Synagogue, London

[1] This talk may well have been given at the 1930 Biennial Convention of the Federation of Liberal Jews in Germany. According to the Liberal Jewish Monthly (February, 1930), Lily Montagu and Israel Mattuck were to address the Conference, held in Breslau, after meeting with the Governing Body of the World Union in Berlin.

[2] Though here, as in her autobiography, The Faith of a Jewish Woman (1943), Lily Montagu cites 1915 as the year in which women gained permission to preach at the Liberal Jewish Synagogue, the Minute Books of the Jewish Religious Union-Liberal Jewish Synagogue reveal that this decision was not reached until June 1916. Moreover, it was not until June 1918 that a woman--Lily Montagu herself--actually preached at the LJS. Lily Montagu correctly identifies this date and its significance in her essay, "The Jewish Religious Union and Its Beginnings" (Papers for Jewish People No. 27) published in 1927. Her sermon, "Kinship With God," is included here on pages 111-119.

THE SPIRITUAL CONTRIBUTION OF WOMEN AS WOMEN

Chicago: Jewish Education Building:
Friday, November 26th, 1948

I am attempting to discuss a subject with you today which is fraught with particular difficulty. To begin with, it is very likely that you as feminists will disagree with my premises. My central thought is based on the idea that although women should cooperate with men in all the activities open to human beings, and that they should recognise no limit except that of incapacity, and that sex cannot disqualify anybody from doing that for which they feel themselves fitted, women have certain qualifications which are different from those possessed by men. Indeed, I am a feminist too and believe in complete equality between men and women in the social, political, economic and religious spheres, but I think that humanity is enriched by the diversity between the two sexes. It follows that they must develop their special qualifications, and they must give as complete a contribution to the world's spiritual treasury as possible, but that it must have a character of its own, and not be an imitation or a replica of the contribution made by men.

Men and women have the creative faculty jointly, but men can work more objectively than women. Let me take a simple illustration. Father and mother want their small son or daughter aged 4 to learn to pray. They want to stimulate the capacity for prayer. Father takes his child to Synagogue while no service is in progress and carries him round and shows him the various features, including his special seat, and the Ark, and explains that the books of the Bible are contained in the Scroll which is in the Ark. He is informative and interests his child. The Sabbath comes and the boy or girl is dressed in his best clothes and accompanies his Daddy to the Synagogue and carries his prayer book. The child sits between him and Mummy. Daddy occasionally shows him the place in the book, and he stops fidgeting for a moment. He is happy and prepared to repeat the experiment on subsequent Sabbaths. Gradually, after a long time, the atmosphere of the Synagogue impresses itself on the child and he feels the inclination to worship. The realisation of that possibility will depend in a great measure on the father's own reaction to the service and what he says about it when he gets home.

The mother has another method. At bedtime she can do many things. The element of thanksgiving is a good preparation for prayer. She remembers a beautiful fungus which she and Johnny admired together while on their walk. The imaginative faculty is strong in her. "Johnny" she says, "do you remember our walk today and that fungus we saw, and the lovely streaks of colour, the red and yellow bits, and the little bits of green and brown, and how we wished we could have found a mushroom, but then we said it would not have been half as pretty?" Shall we thank God for making that fungus?" "Yes, lets, Mummy." "Thank you God for making that lovely fungus, with the red and yellow bits, and the bits of brown and green" added Johnny, "and next time plase make it into a mushroom so that we cn eat it." "Amen" says Mummy. Another night Mummy and Johnny make a list of the people they both love and ask God to bless them. They make their prayers together and they are their own special prayers.

A woman creator gives her own spiritual experience of pain and joy to the progressive conceptions of Judaism. A man analyses and sifts and reasons while with the woman he climbs the mountain of God. I have heard it said how a man climbs step by step until he reaches the level within his reach. His path has been sure but rather slow. He looks round and sees a woman by his side. He did not see her while he was climbing because she sprang from ledge to ledge taking many risks.[1]

In religious discussions on the source of authority in Progressive Judaism, you will find men more interested in external authority than women. A man says: "We shall have chaos unless the men of scholarship and experience get together and decide on specific observances. Does Sunday observance lead to disloyalty? Should we have more Hebrew in our liturgy? Is the Cantor's assistance essential or even desirable? "Well, I don't see that it matters what the big people think" says the woman. "I know I cannot get my young people to service on any day but Sunday. Hebrew may be all right for some people, but it is no use for those who do not understand it. If I want the best singing, I go to the Opera. When I am at a service, I want to sing and join in, and I know my children do. If they can sing, all the better, and if they can't, let the others sing louder and drown my children's voices, but they too are singing." There is an element of practicality in all this, perhaps a little less feeling of responsibility, a longing that her own young people should be satisfied.

We women must approach the question of international peace from, I think, a rather different angle from that adopted by men. In the first place, I think we must lift the problem out of the sphere of politics into the sphere of religion, or, as I would greatly prefer, bring a strong religious influence to bear upon the political issue. Men and women of course know equally well the misery and futility of war, the demoralisation which is part of its aftermath. But women surely realise more fully the affect of war on home life. The responsibility seems to me to rest on them to overcome the sense of defeatism and frustration which is surging over the world. Men are in their outlook more realistic than women. Their vision is blocked by the existence of the atom bomb and the threat of totalitarianism. They have given so much to the cause of liberty, and they see all forms of tyranny flourishing and becoming ever more threatening. They are weary but resolved not to show any weakness. So they turn to war preparations as the only way to secure peace. Here is the woman's part. We have to affirm with all the strength at our disposal that because God is, the reign of peace and righteousness must triumph in the world. If we firmly believe in the wickedness of war, we must turn away from it and find other ways of settling our differences, however difficult the search may be. If we fail now, our civilisation perishes and with it all that is precious in home life. It is only on the plane of religion that we can find the way to restore our faith in man and in ourselves. We can help because we are outside the actual fighting arena. Even though we are in the war unit, our methods are not confined to physical force.

Before I close, I would ask you to consider whether you think you can resist the present drift away from the consecration of home life. Men may make a greater effort even than women to keep up appearances, but you know as well as I do that a rottenness has set in, and the moment has come for you to arise and shine forth. On the stage, in novels and in the newspapers, the idea of the divided home is accepted as inevitable. The children are being sacrificed to the general feeling of inevitability. The natural happy and chaste home life is regarded as exceptional and unexpected. The marriage vow has become loosened. The marriage ceremony is only religious in form. Its significance is forgotten. Men think you feel that this phase is inevitable, that the new code of morality or immorality is likely to prevail; it is in the trend of the times. Business is absorbing. The survival of the fittest is the law of the day, and no other consideration can count while the struggle for existence is so fierce. Here again we must make our faith felt and before we can do this, we must revere it, each for herself. If home and the children are our most precious possessions, if the exaltation of their worth is anything more than mere phrases, we must hurry to the work of salvation.

Yes, friends, in the field of religious education, at home, in the work for peace and chastity, we must work with new zeal and new faith. Our contribution is needed. Our courage must be added to that of our men. We must restore to them some of their lost confidence and hope. We allowed them to lose much through our apathy and inertia. Now we must know that we stand before God and must either perish or be prepared to obey His word. Each must say for herself: "Here am I, send me."[2]

                                Archives, Liberal
                                Jewish Synagogue, London

[1] See "Women's Contribution to the Spiritual Life of Humanity" where this and the above examples are used.

[2] Isaiah 6:9.

RELIGICUS RESPONSIBILITY IN PUBLIC LIFE

                    Interfaith Meeting: June 28th 1950

I am grateful for the privilege of addressing you, my sisters of the Jewish and Christian faiths. My subject is women's religious responsibility in public life, and I am speaking as a member of the Liberal Jewish community. I do not represent the Orthodox section of our community although we hold the Orthodox in the greatest respect as it is the progressives whose system of religion fits in, to quote our leader Dr. Mattuck, with the thoughts and ideals of Western culture.

We believe in certain eternal truths which we seek to apply to the life of the state. God, through His prophets and teachers, has revealed to us an absolute standard of righteousness. Through our belief in the Oneness of God, we conceive the idea of the Brotherhood of man. All men and women have the right then to live, and we must, therefore, see to it that they are supplied with the opportunity to obtain the essentials of life. No man or woman, as a child of God, can be denied the right to a home with air and light; as also the possibility of developing his physical and intellectual and spiritual life. In the light of our faith in One God, body, mind and soul must be reverenced as holy.

There was a time when people no less good than ourselves deemed it necessary to let little children work in mines and factories in order that industrial profits could be increased. God knows what sins we are committing today for the sake of what we believe to be equitable gain while a Shaftesbury is preparing to show us our crimes and bid us change our ways. We shall be judged by future generations even as we judge our predecessors.

Today, since we are aware that children are made in the Image of God, it is necessary for us to reverence them as personalities. This recognition must impel us to try as soon as we possibly can to disallow overcrowded classes in schools, so that each child's possibilities and limitations should be known. Moreover, in order that our children should realise themselves, they must have occasional opportunity to see large stretches of country and sea; that sea which was once described by a child as the one thing in the world of which there seemed to be plenty for everybody, and as she said it, she laughed aloud and rejoiced exceedingly.

It is because we reverence human personality that we also stress the necessity for self-realisation among adults. We know that this can only be secured if a certain amount of leisure is possible for rest, recreation, for study and thought. Woman assists in the function of creation, and it is therefore easy for her to recognise the responsibility of maintaining the value of human faculties. She must throw herself into the arena in which evil is combated until it is overcome. She can no longer find protection by insisting on retirement while her men folk fight in the cause of righteousness. Woman's emancipation, if it means anything, must mean that she is called to cooperate with man in every sphere of life. Because, as I think, her endowments though equal to, are different from those of men, her distictive gifts are needed for human advancement. She must fulfil her responsibility as a citizen and elector, and since she believes in the omnipresence of God, she cannot allow any activity to appear to be outside the sphere of His influence. If there is corruption in the political or civic life with which she is familiar, she is responsible as far as her individual influence goes for securing clear administration. Where oppression or unfairness is observable between employer and employed, between class and class, she must become aware of her own devotion to freedom and work to remove the injustice. The tyrant, whoever and wherever he is must let his people go that they may serve God, the Highest. Woman recognises no other domination.

It is part of woman's responsibiltiy to look after the health of the community. We have grown out of the era when certain classes were supposed to <u>enjoy</u> unsanitary conditions, and so were left to them without protest or relief.

We heard it said that if they had baths, they would not use them, or that a section of the population was so ignorant that a certain measure of infantile mortality was inevitable. No good advice, it followed, was acceptable even if given with the utmost altruism. Today we know that ignorance is not valued as a class privilege. Every section of the population seeks the knowledge which will save them and their homes from disease and deterioration so long as it is given in an acceptable way. We must stress the idea that men and women must be treated as human beings, as striving, aspiring people and not as machines capable only of mechanical advance. The woman voter must introduce into the state policy plenty of love, much imagination, a large amount of understanding sympathy.

I have recently read the story of Bermondsey in the life of Alfred Salter by F. Breckeway. Without accepting his extreme political ideals, there is one portion of his activities which must rouse the admiration of women of every political shade of opinion. It is his faith in beauty as a means of redemption. Not only were the overcrowded and unhealthy citizens of Bermondsey to be carried into the country and allowed to soak in the influences of its beauty spots, but flowers and exquisite shrubs must be brought to the streets and alleys of the slum area and stimulate the spiritual life of the inhabitants. Salter succeeded in his aims to a surprising degree. The appearance of the district was transformed, and the interest of the people in culture and religion was quickened. In the recognition of beauty as a revelation of God, it seemed possible to accept his nearness, to strive to harmonise life a little more closely with the reality of God's being. As citizens we have the opportunity to increase the beauty of everyday life, to insist on legislation which can give opportunity to ordinary men and women to increase their knowledge of art and to have greater opportunities for enjoying it. Certainly, the response to the beauty of art and music is not universal or uniform. But the response does come sometimes from unexpected quarters and everybody must have his chance. I remember years ago giving a talk on the pleasures of life to a group of very poor men and wondering whether they were being bored, and whether politeness alone prevented them from saying so. After the lecture one man got up and said: "I am a great lover of ornithology, are you?" I was not quite sure at the time of the meaning of the word, but I felt humble indeed when he began to express his feeling in picturesque language.

We women must be unafraid to enter public life by whatever door we think fit so long as the light from Heaven illumines our work, and we venture to seek God's guidance in dealing with the problems which confront us. We are hearing on all sides that the standard of morality is being lowered for small immoralities are increasing greatly and are being tolerated. People are hesitant in their resistance to moral deterioration. Even while in positions of responsibility, we women allow such evil to be brought in the holy name of charity. We bribe people by the love of excitement of all kinds to give money to important causes. We allow small personal prejudices to imperil the progress of great efforts in social service. The time has come, I venture to think, when we must remember that our social service can be of little use if its achievements entail the weakening of the social conscience. We who have entered public life know the encouragement to evil given in the three words: Everybody does it. One of the great contributions which we women can make to public life lies in our insistence that our work is worthless if it flourished through cheating or gambling or self-advertisement. Our methods of organisation must be as admirable as the cause for which we are labouring. We are pressing for the better care of children in their own homes and in institutions. We know and are proclaiming from every kind of platform that much of children's delinquency and indeed of their unhappiness can be traced to the broken homes to which many of them belong.

Lady Stanagate has stressed the importance of our influence in home life. The recognition of the moral law must, I think, be carried from the home sanctuary into public life. We must not be afraid either by example or by precept to show our reverence for the underlying principles of cleanliness and chastity. If our principles are old-fashioned, we salute them on that account. They have survived for 3,000 years and their failure will involve the failure of truth and of love.

Perhaps the time has actually come when we should apply our religion, be it Christian or Jewish, to the life with which we are familiar - our everyday life. We do certainly do this up to a point, but generally in such a vague unreal way. People blame religion for the immorality existing in the world. "What has been the good of it all?" they say. "Much unhappiness is caused by religion, but when does it really prevent evil?" In spite of religion people go their own way and try to escape from God."

People blame religion, but should we not blame ourselves for not heeding religion? Certainly, as a Jewess, I know that we have been taught Judaism for thousands of years, but we are often unreceptive and so our standards are still low in actual life. We can proclaim great truths about honesty and cheat the customs officers and smile at our cleverness. We may listen to the command: Thou shalt not commit adultery, but subsequently forget it and our lapses may be condoned, since desire is allowed dominion. We are sometimes unafraid to tell lies because we deem their colour "white." The Psalm which says that God desires truth in the inward parts is very beautiful, but it can be made to seem a little out of date. Are we justified in these small reservations? Who has granted us our licences?

I think that we must really carry our faith into public life and affirm that it is still applicable. Shall we no longer deem the law breaker here who, as a Committee member, sanctions irregularities, and the man who sticks out for the sake of principle a prig? After all, if we are privileged to engage in social service, it is because we want to share the best we know with those whom we are trying to serve. Their moral gift strengthened by grim fights with reality is often greater than ours. Surely religious sincerity must be one of our best qualifications for usefulness; a working religion must express our creed.

It was a practical faith in God's command: "Let my people go that they may serve me" which made liberty for the oppressed true freedom - not licence - one of humanity's most precious spiritual possessions, and it was conceived by a slave people at the hour of their emancipation and applied to life as it progresses through the ages.

There is a tendency in public life today to belittle the possibility of peace by our cynicism and want of faith. Dame May Curwen will deal with our international responsibility, but I should like to suggest to you that here in our own country, we must stress the ideal of cooperation rather than that of rivalry. Her many women's organisations start with high objectives and are broken up into sections because of petty jealousies and rivalries. Such catastrophies can only be averted by the courage and faith of those who value peace as a revelation of God.

May I summarise the ideas I have tried to express in this paper by a quotation by Ramsay in Lord Samuel's book of quotations:

> A nation cannot permanently remain on a level above the level of its women.[1]

I believe, therefore, that there is no sphere of public life in which women are not needed, but the success of their entry depends on their faithfulness to the standards of morality and spirituality which must be interpreted by them according to the teaching of their ancestral faith. This teaching together with its interpretation is progressive in character, and will ultimately bring all seekers nearer to the God of the whole world.

Archives, Liberal
Jewish Synagogue, London

[1] From *Viscount Samuel's Book of Quotations* (London, 1947), a book described by Samuel's biographer, John Bowle, as a "mellow, casual anthology showing a broad worldly wisdom." (Bowle, *Viscount Samuel: A Biography*, London, 1957, p. 335).

JEWISH WOMEN IN THE RABBINATE

London, July 1956

I feel that men and women have a different contribution to make to the spiritual treasury of mankind. Their natures and powers are not identical, but through free cooperation they can develop the best gifts which God gives to humanity.

Men seem to me to prosper intellectually most successfully when they can fully indulge in investigation and scientific reasoning; women do so in imagination and in the full use of the creative spirit. It is said that a man

THE ROLE OF WOMEN IN RELIGIOUS LIFE 183

climbs slowly step by step up the mountain of knowledge only to find sitting at the top a woman who cannot explain how she got there.

We are a people of eastern origin and it has taken us a very long time to arrive at the conclusion that men and women have an equal right to free development and unrestricted powers of service. Through the revelation of God which led us to accept His truths, Jewish women in history advanced more quickly than their contemporaries in acquiring human rights. They have not yet reached the stage when equal rights should be allowed them if they desire to acquire them in all professions.

As a matter of convention, the majority of Jews would not favour women in the Rabbinate, although in other departments in western countries and in India they are allowed without restriction to attain the highest professional dignity. As doctors, lawyers, politicians and actors, they are not debarred through sex of the highest positions. But the eastern idea of physical inferiority still interferes with their position in the Ministry.

One of the objects of the Jewish Liberals in England when they founded their movement at the beginning of this century was to establish the equality of men and women. Their rights to take part in the government of the Synagogue was not accepted in the Orthodox section of the community. In the Liberal division they were fully accepted and their position has influenced the general community which now, in some part at least, allows women as seatholders and as members of Councils. But we owe it to our great leader, Rabbi Dr. Mattuck that the principle of allowing equal status to men and women as Lay Ministers was accorded. There was unfortunately no woman qualified by scholarship and ministerial training to enter the Rabbinate, but a woman Lay Minister was inducted and given the leadership of a Congregation.[1] We are hoping that others will be trained for the full Rabbinate when Liberal Theological colleges are established.

From the practical point of view, we have to admit that today few Congregations would accept the spiritual leadership of a woman if a man were available. So candidates dependent on this work for their living would have to hesitate before accepting the training even when freely offered to them. But prejudice is removed by time. There is little doubt that if women are prepared to recognise that their Ministry must depend on the development of their full intellectual powers, as well as those of heart and spirit, they will before long see their services eagerly accepted by Congregations. If they have a feeling of vocation, their God will help them to develop and use that feeling to the full. They must prove their worth. They must exalt themselves through service, and never rely on any minor personal attraction to render them acceptable for Synagogue leadership. A Minister must share the joys and aspirations, sorrows and frustrations of the whole of humanity. There must be no artificial limitation to their human interests and sympathies. They must learn humbly and reverently to understand some small part of God's revelation of truth and then be prepared to give of their highest thought and feeling to a Congregation who would desire their services. Through service to God, they will find the way to serve a Congregation of men, women and children. If they can do this, they will surely be invited belong long to join the Jewish Rabbinate. Why not?

Archives, Liberal
Jewish Synagogue, London

[1] Here Lily Montagu is talking about herself. See Service for Induction of Lay Ministers, p. 335.

UNIT TWO

RELIGIOUS VOCATION

V. LIBERAL JUDAISM AS THE JUDAISM OF THE FUTURE

INTRODUCTION

Lily Montagu saw as her vocation the bringing of others to an awareness of God. This sense of vocation emerged out of her own vision of what it meant to be not only a human being but also a woman and a Jew. By the age of seventeen, she felt that she had received a Divine call to better the world and to actualize her potential. Alan Mintz, in his study of George Eliot's <u>Middlemarch</u> (Harvard University Press, 1978), has characterized this late nineteenth century merging of the "ideal of service" with the "reality of ambition" as an ambitious calling. Replacing earlier nineteenth century notions of self-denial and selfless dedication, it recognized the importance of self-realization, of using <u>all</u> of one's abilities in the service of God.

Believing that Liberal Judaism was the Judaism of the future--that form most capable of arousing the religiously indifferent and appealing to the young--Lily Montagu felt that her spiritual vocation could best be fulfilled through the advancement of the Liberal Jewish "cause." The sermons, letters and addresses included in this chapter make the relation between Lily Montagu's vision and vocation clear. Her vision, as we have seen, was of a loving, righteous God whose ethical teachings were to be revealed in the conduct of one's life and spread throughout the nations. This vision crystallized in a Divine call that spurred Lily Montagu to action. While believing that it was her mission as a Jew to bear witness to the reality of

God, she maintained that as an individual, it was her vocation to help others actually feel that reality. Though the awareness of God could be gained through many religious forms, it was Liberal Judaism, she asserted, that was best able to awaken this "spirit of religion."

In "Think, Thank and Do," Lily Montagu emphasizes the importance of individual effort in advancing the Liberal Jewish cause. Each one of us, she writes, must be its defenders and champions, working to ensure its success. Believing that Liberal Judaism can best meet the spiritual needs of present and future generations, she claims that the survival of Judaism itself rests in the hands of those propagating its message. The enormity of this task is made clear in "Can We Possibly Be Mistaken?" Here, Montagu compares the comfort of orthodoxy to the greater uncertainty that Liberal Judaism offers. While Orthodox Jews need not think about religion, sure that the teachings they have been given are true, Liberal Jews, she maintains, constantly must search and sift, facing both doubt and affirmation. Orthodoxy gives one a specific spiritual path to follow. Liberal Judaism demands that one create one's own. Yet, she insists, this effort is worthwhile, for only in creating such a path can one truly assimilate the teachings of past generations, transforming Judaism into a personal religion capable of sustaining a living, religious faith through which one can "climb nearer to truth."

Club Letter 56, addressed to members of the West Central Club, attempts to spell out the secret of Liberal Judaism's appeal. Once again, Lily Montagu returns to the theme of Liberal Judaism as the Judaism of the future. She asserts that its principles are worth upholding for it alone "is in harmony with life and truth as we conceive it," a harmony which, "through its progressive power," will always be retained. Here, as elsewhere, Montagu stresses that it is not merely Liberal Jewish leaders who are responsible for furthering its cause. This work, she insists, also needs to be done by "ordinary people," and modestly including herself adds "by you and by me." Best effected through the consecration of one's actions, it reveals the intrinsic relationship between faith and morality. In so doing, it gives expression to what Lily Montagu believed was Liberal Judaism's religious essence.

Developing this theme further, Lily Montagu addresses herself, in Club Letter 165, to those members who remain uninterested in Liberal Judaism's teachings. Here, she attempts to show that such teachings are reasonable, i.e., make sense in light of modern conceptions of religious knowledge and the realities of modern life. One of the examples that she uses to demonstrate this reasonableness is the Liberal Jewish observance of the Sabbath. Offering its adherents several options, Liberal Judaism believes that the Sabbath can be consecrated in many different ways. Thus, for example, it provides synagogue services on the evening, morning and afternoon of the Sabbath (the latter intended for "those who for economic reasons are obliged to work" in the mornings), while sanctioning and indeed encouraging Friday evening worship within the home. To facilitate such worship, Lily Montagu published a booklet entitled <u>Suggestions for Sabbath Eve Celebrations</u>. Going through several editions, it included selections from the Liberal Jewish Prayer Book, hymns, psalms, and other "alternative" scriptural verses and prayers. While it may seem that Montagu is here confusing "Liberal Judaism" with the specific offerings of the Liberal Jewish movement, she is in fact arguing that Liberal Judaism itself allows for such options, that unlike other, more "antiquated" forms of Judaism, it believes that it is up to the individual, given the realities of life, to establish ways in which he or she can consecrate the Sabbath best.

    Lily Montagu devotes the remainder of this letter to other aspects of Jewish life, again attempting to show the reasonable approach that Liberal Judaism takes towards each. Her intent is to convince her readers that it "makes sense" to interest oneself in Liberal Judaism, for its teachings contain the highest spiritual truths that the modern age can offer. She reiterates this point in her 1958 Presidential Address to the members of the Union of Liberal and Progressive Synagogues. Emphasizing the importance of the adjective "Liberal," she describes some of the ways in which Liberal Judaism has and might continue to give credence to the conviction that Judaism is an historical <u>and</u> <u>living</u> religion. Here, as elsewhere, Montagu's concern lies not only with increasing the numerical size of the Union but also, and more importantly, with increasing its spiritual strength.

THINK, THANK AND DO

J.R.U. United Service, January 19, 1936

    I fear the title which I suggested for this address is rather egoistic. For the first two words with an "and" between them - think and thank - happen to be the motto of the Montefiore family. Who chose them, and when they were chosen I do not know. Perhaps for my purposes today it might have been better if, instead of the second word "thank," I had put the word "pray," and so made the title "Think, pray and do." And, perhaps, in saying this, you will all perceive the drift of the remarks I am going to make, and I might stop here and leave the desk. Assuredly the text is often the best part of some sermons; "think, pray and do"; very likely everybody here could fill out the words in the manner most appropriate to him or to her. But it would be too peculiar and too unorthodox if I were to stop at the beginning, and so, for better or for worse, I must continue.

We, who are met here together this afternoon in this Synagogue are members of various Liberal Jewish congregations in London and in the provinces. A certain bond unites us all together. We are the representatives of a single cause, and if the historic truth is to be recalled, it might even be said that we are here as the spiritual children of one particular human being who is worshipping also by our side. This fact - the fact, I mean, of our special position - should, I think, have a double effect upon us. It should make us very humble, on the one hand, and yet fill us with a certain pride, upon the other. The combination is not easy. We have all probably met people of whom their friends say, or have said: "The trouble, or the misfortune, with dear old Robinson is that he takes himself too seriously." By this is meant (more or less) that Robinson thinks himself more important than he actually is. And, in all probability, the criticism was entirely justifiable. Robinson, in relation to the world, to his city, or religious community, was probably of very small importance. It would not have made much difference to the world or to the city or to the religious community, if Robinson had never been born, or had died when he was five years old. And yet - that is not the whole truth. Each brick is needful for the building; each bit of mortar or putty is required. And if the brick is a bad brick, the building, pro tanto, for that brick, is so much the worse; if it is a good brick, it is so much the better. "As God sees things," to use the words of our greatest English poetess,[1] he does, perchance, in some mysterious, hidden, unknowable way, need us all. At any rate, Robinson does well to think that he _has_ importance; that his city, his religious community, - and, therefore, if you like, even the world - are the better for his faithfulness, his industry, his love, his self-sacrifice, that they are the worse for his slackness, his follies and his sins. And so, if we are to be individually humble as regards our puny, unimportant private lives - if we are to remember that, in a very few years, the world, the city and the community will have forgotten our very names, - and yet also, at the same time, to think ourselves of such importance that our slackness and our sins are treason, the like is true as regards our group life, our life as representatives of a congregation, a movement, a cause. Most of us, indeed, have small reason to be proud. Not merely that we never can do much, but also because we have not done all the little that we could do, or because we have done that little feebly. We are conscious - at least, I _hope_ we are conscious - of our short-comings and slackness towards our cause, our congregation, our movement. Nevertheless, we shall not have the spur and the stimulus we might have to conquer, or, at least, to lessen, our slackness, unless we have also a certain pride. However feeble our strength, however inadequate our capacity, yet are we the representatives, the advocates, the defenders, the promoters, of a great cause. Ours it is to champion that cause and to push it forward. And that we are such defenders and champions may legitimately make us proud.

Hence, perhaps, the first, or the primary, direction of our thinking today at this joint service, - and indeed, a primary direction of our thinking generally, so far as our relation to our movement is concerned - should be an attempt to realise its greatness and its importance.

For my part, I hardly think we can put its greatness and its importance too high. It seems to me to be intimately associated with the grim, but by no means chidish, question: Is Judaism, as a distinct and definite religion, going to survive? You may say: "To put such a question is to imply that the questioner is lacking in faith. You may say that it is enough to <u>believe</u> that Judaism will survive; that it has existed for - what shall we say? Well, let us say, for 2,700 years or 3,700, or 4,000 years, and that it will continue for another 2,700 or 3,700, or 4,000 years, and that we can leave the ultimate issue to God. I do not deny the propriety of such a faith. Even more. I have no doubt but that the faith will help to the survival, that it may also help us to play our small part <u>in</u> the survival. But the faith will be, instead of a help, a positive obstacle or hindrance, if we put our hands in our lap and say: "Oh, God will see to it all; Judaism is safe all right; trust God for that. Nobody need worry." I think we <u>must</u> worry; God works through human beings. And if we are all slackers, upon the slackers, He may say, be the responsibility for the fall. That is putting it all very crudely, very anthropomorphically, but yet, I think, not altogether untruly.

Think. Judaism is assailed today by many forces. These forces are of considerable power. The forces are not the same as the forces which assailed it in olden days, but they are, perhaps, more insidious, more seductive, more <u>dissolvent</u>. In the old days the religious power of Judaism was, we might say, assailed by the religious power of the Church, of Christianity. It was a case of one religious power assailed by another, a little power assailed by a big power. And that direct assailing made the little power more resolved to resist; it stiffened its back; it braced its resolve. Judaism is no longer assailed by the Church.

Indeed, the Church and ourselves are now, to a large extent, allies instead of enemies, allies in a defense against assaults of a common enemy or enemies. The direct assaults of Christians against Judaism through the missionary societies, whether Protestant or Catholic, are comparatively negligible. There is, indeed, a certain indirect pressure in countries such as England or America where the Jews, a small minority amid a huge majority, are free and unpersecuted. There is a certain inevitable gravitation towards the religion of the majority. Intermarriages are not infrequent, and their result is usually, though not invariably, disadvantageous to the minority. But this danger, too, is of no great importance, and, as a tremendously keen advocate of the Judaism of the so-called Diaspora, I would add that the danger is well worthwhile, and richly compensated for by its enormous advantages. The forces I am alluding to are very different, and they are mainly modern and new.

There is, first of all, the force of religious indifference. It is a strange force. The very fact that we are here in this building this afternoon shows that we are not <u>entirely</u> indifferent. Nevertheless, indifference is a force which, partly through its many causes, is not only powerful, but very contagious and seductive. It has a strong ally, as well as a partial cause, in that inertia or laziness to which so many of us are subject. It is odd, though, perhaps, in one way, it is rather merciful, that we <u>can</u> be indifferent. You may remember the poet's words, which, though the poet was a sceptic, can affect us all:

> A moment's halt, a momentary taste
> Of being from the well amid the waste,
> And, lo, the phantom caravan has reached
> The Nothing it set out from - O make haste.[2]

Between the eternity behind us and the eternity before us, here for a moment we are. It is almost strange that we can take it so calmly. If this life be the end, it is strange. But if this life be <u>not</u> the end, if good and evil be realities, and even super-human realities, it is still stranger. And for us, as Jews, is not our history strange, our present condition strange? Nevertheless, there is the fact; indifference is a strong dissolvent force; it is our duty to think about it, to fight it in ourselves, to see what we can do, even on the smallest scale, to lessen it in others. Think, pray, and do.

Then there is a second force, rather difficult to describe. It takes two forms. Its first form is what is known as a dislike of, an objection to, all institutional religion. To this objection I would wish to be quite fair. It is sometimes perfectly honest, and may be due to causes for which institutional religion (which, as we all know, may be very unattractive) is itself to blame. Sometimes it is, I fear, only an elegant cloak or mask for indifference. But whatever its cause, and whatever its degree of sincerity, it is a danger to our movement. The Jew and Jewess who hold themselves aloof from all institutional religion are, in most cases, bound to become alienated from Judaism. For Judaism, like other religions, is partly dependant upon a corporate, public and institutional life, and the more that life is weakened, and the feebler it becomes, the more will the religion tend to wither and fade away. I may add that even for the individual's own private religious life and vitality, there are only very few highly gifted and exceptional souls who, without danger or stunting, can do without institutional religion; but I ask you to think not so much of the loss to the individual, as the loss to the community and to the cause.

Another form which this second danger takes is this. There are those who say: "A <u>particular</u> religion is too narrow a religion. One can be deeply religious," they urge, "and yet, for that very reason, be attached neither to synagogue nor church." It would take me too long to deal with that argument and danger; I believe it to be sophistical; but, obviously, those who take this line are useless as Jews, whether to Orthodoxy or to Liberalism. I must, however, say a word about a precisely opposite danger. There are those whose Judaism is confined to, and only shows itself in, an almost fanatical opposition to, and dislike of, Christianity. What good is this? It may, indeed, suffice to keep them, as people say, within the Jewish fold, and our cemeteries may be assured of receiving their bodies, but the enrichment of the cemetery is preceded by the impoverishment of the religion. If ever there was a negative and futile sort of religion it is one the only manifestation of which is the dislike of another religion than your own. It is easy, but cheap; it is simple, but useless. Judaism can only be preserved by the <u>positive</u> affection, by the <u>positive</u> service, by the <u>positive</u> devotion, of its members; mere negative dislike of our neighbour's religion is of no value whatever. To be above creeds and distinctions is dangerous; to be so below your creed that you can only be described as <u>not</u> something else is both dangerous and despicable.

A third or fourth danger is much larger and more ominous. You must all be aware of it. It affects our Christian neighbours quite as much as it affects ourselves. A great attack is going on against Theism - that is, against the sort of God, the Father and King, whom Judaism and Christianity alike dare to believe in, to proclaim, and to worship, - and also against all religion. Theism is on its defence; it is on its defence against Pantheism, or against an impersonal and un-self-conscious God; religion as a whole is on its defence. We are living in the midst of these attacks. We cannot ignore them. Think, pray and do.

This too specially I want to say. You all know what has happened, and is happening, in Russia: something which the world has never seen before. An organised attack upon all religion, conducted, I had almost said, with all the magnificent resources of modern civilisation; an elaborate propaganda of militant Atheism superbly managed upon a gigantic scale, and with admirable efficiency. A whole population is growing up taught, and well taught, to laugh at, and despise, and hate, all religion and the very idea of immortalitiy and of God. Many Jews by birth or race are among the most active in this propaganda. You may say: "Russia is a long way off: What does it concern us?" But today there is no country which is a long way off, and there are no ideas which, active in one country, are a long way off from another. Now here again, for this awful condition of things, religion - not our religion, I think, - is partly to blame. And I want to say this. Our movement is not political. There are Liberal Jews who are conservatives; there are Liberal Jews who are Socialists, and I do not see why there should not be Liberal Jews who are Communists. It is, however, I believe, a fact that 99 out of every 100 Communists of Jewish birth are neither Orthodox Jews nor Liberal Jews, but hostile to all religion. And they are hostile because they say that religion and communism are, of necessity, deadly foes. In these matters I am very ignorant, but I sometimes wish that many ardent religious Jews, whether Orthodox or Liberal, would become Communists, in order that the spectacle of what we have seen and see in Russia might never be seen in England. But whether communism as a social and political system be true or no, the fact of its power, the fact of its proselytising energy, and the fact of its prevailing antagonism to religion, are undoubted: so again I say: Do not shut your eyes or your ears: think, pray and do.

I have to speak now of yet another danger, or rather of two dangers, which I will compress into a very few words. Orthodox Judaism has two sides, each of which should support and strengthen the other. But as things now are in England both are being weakened at one and the same time, and hence the decay of each is hastened and increased by the decay of the other. I refer to Orthodox Jewish belief and Orthodox Jewish practice. As regards belief, Orthodox Judaism depends upon the doctrine of the Mosaic origin, the homogeneity, the perfection and verbal inspiration of the Pentateuchal laws. But that doctrine historic investigation, biblical criticism and the philosophy of religion, make it increasingly difficult to maintain. As regards practice, with the weakening of the doctrine, which is the basis of the practice, the exigencies of modern life put increasing difficulties in the way. Few among us would wish the Jews to live in a segregated ghetto; few would wish them not to take their share in the general life, and in the general culture, of England, their home. One point more; I will mention a highly contentious word, but yet I will avoid everything which is contentious. I name the word Zionism. Now our movement is neutral as regards Zionism. We have among us eager and enthusiastic advocates, and eager and enthusiastic opponents, of Zionism. But what I want to say is this. Even in Palestine, even in the very seat and living centre of Zionism, many of the difficulties which assail Judaism _here_ assail it _there_. Some possibly assail Judaism with even greater power in Palestine than in England. And many earnest Zionists would tell you that if the growing number of Jews in Palestine is to grow up, not a godless and religionless, but a God-fearing and God-loving, community - a community which, in all sincerity and passion, can still call upon Abeenu Malkaynu, our Father, our King, - then it must be some form (and the form is comparatively indifferent) of Liberal Judaism which will save them, some form of Liberal Judaism which must become their religion.

Such are the dangers and the troubles which confront us. I hold that Liberal Judaism, and Liberal Judaism only, can tackle and triumph over them all, but it needs - under the providence of God - all our strength, all our keenness, all our fidelity. Think, pray, do. Think too of a hope which is too sacred to be often mentioned, but is yet deep within our hearts. The present is urgent, but what about the future? How if Judaism, with that name or another, is destined to be the religion and the Theism of the future? What a thought is this: Think. As Jews we are bidden to use our minds. "Give us knowledge, understanding and discernment," says the old prayer. Yes, let us think hard, and seek to realise the greatness, as well as the need, of our movement and of our cause. But, as Jews, there is something else incumbent upon us too. Think and pray. A mere intellectual acceptance of the arguments and of the facts which I have ventured to put before you will not be enough. We must bring our feelings into play as well as our minds. Together with our thinking there must be worship and prayer. For will and mind and feelings must support each other. The intelligence alone can end in apathy. Therefore are we wise, therefore we do well, to come here today for common worship and prayer; joining together, and thereby helping one another, in common devotion to God and in the better dedication of our lives to what we believe to be his service. Let private prayer and public prayer go hand in hand. Each can help the other.

Let us pray to God that we may be receptive to His influence and His inspiration. The Shema bids us love God with all our heart, but to the old Hebrews that usually meant with all our <u>mind</u>; and then we are to love Him with all our soul, that is, not coldly, if a cold love be possible, but with emotion, with our <u>feelings</u>; and then we are to love Him with all our might, that is, with our <u>will</u>. Think, pray and do. But can we all "do"? Yes: in our various degrees we all can. We cannot all be leaders; what is an army without its rank and file? But there is none of us here, no man, no woman, who cannot <u>do</u> something, even if it be only the winning of a single extra adherent to our movement and our cause. In one way or another we all can add one small brick to the fabric. We all can help; we all are needed. The cause needs <u>us</u>. Still more do <u>we</u> need the <u>cause</u>. Think, pray and do.

Archives, Liberal
Jewish Synagogue, London

[1] From Book IX, line 179 of Elizabeth Barrett Browning's verse-novel "Aurora Leigh" (1856).

[2] Lines 189-192 of Edward Fitzgerald's "The Rubáiyát of Omar Khayyám" (1859).

CAN WE POSSIBLY BE MISTAKEN?

November 11, 1939

We are all familiar with the phrase: "I may be mistaken, but," and the conviction that the speaker is certain he is right rings through his words. But the history of nations, as well as the history of individuals, is a record of mistakes, and very frequently it is just out of these mistakes that progress is made. "Every good, that is worth possessing," says Professor James, "must be paid for by strokes of daily effort."[1] It is pathetic to see how much error has been perpetrated in good faith by men and women prompted by the best motives. Witness all the terrible industrial laws which grew out of the error that cheap labour, child labour, was essential to national well-being. So children worked inordinate hours in mines and factories, and even risked their lives in cleaning chimneys, and good people shook their heads over the sadness of these children's lot, but felt it belonged to an unchangeable order of society. It required the illuminated conscience of a Shaftesbury to reveal error, and to demand that this error should no longer be persisted in.

Individuals often fall to their lowest standard of conduct through smugness, or lack of courage, for, having recognised error, they refuse to correct it. Perhaps it looks bad to own ourselves mistaken, and it is only the courageous who can struggle against error, especially if it has the support of the majority. Unless we can accept an absolute standard of goodness, which progresses from age to age, it is almost impossible for us to recognise our errors. Through our natural indolence, and through our inclination to live from hour to hour, without weighing the consequences of our actions, we cherish expediency and revel in compromise.

But it is about the absolute standard that I should like mainly to speak this morning. It happens to all of us, who think at all, to have moments when we wonder _how_ we can continue to believe in God in the face of evil. We ask in misery, and, sometimes almost in despair, whether perhaps after all we are not building up our lives on popular myths and fairy tales. There _can_ be no certainty in the field of religion.

In 1914, a war, it was believed, could only last a few weeks, months at most. We could trust the German people never to harbour hatred against England. The two countries were so intimately associated in friendship and national interest. They could not long be separated. Then, when these prophecies were falsified, we believed that a passion for peace was being developed between 1914 and 1918 which could never again be disturbed. With the fraternising of all classes in wartime had come a new era in the life of the English nation. Class distinction was destroyed for ever. Men and women had discovered the true values in life, and could never again fritter it in vanity, or in the pursuit of selfish aims. We ourselves spoke these or similar words only yesterday - 20 years or so ago - and _now_ we know how false all these opinions were. We were terribly, sadly mistaken. Can we possibly be mistaken in our convictions again? We can endure to be mistaken in our political and social theories, but we cannot let our religious certainties totter. Not those! Surely not those! How can we _know_ there is a God? Is it not possible that in this, as well as in so much else, we are mistaken?

If you were Orthodox Jews and believed in the literal and eternal truth of every word contained in the Pentateuch, you could not accept the possibility of being mistaken. God revealed Himself on Mount Sinai. The Israelites actually heard the thunder and saw the lightning which accompanied the giving of the Ten Commandments. They saw the light on Moses' face when he descended from the mountain, having spoken to God, and been in close contact with His spirit for forty days and forty nights, needing nought else but spiritual sustenance. The eye-witnesses of all these wonders told of them to their children, and those in their turn spoke of them to those who came after them, and so on throughout the generations, even to this day, when we stand together in this place. "Ye are my witnesses," said the Lord.

How is it that even those Jews who call themselves Orthodox begin to hesitate in their convictions, and wonder if they, even _they_, may be mistaken? They do not realise that their doubts are inconsistent with their Orthodoxy. Perhaps they do not often think about religion at all. They are Jews, and it is easier to call oneself Orthodox than otherwise. The Orthodox umbrella covers people and makes them comfortable. They need not think any more about their Judaism. But, unfortunately, for themselves, they are not protected against the disintegrating scepticism of the age, if they only give lip service to their Orthodoxy. Unless they have dared to use their minds in the service of religion, their convictions cannot be real and lasting for all time, as are those of the consistently Orthodox.

You and I who have imbibed the principles of Liberal Judaism, and are determined to give them allegiance, cannot place ourselves, even for our own comfort and protection, under the Orthodox umbrella. We have lost faith in miracles. The Bible, we think, reveals God, and is full of His inspiration, but we cannot believe such parts to be eternally true which clash with our sense of truth, and our conception of righteousness, justice and love. We have learned that the authority for our own belief lies in our own conscience nourished by communion with God, and trained by the scholars of the past. We have to examine our religion for ourselves, anew, today, in this year 1939, in the midst of human upheavals and miseries and desperate conflicts and doubts. Will our religion survive? _Can_ we be mistaken?

Friends, we have each to do our searching for ourselves. Our religion to be worth anything must be our own, the result of our own searching and sifting and striving and doubting and triumphant affirmation. I can only with great deference, and in all humility, explain to you something of my own in case it may in some measure be acceptable to you.

I start out deeply influenced by the devotion of the past. I have read my Bible, compiled by men and women who called themselves, as I do, Jews, and have found in the Bible some teaching which appears to me so perfectly good that my mind cannot conceive of anything better. It seems to me that this teaching is perfect, and I do it homage. "Seek peace and pursue it." "The just shall live by his faith." "Love thy neighbour as thyself." "Love mercy." "Thou shalt not kill." "Thou shalt not steal." "Thou shalt not commit adultery." "Walk humbly with Thy God." These are only a few of the sayings which, to my mind, represent absolute truth.

I read my Bible history, and see the progress of a small group of people. I see how they survived persecution and suffering. I see a purpose running right through their story. I see why they were preserved alive. I recognise the treasure which they have been holding throughout the ages, and how this treasure must serve as a blessed influence in the world for all time. I see the succession of men and women, and how with their aid more and more spiritual truth has been found to serve the whole universe. Then I realise that I am part of that succession of men and women, and I know the purpose of my life here.

Now friends, *if* men and women had obeyed God's law, not intermittently but continually, not in certain spots on the globe, but throughout the whole world, would not our present miseries have to a large extent disappeared? But *why* should men have been so wicked for so long and so frequently? Why should they have acted in defiance of love and justice? Why were certain individuals allowed to set aside the law of goodness and truth which should have enthralled the world, and in their insolence and wickedness have been allowed to dominate instead? Why were not their evil machinations frustrated?

Did God reveal Himself, and then withdraw from our world? I don't think so, but I think that God gave freedom of choice to humanity, and He also gave them the assurance, which is being verified every day that he would strengthen the will of the righteous who seek advance through righteousness. If we obey, we will be allowed to live in peace and security. If we disobey, we lose quiet and peace - see the world today! In quietness and confidence shall be your strength. I dare not call this teaching out of date. I see around me the chaos which results from defiance. I feel sure it was God who set before humanity a blessing and a curse, and said: Choose thou! How can I be mistaken, when I see what disobedience brings?

My faith is supported by personal experience. I have learned to pray, and when I pray I can make an effort to adjust my life in harmony with the spirit of goodness. I <u>can</u> feel the revelation of God, even as my fathers could. I see the wonders of creation, and the uniformity of the laws by which they hang together. I recognise the one mind of the God Creator. I see the marvels of harmony in natural colours and the harmony of sound in the songs of the birds. Again, I bring homage to God the Creator. I see goodness in my fellow men. I experience love. I recognise discoveries based upon the law of truth. I see works of art. I listen to sublime music - God, God everywhere! I hear within myself the voice of conscience bidding me seek to be good and just and merciful. I feel the stings of remorse when I lack courage, when I fail in obedience. My God remains within me when I would ignore

Him. I experience pain. But all this is so difficult. The existence of the perfect God, revealed in the Bible, and in the world, in the lives of others, and in my own soul, makes my own imperfection so overwhelming. I find it so hard to live up to my religion. Can it not be all a mistake, seeing it is so often beyond our attainment?

But how about love? Do you doubt its existence between parents and children, husband and wife, and friends, because it is sometimes absent when it should never fail? How about light? Do you doubt the existence of the sun because it is often hidden? Is there no truth in the world because falsehood is so inclined to vaunt herself? Have you never seen beauty? Ugliness exists, but beauty <u>must</u> prevail.

No friends, I don't think we can be mistaken in the absolute and eternal God idea. When we have failed and uttered such incalculable absurdities, and acted with such unfathomable stupidity, our eyes and hearts were not sufficiently trained. We had not got far enough on the mountain of life to get the right perspective. The light was still shaded; our eyes were still weak. And even today, this is our state - weak, imperfect, in definite and unquestionable need of guidance. It is through our mistakes that we can attain to God. But we must <u>dare</u> to struggle if we would attain. We must <u>use</u> our mistakes if we would climb nearer to truth. In God's light we see light, and away from God there is darkness now and for evermore. God's light must grow more and more until we can reach the Perfect Day.

Archives, Liberal
Jewish Synagogue, London

[1]From William James, <u>Talks to Teachers</u> (1908). This quote also appears in Claude Montefiore's "On Effort and Struggle" in his <u>Truth and Religion and other Sermons</u>

Delivered at the Services of the Jewish Religious Union (London, 1906), p. 138. It may well be from here that Lily Montagu familiarized herself with this quotation.

CLUB LETTER NO. 56

February 1944

LIBERAL JUDAISM AND ITS APPEAL

In my February message to our West Central Liberal Jewish Congregation, I appealed to the members to use their energy in the cause of the Congregation, or rather for the cause for which our synagogue works. I looked up the word 'energy' in the dictionary and found: 'Internal or inherent power', or 'capability for performing work'. A quotation from Tennyson runs: 'My desire like all strongest hopes by its own energy fulfilled itself'.[1] Among the synonyms for 'energy' are 'life', 'spirit', 'resolution'. Here we have matter for a sermon, or for many sermons.

We feel that we have some energy, that is some inherent power. It seems to come of its own accord, and when we consider the synonyms 'life', 'spirit', we realise that this energy is the expression of the God within us. God is eternal, so if we feel slack and incapable of work, it must be because we are trying to suppress the voice of God.

The quotation from Tennyson suggests that if we want something enough, we shall find the energy to fulfil our desire. Now I want to ask you how far you really do care for our cause and are prepared to use your energy in furthering it? What, in the first place, is our cause?

The cause we have in mind is the spread of Liberal Judaism. Why Liberal? Because I think Liberal Judaism is the Judaism of the future, as it is in harmony with life and truth as we conceive it and through its progressive power it will always retain this harmony.

Some people think that one religion is as good as another, and that we have no reason to press for the spread of any particular religion. What do you think? For myself, I hold Liberal Judaism to be true and I see value in truth. I think it does matter incalculably what people believe, because such faith affects conduct. I am quite prepared to agree that every religion produces the finest types of character if it is sincerely held. But I hold that our conception is the one which we hold because we believe in its value. So we who hold it cannot spread any other presentment, for we should not be giving of our best, and you and I are called upon to give our testimony, and we are called to do this by God Himself. Moreover, I say to you that you have the energy or inherent power, or the capacity for this work, and that if you desire to do it sufficiently as to put into it all your strength, your hopes will be fulfilled.

Now I am going to suggest to you some of the ways by which in my view the work can be done, by ordinary people, by you and by me. We have to correct certain misconceptions about Liberal Judaism, not merely by refuting error through argument, but by giving positive illustration of the truth of our religion.

People say that Liberal Judaism is a religion of convenience. We say that it is a hard and exacting religion, as well as a splendid, life-giving religion, a religion which makes heavy demands on us as well as creating for us spiritual joy and peace. How can we prove this? I think we must do this by living up to our standards of goodness and truth. Our Judaism demands that we must work fairly, refraining from acting unjustly towards our employers or employees or the public, that in fact we must be scrupulously honest and honourable people, not because honesty is the best policy (it may or may not be), not because our set includes people of this sort who would ostracise us if we behaved in a shady way in our business concerns (they may be that sort, or they may not), but because the never-changing God requires honour and honesty from us. Judaism requires us to be temperate in our pleasures, clean in our sexual relations, and to refrain from exploiting the personality or gifts or any other human being for our own amusement. Let us follow the practice then of reviving our lives day by day, evening by evening, and by being strict in the judgement we pass on ourselves, feeling in our feeble, human way we are reflecting the judgement of God.

People say that Judaism is an inherited religion which we accept as a birthright, but never take the trouble to appreciate its worth. Liberal Jews however affirm that our religion grows and develops because it can satisfy the needs of every succeeding generation. It behoves us to study our spiritual inheritance with reverence, and then try through prayer and the effort to pursue righteousness to come in contact with the God who gave us our revelation. We have to discover for ourselves how far the lessons of the past are appropriate to the life of today. Have we through standing on our fathers' shoulders the power to see a little further into truth than they were able to see? If so, we must dare to act according to our convictions even though the change in our religious views may give us a certain amount of pain, or worse still, give pain to those we love. We say we serve the God of truth, so we can only seek to approach Him through unflinching devotion to truth.

We consider ceremonials and observances as "aids to holiness." We examine our festival seasons and our penitential days and the reasons for observing them. Sometimes we place a new emphasis on the old teaching, and so pour new wine into the old bottles, but we do find that the Holydays serve as vehicles for enriching our lives with ethical conceptions by which our lives must be improved. Having once decided these points, we must act in accordance with our ideas. Convenience does not enter into our consideration at all where our religion is concerned. We say public worship is helpful, so we must join in public worship. We say that Passover has a life-giving message about liberty and freedom from oppression; therefore, we must observe Passover. We say Pentecost establishes the relation between morality and religion which is greatly needed by our generation. This is fine teaching, so we must observe Pentecost. We say that Tabernacles is the festival of thanksgiving. It emphasises the connection between religion and nature. We need this emphasis; we can find God through reverence for His revelation of beauty. Let us then observe the festival of Tabernacles.

We say that we have given the Sabbath principles to the world and so infinitely stimulated its spiritual life. If our teaching is to inspire others, let us show our devotion at any rate to that part of the Sabbath which we can call our own. Let our allegiance be unaffected by the desire for gain or social pleasures. Let us at least enhance the claim of Sabbath observance, even though to our great sorrow and conscious loss, we cannot retain our economic independence and refrain from Sabbath work.

The New Year and Day of Atonement as the penitential season demand our allegiance. On these days we have to examine our way of life and change it if we think it is leading us away from instead of nearer to God. Let us use these days in spiritual effort and recognise their importance and solemnity. Let us on these days at any rate spend our time consciously in the courts of God.

When considering these observances it will not do for a Liberal Jew to say: "I do believe these observances are good, but this year, I just can't observe them. I am a Liberal, and after all I can make another day or method serve my purpose. It doesn't matter." But, friends, it does matter, and just because you are Liberal, you must be rigid with yourself. You are serving God and you must be prepared to sacrifice yourselves according to the dictates of your conscience, for your religion demands sacrifice in order to gain the fulness of spiritual life. You must be of use to the community which has to speak its message to the generations. You are a link in the great chain of witnesses; you dare not break that chain.

Even if your happiness is at stake, you must be faithful. If intermarriage increases, our message will lose its strength. Our community will disintegrate. You must admit this truth. Then if your turn comes, or the turn of your son or daughter, and these young people stand at the cross roads, and can either deny their obligation to spread Judaism or affirm it, they must if they are Liberal Jews remain true to their faith. We are the children of the Book. We have a certain way of regarding our Bible which expresses progressive teaching. We must then know our Book and understand its teaching and prove its value as an inspiration for our lives and the lives of all humanity.

Such knowledge can be acquired by your children with a certain degree of ease, if it is imparted properly. You can acquire it also, but it will be harder for you. But it must be done if you accept the charge given to you by Liberal Judaism. The future life of the Old Testament should be in your hands, to save or to destroy. It is said that Jews are more ignorant than their non-Jewish neighbours of the Bible. Is that not a shameful reproach? Can we ourselves feel altogether guiltless?

Now, friends, I have only mentioned some aspects of our obligations to our cause. But I think I have made sufficient claim for the moment on your energy, your inherent power, your capacity for accomplishment. And if you use your energy in the way I suggest, will it be of advantage to you? Yes, friends, I believe so. I think you will grow in the consciousness that you are living with and for your God. I think, moreover, that you will feel that you are serving God's holy purpose, for you will be serving your generation and the generations which will come after you. By your faith, your Liberal Jewish faith, you shall live.

Private Collection,
Hannah Feldman, London

[1]From Tennyson's poem, "The Gardener's Daughter."

CLUB LETTER NO. 165

June 1954

I am told that some of you are not interested in Liberal Judaism and do not want to know about it. The second part of this statement explains the first. If you understood the meaning of Liberal Judaism, you would, I feel sure, be interested, and I want more than anything else in the world that you should understand it. Why do I feel like this? In the first place it is because, as your Club Mother, I want to share with you that which I value most in life. Then I believe that Liberal Judaism is the Judaism of the future, that it is in harmony with the best thought of the age in which we live, and that through following its principles you can attain the best life possible.

It is true that I should not trouble to write this letter if the members of our Club whom I am addressing were leading lives according to Orthodox ideas. In that case, I should respect them and quite understand that they did not need my explanations of religion, and I would not wish to interfere with them. But although some of you call yourselves Orthodox, you do not lead Orthodox lives. You do not believe these laws were framed and directed by God Himself, for, if you did, you would not dare to break them. But, except for a very small minority who are truly and sincerely Orthodox in the highest sense of the word, you work on the Sabbath and several of the festivals, and you do not attempt to hallow any part of these holy days through public worship. Many of you neglect the dietary laws when you are away from home. You also ride and go to places of amusement on the Sabbath and even go shopping. You do not wish to break the law, but your lives shape themselves in that manner and you say you follow the ways of your fathers as well as you can and do not think about religion.

Many years ago at Littlehampton[1] a girl of about 20 asked me whether goodness had anything to do with religion. Of course I told her that religion had to do with goodness because it means the binding of the soul back to the God who gave it. God is perfect goodness and through prayer you can gather something of God's being into your own and so have help and guidance in your life. I believe that you people who call yourselves Orthodox, but do not observe Orthodoxy do still achieve goodness through contact with the God of lovingkindness. But I am, in all humility, anxious to show how Liberal Judaism can strengthen your faith in God because it is so reasonable and because it gives you a standard of right living.

I am sure you agree with me that it is not easy to be as good as we would wish to be. So since I am sure you are broad-minded seekers after truth, I want to give you all the help I can. Liberal Jews accept much of the teaching of the past and adapt it to the needs of the present. Since the time of the Prophets this process of development has gone on and we think that each generation of Jews has some particle of truth to add to the great store which makes up Judaism. We Liberals, even as the Orthodox, believe in the Unity of God, and think that we can and should pray to Him directly. We need no intercessor. We try to follow the teaching contained in the Shema and to love God in all we do and try to do and seek to serve Him throughout all our human activities. We believe that Judaism is expressed in honest living and in kindness to all men for all are God's children. We believe that we have a religious contribution to make to the life of the world which will hasten the time when all nations will be at peace and be exalted by righteousness and truth. In this way we help to build up God's kingdom on earth, even to bring nearer the Messianic age.

Sabbath Services.

Liberal Jews lay great stress on the observance of the Sabbath Eve as holy. It should give the opportunity for consecrating family life through the gathering of the family together for worship and intimate talk and joyous recreation. In many of our Synagogues joyous services are held for those who prefer public worship on the Sabbath Eve and a sermon on some topical theme is given. In addition to Sabbath morning services, we have also services on Sabbath afternoons for those who for economic reasons are obliged to work on the Sabbath. Of course we think they serve God through seeking a high standard in their work and so as they pass from their workshop or business house or office to the Synagogue, they are in the House of God all the time.

Hebrew.

In every part of the world we think in the language of our country, and we believe we can pray most sincerely in the language we understand best. In England it is English, in France French, in all the Synagogues in Israel, Progressive as well as Orthodox, it is Hebrew. God understands all languages, even that of silence, which also we use in our services. But in order to preserve unity with all other Jewish Congregations, we retain Hebrew for several of our traditional prayers. Moreover, children are taught Hebrew in our religion schools as without Hebrew Jews cannot get the full meaning of the Bible word which we hold very dear.

Hats.

Liberal Jews wear hats when they pray if they think that by so doing they show reverence to God. Our Ministers always keep their heads covered during the service and it is one way of showing their belief in the unity of our brotherhood. Jews originate in the East where people have to keep their heads covered because of the heat of the sun. Some Western Jews feel that the custom (it is only a custom) means much to them as they have always seen their menfolk observing it. Others who have never seen it in their own homes, feel uncomfortable when they wear hats in Synagogue because they hold that respect is shown to God as well as to human beings when the hat is raised. The custom of wearing a hat or not wearing a hat must be left to the choice of the individual. He must be impressed with the belief that the thoughts which prevail under the hat can lead him to God, not the hat itself.

Riding to Synagogue.

Liberal Jews ride on Sabbaths and Holydays in public conveyances to their places of worship because buses and trains go whether we use them or not. If, however, we have a chauffeur or a horse, man and beast must have a weekly day of rest for we, like Orthodox Jews, accept the principle of the Fourth Commandment. It is surely better to ride to a service which stimulates our religious faith than to cut ourselves off from Jewish public worship because we cannot walk to Synagogue.

Attitude to the Law and the Whole Bible.

We Liberal Jews think that the Bible was built up generation by generation and that some parts contain eternal truth and some were suitable for people of a certain degree of civilisation and living in a particular age, but they cannot be accepted by people of a different stage of civilisation or living in a different age. We follow that part of the Law which we think contains truth which can harmonise with our highest thought. We do not believe that the Law was given on one occasion for all time, nor that God spoke the Commandments Himself and wrote them on tables of stone. We think the Law grew gradually through the works of great teacher-scholars and prophets who were in close contact with God. That is why we see the development of truth in the Bible. Some laws such as those about animal sacrifice can have nothing to do with right living today and could never again become part of religious observance. But we Liberal Jews uphold and try our best to observe the exalted teachings of the Law such as "Love thy neighbour as thyself" and "Thou shalt love God with thy whole heart" and "Seek peace and pursue it". We lay stress on the teaching of the prophets on social righteousness.

Observances.

Liberal Jews value observances as a help to right living and not because of their antiquity or because of certain laws about them which are found in the Bible. They have to ask: Is this law true for me and my children? Does it help me to be a better man or woman? If it seems good and true to me, I must observe it even if I have to make sacrifices to do so. If it does not have a helpful meaning for me, I must have courage, while respecting those who observe it, to pass it by, for my observance would be insincere.

So Liberal Jews call for the observance of the New Year with its message for us to return to God through penitence followed by rejoicing; the Day of Atonement spent in prayer and meditation in Synagogue with, if possible, complete abstention from food. On this day we must try to harmonise our lives with the God idea. Liberal Jews also observe Passover and lay particular emphasis on the need for every individual to free himself from sin, bad habits and prejudices, and to seek freedom for every nation which must be allowed to express itself as it wills in thought, religion and political life; they seek freedom for every oppressed or persecuted individual. They also observe Pentecost with its emphasis on morality on which religion is based, for the good Jew must lead a decent life. They rejoice in the harvest of Tabernacles recognising nature's laws and bounty and her revelation of beauty. They observe the festival of Chanukah with its appeal to courage and its dedication of the human soul. Liberal Jews do not observe Purim because the book of Esther has no historical authority and does not once contain the name of God. It is a story full of cruelty and revenge on both sides.

Dietary laws.

Liberal Jews consider the dietary laws as laws of hygiene which were made part of religious observance in order that cleanliness which is part of religion should be enforced. Also the Bible recommends the most humane way for slaughtering animals known in those far off days. Some of the hygienic principles especially those regarding the examination of animals before they are used for human consumption, have been accepted by civilised people of all faiths.

Circumcision.

Circumcision is considered by Liberal Jews as a health law which is now very generally followed by people of other religions as well as by ourselves. If a male proselyte does not wish to undergo the operation which is quite severe for an adult, Liberal Jews accept him notwithstanding, if, after careful tuition, he acquires the necessary knowledge of Judaism and gives evidence of true sincerity, for he is converted through his spirit, his mind and his heart and not through his body.

Confirmation.

Liberal Jews encourage the confirmation of boys and girls instead of Bar Mitzvah. In Western countries the boy of 13 is happily still a child and we cannot ask him to take religious responsibility or to understand the inwardness of his religion. The Confirmation, including a service, is a most solemn experience for boys and girls of 15 or 16 who are first taught all aspects of the Jewish religion. In this, as in all other parts of Synagogue life, we have equality between the sexes. They are taught together in the religion school and have equal rights as Synagogue members. Men and women become lay Ministers if they are qualified.

It is not possible for me to explain thoroughly in one letter the teaching of a great religion. I can only ask you, if I have been able to interest you at all, to attend one of our services or meetings of our youth group, and perhaps one or two of our discussion meetings. Better still it would please me much if you asked me for an appointment when we could have a heart to heart talk.

The Prophet tells us to live by our faith. Before we can do that we must understand and accept it. Are you ready to do that? Your Judaism should come to life; you have inherited its basic principles from your ancestors and God Himself through His Prophets asks you to seek truth and to observe it.

Private Collection,
Hannah Feldman, London

[1] Site of the Club's summer holidays.

PRESIDENTIAL ADDRESS

Annual Meeting,
Union of Liberal and Progressive Synagogues,
Liberal Jewish Synagogue Sunday,
May 11th 1958

It is my privilege to welcome you all here, and to express the hope that this meeting will give us the opportunity to exchange thought and to make resolutions which will stimulate the development of our Union, not only numerically, though that is important, but particularly in spiritual strength.

Our officers, to whom we owe so much, will give you the factual history of the past year. I want to take the opportunity to emphasise the lesson I have learned throughout my connection with our Union, and which has been especially impressed on me in the last year, that the adjective Liberal, by which we describe our conception of Judaism, is of supreme importance. It is our duty to think about it continually, thoroughly to assimilate it spiritually, and to let its inherent power be for sustenance for our groups, and in time serve the whole of our community.

Today, we hear people say that so long as they profess to be Jews and are loyal in their professions; so long as they through their daily conduct bring credit to the community as a whole, it is not important that they should define their religion more closely. I venture to differ from these views. I believe that Liberal Judaism is the Judaism of the future, and I even dare to say that its main tenets will ultimately illumine the lives of all people. I do not affirm that our present <u>form</u> of Liberal Judaism need necessarily be the religion by which men and women will live some decades from the present. For myself, I cannot conceive better externalities than those we use in our methods of worship, without however waiting for the future. I should like to see now, today, a new festival, contemplated, a festival for the better understanding of self-dedication to the cause of peace, a festival in accordance with our principles, to satisfy the spiritual yearnings of the present and to be an aid to holiness. If we honestly believe in progressive revelation, we have the right to create as well as to discard. Perhaps such a festival might in time replace Purim,[1] as it would be on an advanced ethical plane, and we, seekers after God, might express our faith and hope in prayer and music, using silence also as a medium for approaching the indefinable God of the universe, always rejoicing in the teaching of the past to give us the peace ideal which we expect to realise in the future.

Would you not like to observe such a festival, since peace is of such important to us, and we could embody in our worship the best we can find for our approach to God in art and above all in complete self-surrender to God? Why should we not on special occasions hallow our thoughts and aspirations on international relations which affect all mankind?

I claim that our religion, by its very nature, must develop in its expression in order to satisfy the present seekers after truth, even as it did in the past. Judaism will not change its fundamentals. To be a Jew, a man must always believe in God and in direct communion with Him. And we say today, at this annual meeting of our Union, that this faith gives us the obligation to seek new truths, to adapt our spiritual faith to the needs of our day, and to prepare and work for the time to come which will ultimately merge into the Messianic Age. Through our efforts, we must render the observances and ceremonials which we have inherited from the past meaningful to ourselves and helpful to our children. There are thousands of men and women who call themselves Jews because of their birth from Jewish parents, but they are entirely indifferent to the principles and practices of Judaism. We think that we Liberals have a treasure. As Liberal Jews, we can share this treasure with others because we are convinced of its value. Through our interpretation, we can, in all humility, testify that the ancient observances are aids to holiness. I cannot call indifferentists my co-religionists. They may be very good people, far better than I am, but I acknowledge this fact with shame as Judaism does not help them at all, and Judaism, prefaced by the adjective Liberal, is my most valuable possession, and should prove an inspiration to all who share it.

Again I insist that unless Judaism is a historical <u>and</u> living Judaism, it cannot be a formative influence in our lives. We cannot consciously seek the privilege of working for a Messianic Age merely in the name of our ancestral faith. Our religion must fill <u>our</u> hearts also. It is ancient, of course: it has stood the test of time, but it is alive. The adjective Liberal is of infinite importance because it shows us the way to adapt our faith to the life of an ever-changing world. The Orthodox accept revelation as given in the past, and the more enlightened among them admit also that the work of adaptation used in the past is still of value to us. But Liberals emphasise the here and the now. The Conservatives, as far as I understand them, accept useful changes in religious externalities, but do not care to enunciate the principles which inspire them. They polish the surface of the table, but do not examine the feet on which it stands. They invite Jews of all shades to join in a happy fellowship with them, and lay little emphasis on the meaning of Jewish ceremonial as long as it is decorously observed.

Our Union cannot identify itself with either of these great sections of Jews. I say this with the greatest respect and no false superiority. We must serve God with the truth which we conceive with our own hearts, not the hearts of others. I do not feel I could fulfil the purpose of my life if I were not a Liberal Jewess, with emphasis on the adjective.

Needless to say, I wish we were all less ignorant, and more powerful through knowledge; much more righteous, with a higher sense of truth than we actually possess. Then, indeed, we should be walking sermons, irresistible in their appeal. But we can connect with our Liberal faith the possibilities of our lives. I dare to think, moreover, that God gives to every man and woman, however weak, humble or ignorant, the command to work with and for Him in the building of His Kingdom. You will hear from our Minister to the Union, and from our Secretary, that our Union is growing. It must become, with your help, an instrument in God's hands for spreading truth. We offer the coming generation a growing religion. It is your responsibility to express the spiritual teaching of your time. You look back and gather the highest traditions of Judaism. You meditate over and over again on the prophetic teaching of the past. Then you interpret these lessons anew and make them part of your new life. The world needs authority for right living. There is a hunger among men to return to God from whom many have strayed. I ask you to consider anew your duties and privileges as Liberal Jews.

The Union of Liberal and Progressive Synagogues is a constituent, a real part of the World Union for Progressive Judaism. Your deputy President, Rabbi Leslie Edgar, is the much loved and valued co-chairman of the Executive Committee of the World Union. We are not working merely as an organisation useful to the communities of today. We received a message which we are trying to fulfil. We are trying to gather together all the Jewish progressive forces in the world in order to teach a living Judaism. It is because we believe our conception has the power to serve humanity. We rejoice in its vitality.

I would beg you not to be detracted from our purpose by the popular appeal for uniformity. The expression uniformity may serve as a big umbrella to cover all types of a dead religion. It may shut out thought and faith as well as beneficent doubt and struggle. Liberal Jews pray that they may be conscious of being part of God's life. They seek authority from God to direct their inner spiritual life and its externalities. We share the general desire to cooperate with all those who seek to live according to the truth which is within themselves. But Liberals have their own conception of truth. It is as seekers that we ask the cooperation of all who attend this meeting and who desire to speak of their faith to the generations who will follow them. So their faith must be alive to themselves. We must be true to the integrity of our thought. We must try all the time to climb upwards, for God is infinitely beyond us, but we believe He is also within us, and, by the light of religious progress, we can pursue our way, respecting the views of others, but believing with passionate sincerity in our own Liberal presentment of Judaism.

Archives, Liberal
Jewish Synagogue, London

[1] The Biblically-based holiday celebrating the victory of the Jews over the wicked Haman who sought to destroy them. Lily Montagu thought the celebration of Jewish revenge against Haman, his sons, and his would-be supporters cruel and not worthy of celebration.

VI. SOCIAL SERVICE

INTRODUCTION

Lily Montagu's earliest involvement in the Anglo-Jewish community lay within the field of social service. The West Central Jewish Girls' Club, founded by Montagu in 1893, was not the first educational and social club formed in England, but it was the first such club founded specifically for Jewish girls of the working classes. At that time, the British club movement was still in its infancy. There were no courses offered either on theories of social work, types of club management, or forms of social organization. For the most part, club leaders were amateurs who tried to develop (often through trial and error) ways in which the intellectual and cultural needs of the working classes, at least as they understood them, could best be met.

What made the West Central Club unique was the religious basis on which it was founded and the religious spirit that Lily Montagu sought to infuse into the Club's daily life. While recognizing that most of the Club members were religiously indifferent, she never tired of trying to awaken, within each one of them, an awareness of the reality of God. She saw the Club as an opportunity to share with Jewish girls less fortunate than she the things that mattered most to her, namely, faith, education and friendship. Though Lily Montagu remained indebted to many, including several of her relatives, for helping to develop the social and educational aspects of the Club, it was she who assumed responsibility for its early religious life.

Through prayer, discussion and personal example, she sought to interest "her" girls in religion. Believing that faith could best be stimulated through prayer, she created special Sabbath and Holy Day worship services that she hoped would appeal to Club members. In addition, she ended "Club evenings" with a brief religious service and on Club holidays, besides morning and evening prayers, organized nightly "talks under the trees" again, on religious themes and not infrequently, on the subject of Liberal Judaism.

Lily Montagu continued to concern herself with the Club's religious life even after 1924, when Nellie G. Levy took over as Club Organizer and Leader. By then, the worship services that she held had gained formal recognition as the West Central Section of the J.R.U. By 1928, these services were incorporated into the newly-established West Central Liberal Jewish Congregation. During the Second World War, Montagu began to write monthly letters--brief addresses, really, on religious subjects--to the now male and female members of the West Central Club. The initial purpose of these letters, as described by Lily Montagu in Club Letter Number 64, was to awaken and sustain the spirit of religion among members who were "at home or on service." They were also sent to a "wide range of friends . . . living away from London." Lily Montagu continued to write these letters even after the war, for as she wrote in Club Letter 100, dated February 1948, these letters (eventually totalling 250 in number) provided her with a continuing means of sharing with Club members "her faith in a living Judaism."

The letters, sermons, and addresses that are included here describe Lily Montagu's work in the field of social service. At the same time, they reveal the sense of vocation that accompanied these efforts. "The Responsibility of Leisure," delivered at a Conference of the National

Union of Women Workers in October, 1912, emphasizes the importance of work as both a means of self-expression and a means of serving God. Lily Montagu admonishes her listeners who, like herself, are members of the so-called leisured classes, to use their free time constructively, helping those less fortunate than they. Putting her message in religious terms, she maintains that it is their responsibility to live and work in ways that "reflect a true relationship with the God Without" whom they have been called to serve. She makes it clear, however, that this call extends beyond the wealthy classes. All men and women, she concludes, have the responsibility of serving others and of acting in "conscious cooperation" with God.

This point is reiterated and developed in "A New Years Talk To Girls," delivered at the West Central Club in January, 1912, and in the addresses given at Littlehampton in August of 1916. Seeking to awaken a spirit of devotion within her listeners, she stresses her conviction that worship is not confined to any specific words of prayer. "Life," she said at Littlehampton, "is full of worship if it is full of aspiration and longing, and the desire to rise by service." In other words, it is the desire to fulfill one's potential and to use that potential in God's service that makes one religious. Even developing a true and sincere friendship can make one holy, for such relationships, she maintained, are "pierced by the flame of God." Here, as elsewhere, her intent is to interest her listeners in religion. Her aim is to show them that religion can be, and should be, co-extensive with life.

Club Letter Number 26 reveals, perhaps more than any other of her writings, the unshakeable nature of Lily Montagu's faith. Written after the bombing of the West Central Club, Synagogue and Day Settlement in 1941, it emphasizes the importance of strengthening one's faith in times of adversity and recognizing that it is not God who is responsible for evil but we who have not sufficiently spread His moral teachings. Though devasted by the destruction of the Club and the loss of twenty-seven workers and members, she refused to hate those responsible for this action. Regarding the man who approached her after the Club's memorial service and said, "Miss Montagu, we shall have revenge," she wrote that he offered her little consolation if he meant that a German woman who similarly had given nearly fifty years of her life to something should experience her kind of sorrow. Lily Montagu concluded that the only possible consolation she could receive was the knowledge that others were willing to help her revive the "Club spirit" that had been given them by God. Urging her readers to cast hatred out of their hearts, she asked that they express, in their words and their conduct, their "highest conception of Judaism."

In Club Letter 118, Lily Montagu discusses the life of service open to single women. While upholding the view that a "happy married life" is best, she points to "self-respecting independence" as a second best form of life that allows the single woman to devote herself completely to God's service. The joy and sense of fulfillment that Montagu herself discovered is made clear in Club Letter 154, written on the occasion of the West Central's Diamond Jubilee. Recalling all that she and her sister, Marian, had tried to accomplish, she describes the Club members as her children, they who enabled her to express the "mother love" given to all women as a special gift from God.

THE RESPONSIBILITY OF LEISURE

Conference of the National Union
of Women Workers,
Oxford, October, 1912

In these days when work is so absorbing, and pleasure is pursued so strenuously that it partakes of the nature of hard labour, we ask, <u>what</u> and <u>where</u> is leisure?

Am I about to write concerning a state which belongs to an archaic era? As I say these words I remember that most of us here assembled, and even I myself, are supposed to belong to leisured classes. As we are not driven by the grim necessity of getting food and lodging, we are called "leisured." It is believed that within certain limits we women can arrange our own lives and direct them to whatever purpose we desire. But I imagine that the majority of us are nevertheless workers who devote the greater part of our time to the fulfilment of definite duties by which we attempt to justify our existence. I believe too that among us there is no distinction between the paid and the unpaid. There is no coin of the realm which can pay for that <u>self</u> which must be given if the work is to be efficient as well as salaried. The so-called voluntary worker, on the other hand, must be trained to achieve that degree of usefulness which will make her cheerfully accomplish all parts of her service, even the most monotonous and mechanical. Our freedom of choice gives us the opportunity to seek our vocation, and having found it, to follow it with a full sense of responsibility.

The woman who dissipates her entire energy in frivolity is, I venture to say, almost extinct; at least I am sure she is not represented here. But a far pleasanter variety of woman is coming to take her place. I refer to the girl, who is frightened by the high standard of efficiency required from social workers, and who, having seen in her aunts or elder sisters rather sombre specimens of strenuous womanhood, forswears altogether the hope of a career for herself. She wants to be free from many responsibilities and able to go to lectures and concerts and parties and away for week ends, just when her charming fancy pleases. Of course she is ready to do just a few nice kind things when they come her way, without troubling herself further with the pain of the world from which she can keep herself at present so delightfully aloof. I am not attempting to justify this class of girl, although I do seem to understand her and know why she came into being. I look forward to the time when her type will be impossible, because life's opportunities must be better equalised, and her excess of leisure must be corrected by some contribution of her time, character, and even charm, to the needs of the State. This era must come, because on the other side of the scale there is the sweated, over-strained piece worker, whose charm is completely crushed by the excessive load of toil to which the over-leisured girl contributes through her very irresponsibility. But even to this over-leisured girl I will make an appeal tonight, and point out that so long as the conditions of life, which she has chosen, are tolerated, she cannot <u>free</u> herself from the claims of a certain "moral thoughtfulness" which may render her life sacramental. Indeed, if she can discipline herself under the great Ideal of Truth and Holiness, - she too may fasten one more link, however small, in the growing chain that is ultimately to bind humanity to God; if she can act with sympathy and intelligence, patience and hope, "she may bring up the lagging side in all the vitality around her to show to every man the worth, the meaning, the possibility of this his human life." Thus she may effect more through her <u>Being</u>, than another girl might accomplish by <u>Work</u>, however big a capital the work might possess.

Certainly if we have the power to direct our lives we have necessarily the opportunity to seek our chief happiness in work, and we know that this happiness is not given unconditionally, but depends upon the spirit in which the duties are undertaken and the degree of efficiency with which they are accomplished. If we desire to take up work for which a salary is paid we owe it to our generation and to posterity to accept only the highest standard of payment obtainable in the market. It is because of our free choice that we can raise the scale of payment for our class of work. If we use some of our leisure to earn pocket money in trades or professions to which other women go for bread, we deserve annihilation, for no other punishment is at all adequate. If we define "leisure" as a state in which we can choose our own form of activity, there are certain general principles which should control this state, whether we can enter it for few or for many hours in the day, whether we have earned it by our own labour, or whether it has been given us by a questionable ordering of society.

I have just touched upon the need for training and efficiency, and the standard of payment, but we have also a special responsibility with regard to our colleagues, either paid or unpaid, and it is this responsibility which the leisured woman is sometimes inclined to ignore.

We all know how painful it is to be treated as machines in our work, but we do not, I fancy, always remember that this same feeling weighs with some of the officials in the Societies to which we belong, and that the most efficient work can only be accomplished when the spirit of true comradeship is instilled.

We want our personal life and also our home life to be in harmony with the Perfect Spirit of love and righteousness from Whom we draw our inspiration. The woman of some capacity who rushes breathlessly about the world, supporting causes without understanding their full reasonableness, incurs a heavy responsibility. Because of our free state we have time to be sane - it is part of our obligation - the world needs sanity, and sanity is produced by harmony between the seen and the unseen.

Probably most of you are familiar with a paragraph in Deuteronomy (vi.) which contains the essence of the Jewish faith. Here the command is given to use love as the basis of right living, whether we go out or come in, whether we lie down or whether we rise up. This love inscribed on the door posts of her gates must fill the woman worker's home and refresh her hours of leisure; it must cover her eyes, so that she may see the divine in all human beings, and most difficult of all, in her colleagués; this love must cover her hands so that her actions may be pure; it must fill her heart and rise to her lips so that she may teach it to her children and to all others who come across her path.

If our days are full to overflowing with special duties in connection with our work, it requires considerable effort of will to get a little time for daily meditation, and to review the tendencies underlying our lives. But it is during these times of meditation that we find opportunity to consider the needs of future generations, and it is through this exercise that we discover what is trivial in our work and obtain the right sense of proportion.

Canon Barnett says, in one of his essays, "triviality is the modern equivalent for worldliness, the regard for the outward and visible. The trivial mind is at emnity with God, and it is of many kinds."[1]

Besides we all know how often we work ourselves up to a state of white heat in our own special corner of activity because we have become keen on some issue which has no real importance in the light of future generations, but which acts like an obsession on our minds and interferes with calm reasoning and good temper. Splits in philanthropic organisations occur just because of these unfortunate failures through want of time to weigh ideas in their right values. Surely our ancient Law Givers had inspired foresight into the rush of modern life when they instituted days for fasting and meditation. The ancient institution of the Sabbath satisfied a need in human nature, which we have not out-grown and which we neglect at our peril.

Is it not through want of thought that the irony has become possible, of men and women trying to improve conditions of work in general while they themselves ignore the needs of those whom they employ?

"The ruin of many a woman," to quote the words of Stopford Brooke, "lies at the door of the fine lady who hurries her work-woman to finish her dress, or who, to save herself a little trouble, or that she may indulge a momentary extravagance, refuses to pay her bills. One would think from the way in which the payment of debts has to be dragged out of the rich, that they think tradesmen can coin money to pay their underworkers. The wages of poor women are kept down and their money held back by this selfish thoughtlessness, and when wages are low women are driven to ruin."[2]

A few weeks ago I was asking a small girl clerk of sixteen whether she was likely to get a raise, upon which I knew her hardworking mother and an invalid father were counting, and she answered, "Oh no, I am afraid I cannot get one yet awhile, for we are owed at least £200." She then gave me the names of one or two well-known social workers with whom her firm had contracted bad debts which were to be paid in the nebulous future. I am quite sure that these men and women had not given enough time to consider that their thoughtlessness affected the entire firm, even the smallest employee of the business house which they were pleased to patronise.

Alexander Paterson in his wonderfully realistic picture of life in South London says: "No employer can afford to give one guinea to charity till he has so recast the system under which his labourers work for him, as to be assured that in serving him they sacrifice unduly neither faith, nor morals, nor religion. The housewife, who governs her little kingdom on the other side of the kitchen door with wisdom and sympathy, the man of leisure who is satisfied as to the conditions of his golf-caddies, and the page boys at his club, have fulfilled their primary social obligations."[3]

With time for meditation grows up the desire for self-development in all directions. But we have to remember that self culture, unless consecrated to a high purpose is nothing less than self-idolatry. The ultimate secret of culture is, as Emerson says, "to learn that a few great points steadily appear, alike in the poverty of the obscure farm and in the miscellany of metropolitan life, and that these few are alone to be regarded: - the escape from all false lies, courage to be what we are and the love of what is simple and beautiful, these and the wish to serve, to add somewhat to the well being of men."[4]

So much of the real importance of a _simplified_ life has been lost through the jargon which has been spoken about dress and food, that we are apt to forget that the right form of simplicity, which is the quality of the soul, can be reached, not by "a bound, but by a steady obedience

SOCIAL SERVICE   235

to the well-known principles of the moral and spiritual life. Our best modern word for it is, perhaps, sincerity."

But from another point of view the practical simplification of life would also seem necessary.

We are all dimly aware of the terrible pain which underlies the life of our community, and it is well that our perception is dim because if it became rather more realistic, the burden might be too great for some of us to bear. But I feel that we should to a certain extent be influenced by this perception and perhaps rather more aware of it.

A few months ago as I left a London Hospital, where I had been visiting a patient, I was met by a woman who asked me to let her have a halfpenny for a lotion bottle as patients had to bring their own bottles to the door of the Dispensary. She showed me her finger which needed dressing. She had been told to get a bottle and she had only a halfpenny with which to buy it. The scientific training which leads us to expect some fraud in casual appeals, made me hesitate before I gave her two halfpennies. She lifted up her eyes to me in gratitude for the extra coin and I felt thoroughly ashamed that I had not given her more. I watched her go back to the dispensary and get her lotion, and it seemed to me so horrible that in our civilised town today a woman should be lacking the necessary half-penny with which to get a lotion bottle. In the face of such abject povery it would appear almost criminal that people should excuse absurd waste and unscrupulous extravagance.

The ideal of some wealthy people seems to be to furnish their homes and to arrange their lives so as to introduce every form of elaboration which makes sincerity impossible. The absolute necessity for buying costly materials, which cannot have even the usual justification that it gives employment to people, is the expression of one of those fashions which make us grieve. But still worse, I think, is the apparent devotion to costly foods which renders it necessary for so many people to leave their comfortable homes and break up family life in order to indulge themselves in restaurants.

If we seek our recreation in excitement, whether it is the excitement of the bridge table, or the race course, or the West End shops during sale time, we incur a heavier responsibility than that shown in our private ledgers.

We give a false impression of ourselves to those among whom we work. If we have succeeded in gaining their love and admiration, our ideals have necessarily a strong influence over them and we must not have them believe that we prize above all else, our dress, our jewellery, our rich foods, our gambling instinct, or they will only look forward to the time when they may have similar happiness in their lives.

It seems to me that, as leisured people, we are responsible today for showing the world a truer conception of happiness. If after honest examination we can say that we find our greatest happiness in that which can be bought without money and without price, surely a better time is in store for the weary toilers who look to us for advice and inspiration. But although our conception of happiness should be coloured by our sense of responsibilty towards those whom we can influence, there is room in all our lives for the sense of joyousness, which appears to come straight from a source above the world and unaffected by its pain. I am sure this joyousness of spirit is part of the necessary equipment of a successful worker.

Marcus Aurelius says: "Such as are thy habitual thoughts, such also will be the character of thy mind, for the soul is dyed by the thoughts. Dye it then with a continuous series of such thoughts as, for instance, that where a man can live, there he can also live well."[5]

Since we pre-suppose by our definition of leisure that we have the ordering of our lives, it should be possible for us so to live and work that we reflect a true relationship with the "God Without." And this reflection will awaken the confidence of those whom we seek to influence. Are we not often troubled by the weakening of the sense of truth in the community as a whole? To people who are in business, business lies are said to be completely necessary, and since the term "business" is used so widely as to cover many of the world's activities, modern men and women are apt to give themselves a vast measure of indulgence. However, they cannot pigeon-hole their lives into separate divisions, and their sense of truth suffers, because it is juggled with at certain periods of the day. When we enter the state of leisured women, devotion to truth should have our whole hearted allegiance, but we are startled by the amount of exaggeration which is used as a matter of course in order to gain a point in debate or discussion, or to save us from bearing testimony to our highest convictions. Again and again among the leisured, who by our definition are free to control their own lives, falsehoods are deliberately spoken to cover an uncomfortable position or to snatch a social triumph.

How can we train our habitual thoughts? I have already suggested that the retention of a certain amount of time for meditation, which to all of us includes prayer, in some form or other, is likely to give us the opportunity to get a proper sense of proportion into our work. But there is also the need for definite intellectual training, and <u>here</u> it is that most of us fail so ignobly. <u>Here</u> I am preaching to myself far more than to most of you, but I feel more and more convinced that if our social work is to attain any useful end, we ought to devote a certain time daily to studying the great issues which lie behind it, and this study cannot be done through newspaper reading. It also cannot be included in the general reading in which we all delight.

We have to rid ourselves of cheap platitudes, which ignore the reverence we owe to human nature - that reverence which is the basis of modern morality - and replace them with sound fact. We have to remember - we people of leisure or liberty - that others prize their liberty too above all else in the world. So we must avoid fallacious theories which attract our superficial approval by soothing our sense of responsibility. For example, it may be comfortable for us to think that A, or B, who is starving in a city slum, can emigrate if he chooses to uproot himself; or that C, or D, who has been out of work for months would find domestic service not over supplied if she desires to enter it. We must get at some deeper truths, less palatable perhaps, before we discover why the factory girl does not become a good servant - and why emigration is sometimes an undesirable escape from misery.

There is absolutely no reason why the social worker should ever grow old as she stands with her eyes always fixed on a better time, and this hopefulness is characteristic of perpetual youth, but we do find that her mind tends to become somewhat slack and groovey, and I venture to think that the only corrective for this is careful and patient study.

There is another aspect of my subject - the responsibility of leisure - to which I want to draw your attention quite cursorily before I finish tonight. We have to remember that when the working girl's hours are over, she joins the leisured classes with an abandonment which some of us are inclined to envy. If we have ever stood outside some of our factories and seen the gaiety which arises with the sound of the dismissal bell, we dimly understand the force of reaction which restores the lost power to nerve and limb. In these days no public cry is heard with greater sympathy than the cry for greater leisure, but it is for us social workers to ask how this leisure should be used for the permanent advantage of the worker. Greater leisure is bound to come with legislation - we already hear the flutter of its angel wings. In all classes of life there is a yearning for a fuller existence, which expresses itself in the unrest with which we are familiar. Every normal man or woman desires the opportunity for self development. "Let my people go free, that they may serve Me," was God's command through Moses, and when the command was obeyed a nation of slaves placed themselves under bondage to the Highest.

We want to affect all classes with our enthusiasm for social service, for intercourse with friends, for the joys of country life, for the influence of works of art, for the pleasures of books, and we can only do this by sharing our greater freedom with those who have as keen [a] latent appreciation but fewer opportunities of developing it. I have known institutions in which working people have had the opportunity for intercourse under the most satisfactory influences, but these institutions have been sometimes established in the teeth of considerable opposition. We have been told by the very people whose daughters love dances and engage in all sorts of work in cooperation with men, that it is dangerous to mix these young people. We have occasionally been asked in the past why we needed money for such purposes, seeing that there are so many starving poor in our midst, but we have of course persistently answered that hunger for bread is not the only hunger which must be feared in a civilised age, and in the end the institutions have justified their existence.

But the sights and sounds of our city streets today, and the longing for excitement in our country villages, surely tend to prove that the need for proper recreation - that sort of recreation which prevents vice - is still far from satisfied. Our girls and boys who labour with their hands the entire day demand some sound intellectual training at night, and the Workers' Educational Association and the great Club and Evening School movement are still insufficient to cope with this healthy craving. Even in our Clubs, some of us who love power, forget that it is part of our duty to share the joy of service with those whom we desire to befriend. In every Club, where young people congregate, the call to service should be heard and answered, and it is in giving them the opportunity for managing themselves, and in developing the corporate life, that we have the chance of creating real citizens.

It is in these Clubs, too, that we can draw from our studies in social science material for citizenship lessons. Here also by spending our leisure with other classes of workers, we can often correct our own standards by comparison with theirs. If we have out of our treasure house to replace the penny novelette with examples of real literature, we have on our side often to purify our conventional prejudices in the fire of life as lived by those at close grips with reality.

The responsibility of leisure rests with all classes. The measure of responsibility is, of course, affected by the size of the gift, but seeing that we have to account for its use or misuse to our Father, who brings every deed into judgment, whether it be good or whether it be evil, it is desirable that we should tonight search ourselves earnestly and discover how far we are consecrating our gift to the highest use; how far, behind all our various activities, we are living a life bound by intelligible bonds to every suffering, sinning man and woman; how far by earnest meditation and by an effort after sincerity we are helping to establish the right relationships between man and man; how far, while dealing with the things we see, we are influenced by our faith in the unseen. As witnesses to this faith we make our lives beautiful and blessed through conscious cooperation with the God of love and liberty.

Archives, Liberal
Jewish Synagogue, London

[1] From Barnett's essay, "Neighbours and Neighbours" in his The Service of God, London, 1897). Lily Montagu's use of this essay is highly selective as the essay, in its entirety, is an explicitly Christian address on the presence of Christ in every age.

[2] For a further explication of these ideas, since Brooke's The Old Testament and Modern Life (New York: Dodd, Mead and Co., 1896).

[3] From Paterson's Across The Bridges: Life By the South London River-side (1911).

[4] From Emerson's "Considerations By the Way," in his The Conduct of Life (1860).

[5] From his Meditations.

A NEW YEAR'S TALK TO GIRLS

January, 1912

Last year, at this time, we looked forward into the New Year, hoping for many things and longing to know what was in store for us. I, for one, am now infinitely grateful I could not see what the months were to bring me.

I am infinitely glad for the power of hoping, fearing, loving and trusting, which have not failed me.

Last year we all felt that we wanted to do so much, to grow so far. Some of you on looking back, have reason to rejoice in certain achievements. Perhaps you have advanced in your work; perhaps you have become more efficient, more interested; perhaps you have advanced on the path of self-conquest, and thrown some weaknesses away. When we stood at this place last year, we prayed that bitterness and reproaches, which spoiled friendship should be cast away from our individual lives; that we should learn to value the essentials of life, the things that matter now and hereafter, not only <u>now</u>; the characteristic which we shall take with us, when we go down the dark valley, the power of self-control and perseverance, of unselfish love, of purposeful concentration; the power of self-respect and humility. How far have we attained?

All I could never be,
All men ignored in me,
This I was worth to God.[1]

In club land we prayed last year, at this time, that we should all work more faithfully together; that each girl's ideal should be self-development and service, self-development in service; that she should use the opportunities given her here, in order to be of use to her neighbours; that she should never attribute unworthy motives to other girls or doubt their sincerity in serving, while she herself should never cease to work without expectation of honour or reward. Have we attained?

In our home life, did we not determine that there should be greater harmony, more real love? Did we not desire greater simplicity and stronger mutual attachment, more forbearance and mutual confidence? Have we attained? Were we not resolved to combat circumstances and force them to bless us, whatever the circumstances might be? Did we not see how struggle, poverty, disappointment and unsatisfied longing, could all become with the help of the divine Alchemist a source of blessing, a guarantee of infinite life? Have we attained? Did we not last year, at this time, resolve that our Judaism should become a living reality to us, that it should consecrate our lives; we hoped to try to understand its meaning better, and to learn how scholars were trying to make it consistent with the highest truths known to their generation. Did we not determine to cut off from our Judaism some of the outer growths, which conceal its beautiful light, even if the occasional cutting process were painful and difficult? We were prepared to make sacrifices for our brotherhood, and to rejoice in the burdens which we were called upon to endure, in order to testify to the truths which we have inherited from our forefathers, and which we have realised anew for ourselves. Yes, we resolved to make sacrifices for truth, and to ignore convenience. Have we attained?

During this last year have we as citizens cared sufficiently for the interests of the general community? Have we tried better to understand the great world outside our little groove? Have we cherished principle, even at the cost of individual loss? Have we attained?

Here we stand on the threshold of a New Year, hoping new hopes, or reviving old ones; making new resolutions, or renewing old ones; and we will say with courage and conviction:

    The New Year met me somewhat sad,
        Old year leaves me tired;
    Stripped of favourite things I had,
        Baulked of much desires;
    Yet, further on my road today,
    God willing further on my way.

New Year coming on apace,
    What have you to give me?
Bring you scathe or bring you grace,
Face me with an honest face,
    You shall not deceive me.
Be it good or be it ill,
Be it what it will,
It needs shall help me on my road,
My rugged way to Heaven, please God.

But I do not feel that today, as we look forward, the note in our song, should be a sad one. Rather let us say with the poet:

Ring out, wild bells, to the wild sky,
    The flying cloud, the frosty light;
    The year is dying in the night,
Ring out, wild bells, and let him die.

Ring out the old, ring in the new,
    Ring happy bells across the snow;
    The year is going, let him go;
Ring out the false, ring in the true.

Ring out the grief that saps the mind,
    For those that here we see no more;
    Ring out the feud of rich and poor,
Ring in redress for all mankind.

Ring out the slowly dying cause,
    And ancient forms of party strife;
    Ring in the nobler modes of life,
With sweeter manners, purer laws.

Ring out the want, the care, the sin,
   The faithless coldness of the times;
   Ring out, ring out my mournful rhymes,
But ring the fuller minstrel in.

Ring out false pride in place and blood,
   The civic slander and the spite;
   Ring in the love, and truth, and light,
Ring in the common love of good.²

Yes, if we ourselves wish to attain - and we <u>do</u> wish to attain - I believe we must take with us into the dark, mysterious 1912, the fear and love of God.

Whoever lives and loves
   One God, one law, one element,
   And one far-off Divine event
To which the whole creation moves.³

I have said "fear and love," but in Judaism these words seem to be almost interchangeable terms, and the fear of God is regarded as synonymous with religion. What is the fear of God? It is something so personal, so difficult to define, that I hesitate before attempting to do so.

The Psalmist says: "The secret of the Lord, is with them that fear Him."⁴ If we can really commune with our Creator, we attain a secret which it is difficult to communicate to others. If we can live conscious of His presence in big things and in small things, we shall find that God is as near to our human soul, as if "it alone existed in immensity." The <u>Yiras Adonai</u> [fear of God] is the mainspring of the Jewish Religion. It suggests that ideal of righteousness through abstention from evil which is the essential part of Judaism. The fear of God is not like physical terror. We experience reverential awe when we consider His goodness and His power, but we have no desire to run away. Indeed, when we feel this fear, we are drawn nearer to the Spirit Who awakens our reverence. The fear of God impels goodness. We <u>wonder</u> at God, at His Goodness, His Beauty, His Holiness and His Truth, until we seem to bring some reflection of them into our lives. Do you not see, that as our conception of God develops, so the fear of God leads more and more to Goodness. In mythological times the gods were endowed with loose ideas of morality. Their devotees shared these ideas. They brought expiatory offerings because they were terrified by these cruel gods, whom they could not respect. They were afraid of their god's revenge if they were successful or happy, and so they bribed him into leaving them alone.

The Jewish idea of God is that of the Spirit of Truth and Holiness, and as you progress from year to year in your search after Truth and Holiness, your reverence for God helps you more and more to attain. If you worship Him because you fear His anger, or expect His reward, you will not attain to righteousness through your fear. The God whom you fear, is the God with whom you can come into communion; the great God outside, Who lives also in your hearts when you truly and unselfishly love, or when you seek truth and self-conquest. The reward he gives is the power to renew your life and strengthen it. He does not give you material benefit because you fear Him. He is not a glorified Santa Claus giving presents to His grateful chidren; He is the God of Righteousness and Truth, showing those who love and fear Him the meaning of infinite hope and of true peace; the peace which comes <u>after</u> conflict, and <u>during</u> conflict with unworthy desire; the power to attain, not only <u>now</u> or <u>here</u> but also hereafter; yes, the <u>power</u> to attain, the power which comes from self-discipline and the cherishing of ideals.

In seeking to take with us the fear of God into 1912, we must first concern ourselves with the <u>conception</u> of the

God whom we would fear, and secondly with the <u>character</u> of that fear. The fear of God is different from the fear of man, Isaiah tells us: "Say ye not a conspiracy concerning all whereof these people shall say 'a conspiracy,' neither fear ye their fear, nor be in dread thereby. The Lord of Hosts, <u>Him</u> shall we sanctify, and let Him be your fear, and let Him be your dread."

The fear of God is reverence for God, the highest conception of God we can attain; the reverence for Goodness, Beauty and Holiness and it is at the basis of love. Indeed, we cannot have even human love without reverence. If we look at a work of art, and feel a glow of affection for it, it is partly because we recognise that the artist possesses a secret which is full of mystery to us, and we respect that mystery. When we see ice hanging in the form of jewels in a cave, which has been formed without the help of man, we wonder at the beauty of the natural formation, and we are conscious of the mystery, and it is partly because of this mystery that we are filled with delight. How came the woods and fields to look as they do? We worship while we wonder at the Force which brought them into being. Again surely we are filled with reverence as well as love for our parents and friends. We respect their qualities, and wonder at their individuality, which in some degree must be different from our own, and in spite of our intimacy, respect sanctifies our affection.

If we would truly love children we must reverence them; we must reverence the frail undeveloped life; we must wonder at the mystery of its creation. Without awe we cannot get to the highest love. When we admit the existence of Perfection which on account of our imperfection we cannot possibly understand completely, we love It, we are thrilled by It and we bow before It. If we do not bow our heads and worship, if we do not revere, we miss the joy of the inward vision. We speak about reverence in public services; in fact, public worship is the spontaneous outcome of sincere reverence, and we believe that in our little services here, this spirit finds expression. If you compare the atmosphere of our Sabbath Afternoon Services, with the atmosphere at the club on ordinary club evenings, you feel that many of those who join in prayer every evening are not conscious of the inward vision; they are not conscious of any real spirit of reverence. It is therefore easier to pray together at the Sabbath Afternoon Services, for as we pray, we contemplate in our feeble way the Spirit of Truth, of Goodness and Holiness. Would that this feeling of reverence should enter the hearts of <u>all</u> our members whenever they seek to worship their God.

The fear of God implies the hatred of evil and wrong. The prophet says: "Thou shalt not curse the deaf or put a stumbling block before the blind, but thou shalt surely fear the Lord thy God."[5]

I read a story, the other day, of a salvationist who worked in a back street of a big town, a street which even men were afraid to pass down at night. She obtained the sympathy of a prize fighter who controlled the neighbourhood by fear, and secured his cooperation in gaining the respect of some of the roughest characters in the town. He recognised in her a force which he himself did not possess, and gradually through reverence for this force she drew him to the bench of penitence, and made him confess the iniquity of his past life. For a time he altered his mode of living, because he saw dimly the light which illumined her life. Again and again he went back into his former darkness. A woman came into his life who led him further astray. The salvationist got the woman to leave the man for a while, but she went back to him, to draw him again into darkness. But because he had recognised the power of the fear of God, even for a while, his darkness was not what it had been, for now he was conscious of the existence of a window, which let in light, if only he had the strength to look through it.

"The fear of God driveth away sin." It is because God stands for Goodness, that worship of Him, without the effort to be good, seems blasphemous. We are occasionally worried because there are so many signs of hypocrisy around us. We see men and women bowing in places of worship, muttering many prayers, but yet we know they do not really attempt to live good lives. "If this is worship we will have none of it," we say, but in reality there is no worship here, for there is no real reverence; there is no conception of a living God, who can only be approached through righteousness.

The fear of God implies regret for the sorrow we cause Him though our faults. Indeed, we may believe in all humility, that the God who gave us life, sorrows when He sees us misusing it.

How do we obtain the fear of God? "Everything is in the hand of Heaven, except for the fear of Heaven" said an old Jewish Sage,[6] and indeed it does seem that we must make real personal effort, if we are to obtain the fear of God. We have to feel that there is a greater Life than ours, outside ourselves, and we must learn to respect the attributes of God, with which in an infinitely small degree we can become familiar as the attributes of men and women. I do not suppose real reverence can ever be experienced by the man or woman who has no respect for love, strength, truth, wisdom and self-sacrifice as abstractions, or when seen in connection with the people whom we meet in ordinary life.

The fear of God is established in those homes in which sacred things are treated with real respect, and in which children are made to understand the meaning of obedience. Parents do not always realise that when they "give children something" in order to bribe them to obey they are making it more difficult for these children later to submit to those inexorable laws of life to which they should do homage. In our home life we must reverence individuality, even when the qualities of our brothers and sisters differ from our own, and above all, we must observe scrupulously the commandment, "Thou shalt not take the name of the Lord thy God in vain." We must remember that when we use God's name lightly, or speak flippantly about the great mystery of birth and death, of which He alone has the key, we are committing a real wrong, and spoiling the tone of our family life. It is also painful indeed to hear Jewish people speaking lightly of the faith of their neighbours, and making mockery of the symbols which they hold as sacred.

I believe we are justified in praying for the fear of God, and if we cultivate reverence, we may hope that our prayers, which today are inarticulate, may form themselves into words. I really believe that if we will stop for a few moments every day, to contemplate the greatness of God, and meditate on His work, words will form themselves on our lips as we attempt to draw some of the divine spirit into our hearts.

I will just tell you, in conclusion, a story which explains to some extent the "fear of God," although the explanation comes from a poor illiterate young girl. There were two brothers once, who, when they were children lost their mothers, and were placed in a school by their father, who paid their fees through a lawyer, and knew nothing or cared nothing about them. The boys grew up, and left school and positions were found for them in the same office. They worked their way up and started business together, and were inseparable. Then came a terrible cleavage. The one brother contracted a marriage which was repugnant to the other. They drifted apart, and the one brother went abroad. News became scarce, and even scarcer, and then ceased. At last the one man who remained at home received a letter from his brother's wife which told of catastrophe. Her husband was in an asylum, and had left her with one child, a boy. The letter contained no term of affection, no appeal for help. The man sent no reply. Meanwhile he prospered, married, and had children and was happy. Now this man was stopping for a holiday at a small village on the Cornish coast. News reached him of his father's death, the mysterious father of whom he had never been able to get news. Money had been left to be divided between the two brothers. The man alone knew that his brother was incurably ill, where his wife lived who had caused the separation, and the child to whom he was utterly indifferent. Why should he tell the secret? The money would be useful to him and his family; why should the money be divided? The man lay in a nest among the rocks unseen with the evil feeling in his heart. Suddenly! the peace was broken by a strange sound. He heard a girl's voice, pleasant in sound, but the words which came to him were curses, three or four times repeated; then - silence. The man peeped out, and saw a girl in shabby clothes and with rather wild hair, seated with her head in her hand, her knees drawn up. It was this girl who had cursed. Suddenly she stood up and stared before her, giving a long-drawn ah! of satisfaction. Alone she stood quite hidden for some time. "What are you doing?" the man asked. She turned round, and stared resentfully with her big, soft, dreamy eyes. "What is the matter, what are you doing?" he asked again. There was insistence in the voice and some kindness. "I was cursing her," the girl said. "Who?"

"The boss, who keeps me slaving night and day in that shop over there," jerking her head backwards. "I came out to curse her; the words had to come out, but then I wanted to look, and so I had to stop." "Look at what?" "Oh don't you know, well! if you don't, you must be a bad 'un like me. You must have evil thoughts in your heart, there - over there." The man stood up, next to the girl with the dreamy eyes and shabby dress, and looked at the glorious colour of the sunset; at the blue, green, mauve and yellow, all exquisitely blended, with the sea in front with its shades of green and blue and grey. Then he looked in the girl's eyes and saw a rapturous glow of joy and hope. "Don't you see," she said, "it is God, and yet it is not God. It comes from Him, and it is like Him; it goes on and on, whether we are good or wicked, but while we are wicked we cannot see it. I wanted to see so badly that I stopped cursing. If you do not understand, if you do not see, it is because you are wicked, but the sky will go on just the same, in spite of you. I must go back." She turned and fled from him, but he stood and looked, and the wickedness passed out of his heart. The glory of the sky was for him! The fear of God had cast out sin.

Let us pray that during the New Year that is before us we may see that God's goodness, love and truth may be <u>for</u> us; that we may reverence these attributes until we seek to connect them with our lives. Then all evil and all lesser fears will be banished, and with the Psalmist we shall each of us be able to say "I will fear no evil, for Thou art with me"; and again, "Except the God of my father Abraham, He whom Isaac feared, had been with me, surely now hadst Thou sent me away empty."

If we want to know God, to commune with Him, to have His help, we must reverence His goodness until we seek to

SOCIAL SERVICE   253

imitate it; then the fear of God will cast out evil by replacing it with good.

> Archives, Liberal
> Jewish Synagogue, London

¹From Browning's "Rabbi Ben Ezra."

²From the 106th section of Tennyson's "In Memorium." Significantly, she omits the last stanza of the section which reads: "Ring in the valiant man and free, The larger heart and the kindlier hand; Ring out the darkness of the land. Ring in the Christ that is to be."

³The last stanza of Tennyson's "In Memorium."

⁴A rare example of Lily Montagu's attributing a source incorrectly. The line is not from Psalms but from the Book of Leviticus, Chapter 19, verse 14.

⁵This too is from Leviticus 19:14 (and not from "the Psalmist").

⁶Rabbi Hanina, Babylonian Talmud, Berakot 33b. Lily Montagu undoubtedly took this quote from H. Loewe and Claude Montefiore, <u>Rabbinic Anthology</u> (Philadelphia, Jewish Publication Society, 1960), p. 285.

ADDRESSES

GIVEN ON THE CLUB HOLIDAY AT LITTLEHAMPTON
AUGUST, 1916

August 5th, 1916

"O, worship the Lord in the Beauty of Holiness."

As we sit here in this beautiful spot, feeling that it is in reality a Temple of the Lord, we will try to discover the real meaning of Worship.

Our first impulse is to lift up our soul in praise and thankgsiving. We feel wonder for the beauty of God's world, and we are conscious of our own insufficiency, our own incompleteness.

Every girl and woman in this place knows best the yearnings in her own heart, and they make her recognise the need for a Perfect Spirit Who satisfies these longings, so far as they are good and worthy.

We must not be afraid of the yearnings which brings us to the steps of God's throne. They are of His own implanting. Even as we formulate them, we feel God's love within us, soothing away the "infinite pain of the finite heart that yearns."[1]

While we pray we become conscious of our brother's need, and our souls are filled with a desire to serve him.

We seek to worship our God in the Beauty of Holiness, whether we pray in private or in public. The sense of holiness can only come to us when we give ourselves completely. We must have one thought, one desire, namely, to rise by service nearer to our God. He has told us that He accepts the humble and contrite heart, as the right form of sacrifice. When we dimly apprehend His perfection, we are conscious of our own imperfection, and repentance once more leads us to our God; and we may be sure that He does not let us grope towards Him without giving us His help. He reaches down to us even while we strain towards Him. While we worship God, we must see to it, that our hearts are pure, free from any spirit of hatred, or jealousy which may separate us from Him. We want to be at one with Him, for in the sense of that oneness we feel the beauty of holiness.

But I do not think we should confine our text to the actual prayer service; life is full of worship if it is full of aspiration and longing, and the desire to rise by

SOCIAL SERVICE

service; if we can live, conscious of the presence of God in our midst, even while we go out and while we come in. There is one of life's activities which is full of worship because it is full of aspiration, because it causes us to know our incompleteness, because it brings all that is good within us into harmony with the best outside ourselves, because it humbles us, even while it comforts us, because it stimulates us to great efforts, even while it causes us to know our own weaknesses and limitations, because it frees us from self and fills us with a desire to serve. I refer to the activity of Love. Yes, Love must be full of aspiration and reverence; it must be pure, being cut through with the flame of God.

There is an old Jewish legend which tells of a man who went to sleep for 70 years, and when he awoke he could find no one near who was his friend. "Not friendship!" he cried, "then death"; and he slipped back again into a sleep which knew of no awakening. So friendship was valued of old. What do we think about it today? Sometimes we hear parents say, "I don't encourage my girl to make friends, I don't believe in them. I like her to keep herself to herself." Just consider the narrowness of a life like this - a life which is kept to itself. Emerson has told us that a friend is one before whom we can think aloud.[2] The fact that she understands, that she forgives because she loves; that she hates the fault, but loves the one who commits the fault; all these facts draw the best from us. We want to be at our best with our friend because she understands our smallest effort after good. All joy seems more delightful, all sorrow seems more tolerable, when our friend shares our joys and sorrows with us. Sometimes it has happened to you to find that the friend on whom you counted, whom you knew and loved as a little girl, no longer interests you. Your paths have drifted; you have grown away from one another, gone up different ladders. You cannot help this state of things. For awhile you still cling to one another for old sake's sake [sic], and because you do not want to hurt one another. You do not want to have an explanation with your friend, and so you keep up a shadow, even though the reality has gone. This effort I believe to be a failure. Friendship should be holy since it is pierced by the flame of God; it must be true and sincere or it is valueless. Better suffer the pain of explanation and face the fact that you have drifted one from the other. Better move away, sending out behind you kind and tender thoughts to the one who once stood for so much in your lives, but pretend no longer!

Some of you have known a friend to be false; you have felt a lump in your throat and a smarting pain at the back of your eyes, as you doubted her, and said you did not care. Do you remember? Are you quite sure you were right? Was there no explanation? Did you seek one? I am sometimes much puzzled by the triviality of the quarrels between girls. It does seem such a pity that they have not the courage or the generosity to ask or give an explanation. No holy friendship can exist where there is no power of forgiveness. Never speak disparagingly of one to whom you once gave your love. Such conduct degrades the possibility of true friendship. Human love dimly reflects the Divine Love. Think of God's infinite patience with us who aspire to receive His friendship. Think of this when you feel impatient with your friend. If you give love you give some of yourself. If you accept love you accept some of another person's soul. These gifts which you exchange are from God; they are part of His spirit. Tread carefully, reverently; the place on which you walk is holy; and friendship, real friendship, is the most glorious activity of the human soul. Be worthy of it, hold it fast, let your souls grow in power as your power to use it grows. Treat friendship reverently; know that it is holy.

There are many other aspects of love, but I can only speak of a few more today, and of these quite shortly. There are the friendships between a boy and a girl, a man and a woman, a husband and a wife. Just think of some happy marriages which you have known. I believe you will agree with me, that they were holy because they were full of aspiration, because the man and woman felt reverence one for the other. A high conception of marriage is perhaps the best inheritance which humanity possesses. The world believes in it as the finest experience of which the human soul is capable.

The man and the woman expect the best of one another, and are tender to the weaknesses they fully recognise. They live in close harmony with regard to the essentials of life, with regard to religion and the religion of the individual to the general community.

Why is it that we know few wholly successful marriages? I believe it is because public opinion has not always held the married state to be holy. It is entered upon without preparation carelessly. Before it came, perhaps the girl held herself cheaply and indulged in larks which left a bad taste in her mouth. Perhaps little was expected of the man excepting that he be able to keep his wife in comfort. It seemed to matter little whether he felt the respect due to her sex, whether he reverenced life, whether he needed to link her individuality to his, so that together they might progress, or whether he merely wished to absorb her individuality for his own purposes. It seemed enough, perhaps, that he should take her and make a home for her. There is no true marriage, no aspiration, if soul is not linked to soul.

Since marriage may be holy; since love is a form of worship given to us by God, let us cherish the ideal; let us beware of cheapening it by thought or by word or by deed; let us never speak of it lightly, or joke about it profanely, for if we do, we degrade ourselves and wrong humanity.

There is the friendship between parent and child. We know of nothing more beautiful than that kind of love which involves perfect confidence and understanding sympathy, and when we miss it in a family, what has happened? Perhaps it is just the time-force which has pushed the parent from the child. The parent has not understood the change in the child's outlook. The child made no attempt to bridge the chasm by her love and consideration.

I read a beautiful story the other day of an old musician, who had adopted a boy and taught him all he knew of music, and sent him into the great world to study from celebrated masters, and to mix with the musical public. He himself had felt music in his soul and had tried hard to produce a great composition, which would be called the "Song of Life," but the power of expression had been denied him. The young man progressed, and the old man watched and hungered for news of the boy's success. He hid his own bits of manuscript away and lived only in his pupil's triumphs. Then one day he attended a concert at the Queen's Hall where the young man conducted an orchestral piece of his own composition. The enthusiasm of the public was wonderful, and the old man fainted through sheer emotion. That evening the son went to his father's lodgings and found the old man had gone out again to think and to enjoy the night air. The son sat by the piano in his father's little room and picked up a piece of the old manuscript and played it. Where had it come from? What was it? With astonishment he recognised the theme of his own great orchestral piece. He had picked up a page of this old manuscript in a bundle of waste publications in Italy - a scrap of manuscript from his father's work had given him the idea for his piece. But it had been such a thin, feeble bit of harmony that he had forgotten that it ever existed, even though it was so exquisitely beautiful. The writing was not governed by any rule of composition. He had worked at it, nevertheless, in spite of its slightness, and the result had been revealed at the Queen's Hall that afternoon. When the old man came into the room, his pupil sprang up to explain. The old man's face was radiant; he was overwhelmed with his own great joy; his whole being seemed uplifted. He threw his arms round his son, and his soul went out in one long song of praise; as he clung to his boy he whispered: "You have taken my 'Song of Life'; you have sung it for me; I could not sing it, I had no strength. You have taken my theme, my boy! and made it understood by the world. Thank God, thank God!"

Yes, our parents give us their song of life. We receive it from them and work on it, and will hand it down to those who follow us to make of it a new and better thing, to make it understood by their own generation. Let us be careful to take the song reverently, not to snatch it ungratefully, lest we break the hearts of those who conceive it. Let us accept the gift thankfully, and keep it pure and clean and altogether beautiful. Let us worship in holiness.

God starts the Song of Life which our parents hear, and which they sing to us so that we may live.

I must keep for next week a few thoughts on some other relations of life; on the love between sisters and sisters, and sisters and brothers; between strangers; between man and God.

Let us end here with the thought with which we began; Love is a form of worship and must be consecrated to God. It must be full of aspiration. Since it is part of the spirit of God, it can never be complete until it finds its fulfilment in God.

August 12th, 1916

"O, Worship the Lord in the Beauty of Holiness."

Last week we spoke of worship as aspiration. We spoke of the raising of all that is good within us, and the letting it come into touch with God, the Author of all good; and we spoke of Love as a form of worship; and we dealt with the various aspects of love - the love between friends; the love of parents for children; the love between boy and girl, man and wife.

Today we must deal briefly with the love between brothers and sisters; the love of our neighbour, and the culminating love of God.

What is it in a home which binds sisters and sisters and brothers and sisters together? There is first the bond of blood, mysterious though it may be. We are drawn by the law of our nature towards the child of our mother. But apart from the physical tie, which affects us whether we will or no, there is the tender bond of memory. We have the same past as our sisters; we have seen life from the same starting point; we have known the same limitations. There is no separating gulf here created by the time-force. To sisters the present bears the same relation to the past, and the future hold the same kind of possibility.

Friendship between sisters is one of the most satisfying that life can afford. Our sister understands us thoroughly; she does not expect more than we can give. We both feel the same tender, yearning love for home, and all it stands for. <u>She</u> misses an incalculable happiness who takes her sister as a matter of course, and ignores the opportunity for friendship which she is ready to give; who instead of sharing the joys and burdens and aspirations of home life with her, thinks that her friendship cannot count, for she is only a sister.

I have seen, have not you, sisters grow up like strangers, never taking the trouble to speak to one another; and I have seen the best friendship grow up on the sure foundation of complete sympathy and understanding. Our sister knows us on our effortless days. She knows us as we are with only the stimulus of home's realities in our hearts. She knows why we feel insufficient to ourselves. She is the first to know when we begin to formulate our dreams for the future. In most Jewish homes it is different with our brothers. Somehow in the past they have been placed from the beginning on a different platform from the girls, and having been placed there by the parents, they take full advantage of their position, and regard themselves as people of a superior clay. I do not know the origin of the mistake, for mistake there has undoubtedly been. I rather suspect it is due to the fact that in the past, the girl's place in the Jewish community has been inferior to that of the boys. Of course, she was cherished and protected from harm as far as possible, but there was no place for her in the Synagogue, and the Synagogue was the factor of supreme importance in moulding the life of the Jew. The boy was taught his Hebrew prayers, and it mattered very much that he had a complete Jewish education. It was hardly to be expected that the girl would need much Hebrew. Her life would be led, so the parent anticipated, mainly in the home. Her mother would teach her domestic observances, and beyond that, why, she did not help to make up a congregation. Ten men over the age of 13 were needed for a congregation. The girl was of no use. This conception was entirely wrong, and the fruits of the wrong have been evil, bitter fruits. Today girls are beginning to realise that they need the help of religion quite as much as do their brothers. Judaism is a living religion, consecrating her youth and satisfying the innermost yearnings of her soul. Judaism, therefore, makes a claim on her life, demanding from her even the best she has to give. Side by side with this new conception arises the possibility of friendships between brothers and sisters. As the feeling of contemptuous condescension is removed, it is replaced by affection and respect. It was only when the boy was allowed to regard his sister merely as a useful domestic appendage that he lost the privilege of her friendship, for he became too conceited to recognise her worth.

In the most beautiful Jewish home I have ever known there were two girls and five boys. The friendship between these girls and boys has supplied a vision which the ravages of time and death cannot obliterate. These girls and boys simply revelled in life because they revelled in each other's society. They were just splendid comrades, and no joke was too trivial for home appreciation. No pain was too slight for home sympathy. Together they walked up life's roadway, expecting the perfect sympathy they received. A family meal in that home seemed indeed a holy affair, because perfect joy was present, because no unkind word or thought could ever possibly enter, because the whole atmosphere was one of tenderness and aspiration. The sister, who was my friend, used to say first of one and then of another of her brothers, "One cannot help wanting to be at one's best when he is near, he draws the best from one. He is so good and he understands." This best, you see, was drawn out at home in a sister by a brother. How merry they were, how kindly was the chaff between them.

How tender the solicitude one for the other. Mazzini tells us that the home should be the temple in which the sacrifice of happiness is placed before God's altar, and then carried into the world to make it beautiful. From the home that I have described went forth the sacrifice of happiness.

Today for you all there is an opportunity more important than any that has ever before been given to you.

The boys out in France and Egypt are learning the value of their homes. We believe that they will have learned before they come home to expect more of girls and women. We must see to it that we do not fail them. If the standard of respect is to be raised; if the ideal of marriage is to be lifted, then our boys must learn, from their reverence for their sisters, the reverence which is due to any and every woman. We must try to get more of our brother's confidence, to make them know that we are sisters to the outcast woman, and that in degrading her they degrade us.

Do we deplore the fact that so often the religion of our brothers is external and perfunctory? Let us make our own religion part of our every day lives; then it will seem so good to them on their return that they will want to share it. Let the flame of God pierce our hearts; let it fill our homes; even the boys will recognise it and will accept its influence.

Our Bible Word teaches us that we should love our neighbour as ourselves. This is a different love from the love of the sisters for sisters, and sisters for brothers. It is the love of strangers one for the other. Did I say strangers? Here we must tread warily, for here we feel the impelling hand of God. He has united man to man by giving all men the common need for loving. Since human legislation is possible, since the same joys and sorrows affect us all, even though in different degrees; since we all have the same kinds of aspiration and hopes and aims and difficulties and sorrows and disappintments, there are no strangers. Life is one for God is one.

Olive Schreiner has taught us in one of her beautiful dreams, how a man could not pray because he could not overcome the injury done to him by another man. He cried to God in agony, asking Him for the power to forgive, and God sent His angel to help the man. He suggested that the man should speak well of his enemy when others spoke ill of him; that he should share some good with the man; and while conferring some benefit on him, he should learn to love him. But still arose the wild cry, "I cannot forgive." The man was reminded of his own past, of his many follies and weaknesses, but still he felt that his own sins were different, that this man's sin he would not forgive. Then he was advised to <u>forget</u> if he could not forgive; but bitterness remained in his soul. At last God allowed His angel to take the man, with his great hate, and lead him to a valley, where he could see the soul of his enemy unveiled, just as it was at the beginning. The man gazed and thought, "How beautiful my brother is." For the enemy's soul seemed like to his brother's soul; and so they recognised one another and walked together in the sight of God.

It is because we are all children of God that we can care for one another. He binds us together, He gives us the same needs, His bonds cannot be broken. Do you want greater opportunities for yourselves, better education, wider recreation, better housing, a freer life? Your neighbour wants these blessings too. Do you value the joys and opportunities of life? So does your neighbour. The knowledge of our neighbour's need makes us feel an obligation towards her in our industrial and business life. Our neighbour wants better wages, better hours, better relations with her employer; we dare not weaken her claim by disregarding our own conditions, and thinking them of little importance. Just now, while women are replacing men in so many industrial activities, it is of importance that they should preserve their womanliness and the respect due to it, while, at the same time, obtaining the best possible conditions, which will help the men in their demands when they return to civil life.

If you are satisfied with bad conditions; if you have not the pluck to ask for better, you dare not say that your neighbour's affair is not your own, or that you cannot help her trouble. You know that "we have all one Father; that one God made us all," and that we are responsible for our neighbour's well-being in so far as our mode of life must necessarily raise or lower hers. The love of our neighbour also shows in our attitude towards the great mysteries of life. If we should talk lightly of these in a club-room, or bed-room, or even in a street, it may be that some ugly word, thrown out carelessly, will cling to an innocent mind, which has by chance received it, and will spoil the purity of that mind for ever.

It matters infinitely that you should reverence the eternal truths of life, because your neighbour needs to reverence them as well as yourself, and you must cherish her ideals as these are inseparable from your own.

We hear of men laying down their lives to save the lives of others whom they have never seen, but who, they know, love life.

We hear of a doctor who travels in India and discovers plague germs and brings them home to analyse in order to find the serum, which shall nullify their injurious properties. We see the laboratory attendant sicken and die, while the doctor and two nurses voluntarily attend him. We see the doctor placing him in a coffin to insure that no other lives are imperilled. He finds himself infected, he takes himself away, sending notes of farewell to his parents and friends; he is ready to die alone, for he has laboured to save lives - the lives of strangers. Strangers, yes, so far as actual human knowledge is concerned, but brothers and sisters in the sight of God. We could multiply these instances, but I have said enough to show that the cry of humanity is a cry to which the normal man or woman must attend. If they are callous or neglectful, the pain in their own souls will become intolerable. They will starve their own lives, if they leave their neighbour's wants unsatisfied.

Finally, I would speak a few words about the love of God, and here I would venture to speak from personal experience.

The more I think of God's Love and Beauty and Truth, the more I need it, the stronger is the appeal which it makes to me. We reverence and admire all that God stands for; we reverence Him until we love Him. While I raise my heart in the act of adoration, I place my spirit in the reflection of His attributes. Having apprehended the reflection I crave for the reality, and then begins the experience commended by our Jewish teachers; - I humbly seek to imitate my God.

God is righteous, and loves righteousness. He has given us something of His Being, and tiny creatures though we are we know love, because God loves, and He has revealed His love to us.

They that love God, says an old teacher, are like the sun when he goes forth in the night; like the sun, they are gentle and strong; like the sun, they carry healing in their hearts. Love God, and make Him loveable to others.

You remember that sweet incident in the story we have been reading, when the old farmer told David that he must not play his violin on the Lord's Day, because God would not approve. David cried delightfully, "Oh, that is all right, _my_ God would approve, and so we do not worship the same God." The God whom David worshipped was a God who loved happiness and beauty, and the child was prepared to show his faith in God's lovingkindness by following his own conception of happiness and beauty.

We are taught not to be ashamed to proclaim God in public. It is also hard not to be afraid to love Him in private. Sometimes we are afraid of our own selves. Let us be very quiet now and listen to His message. Just let Him enter into our hearts, for God casts out fear, ugliness, hatred and impurity. If we are very quiet and rest faithfully on God, if we clear from our hearts hatred and anger and any form of impurity, God's love will enter into our being, and we shall be at peace.

What can we do to show our love when we have received it? We can only attempt, humbly and dutifully, to lead clean and pure lives, to be truthful and honourable, yes, and enthusiastic for if we are once filled with the love of God, we shall desire to draw others to worship Him. We shall disregard failure; we shall be prepared for sacrifice because we shall want to show how much we care, and by the testimony of our own faith we shall cause others to believe.

We have travelled far, and now we must end; we have found that God sanctifies family love and that love is the foundation of social life. Love for God brings us into touch with all that is good and noble and beautiful in life. It robs death of its terror, seeing that it gives to man a share in the life of God, which is life eternal. Let us pray that we may experience love.

Archives, Liberal
Jewish Synagogue, London

[1] A paraphrase of the last line of Browning's "Two in the Campagna."

[2] From Emerson's essay, "Friendship" in his Essays: First Series (1841).

CLUB LETTER NO. 26

May 1941

I had written my May letter, as I always do, a few weeks in advance, but it is lost through enemy action. That phrase has unfortunately become rather familiar to us. It sounds specific and business-like, but it covers up an infinite amount of human suffering. In our case, the destruction of our beautiful Settlement, Club, Synagogue and offices, with all their wealth of important records and reports, precious letters and documents, collected during forty seven and a half years, cannot be thought of without a sense of utter devastation. It is not merely the outer shell that we have lost, but vital information gathered from past experience and necessary, as we thought, for the guidance of those who will continue our work when we lay it down. I suppose records and reports must have taken years of my life, when the separate hours are added together which I worked on them. Then, there were the religious papers produced in connection with the various societies to which I belong. They have all gone. The records of Club work, which Miss [Nellie] Levy has built up during the last sixteen years, the health and other records written by Miss [Olga] Lazarus, the statistics of the Employment bureau - all have disappeared in the wreckage.

All these losses are shattering, but they sink into insignificance when we remember that so many people (twenty seven) lost their lives in that fatal night of April 16th and 17th. These included some precious Club members as well as our beloved Settlement Secretary, Miss Winifred Paynter.

Now I want us to consider some very important questions. How are we going to allow this disaster to affect our lives? How are we going to honour the memory of our beloved dead? How are we going to make the Club spirit increase in strength? There is obviously no use in calling ourselves Jews unless in this hour of disaster we feel that God, our Guardian, neither slumbers nor sleeps. His spirit fills the universe. Our tragedy does not affect our faith. How can it? God has shown us what is good, i.e. to do justice, to love mercy, and to walk humbly with our God. War is a denial of God's teaching, and war created our tragedy.

The international situation was such in 1939 that we had no alternative but to go to war. Brute force was let loose in the world and could only be overcome by brute force. Oppression, cruelty, persecution and tyranny threatened civilisation, and had to be overcome. The world had ignored the leadership of God, and so it had been swept into a state of conflict and disaster. The challenge has come to us, unmistakeably, to order our own lives anew, to turn our hearts Godward, to listen to God, and to dedicate ourselves more earnestly than ever to the cause of peace and freedom. You who read this paper, as well as I who write it, belong to a small group of very ordinary folk, but if every small group feels as we do - and God forbid that they should need our suffering to rouse their feeling of responsibility - there _is_ no doubt that a better life will be established. Many of our friends who have passed out of our sight cared intensely for the welfare of the Club and its ideals. I believe that even now they will help us to progress, for they are nearer to perfect goodness, and they will influence us so that we may become better and more useful people.

The Club stood for happiness. Let us remove little bits of pain from the world by helping "everyman" to be just a little more joyous. The Club aimed at raising our standard of citizenship. We must take all the opportunities that are given to us to understand some of the economic, social and political problems affecting our national life, always remembering that "righteousness exalteth a nation," and that good citizenship required besides much else integrity in business and a high standard also of popular recreation.

Our Club gave us fine opportunities to cultivate friendship. It was a democracy in which each individual counted and was given affection and encouragement to realise as fully as possible the powers of her or his personality. The Club asks each one of us to give the best service we could to the welfare of the whole. Above all, we were offered the conception of a living Judaism, and were expected to express our religion as fully as possible in our lives. The friends who have been taken from us shared these Club ideals, and in honouring their memory I ask you to be more zealous in your loyalty.

As I left Whitefield's[1] after our beautiful service on Saturday, April 19th, a man pressed my hand in a kindly, sympathetic way, and said: "All right, Miss Montagu, we shall have our revenge!" If he meant that a Berlin woman who had given her life to some piece of work for nearly fifty years should experience my kind of heartache when she saw the outward shell destroyed in a few minutes, if he meant that another woman should see the place shattered which had echoed night after night for twenty seven years with the joyous sounds of young people bent on recreation and education, and revelling in activity; if he meant this, then indeed he offered me a poor form of consolation. In memory of our dead, I would urge you to cast hatred out of your hearts, as hatred is destructive, and through hatred we lose our standards and aspirations. We love our country, our England, and insist that she must never do the dastardly things which the Nazis are doing today. If she does yield to the popular cries of revenge, she will have to lower her standards, until they cannot be distinguished from Nazi standards. Not so can our dear ones be honoured. By their graves, we dedicate ourselves to the uplifting of our thoughts and feelings, to the purification of our conduct, to the furthering of deeds of love, mercy and goodness.

I have received from a vast number of our Club members, past and present, offers of help, as well as the expression of loving sympathy. I am deeply grateful, as of course I rely upon each one of our Club children and grandchildren to make it possible to reconstruct our West Central Club. Above all, I rely upon you to rally round your Club leader, Miss N[ellie] G. Levy, and to perpetuate the Club spirit. Your affection and loyalty and courage give us hope. Many of you have told me that the Club spirit cannot die, and I fully believe this, even as you do. If we could be shaken in our belief, it would mean that we had accepted defeat at the hands of the Nazis, for it is their wish that our spirit should be conquered. They have shattered our building and thrown it to the ground.

But the Club spirit has been given us by God, and human tyrants, however powerful, cannot take it from us. God gave us this spirit when we showed ourselves ready and eager to receive it - by seeking after justice and truth and trying to be loving and to live righteously. Again and again we have failed, but our spirit was renewed through prayer and unceasing work.

We are all mourning and our sense of loss is full of acute pain. But for myself, I feel more strongly than ever that God is allowing us the wonderful privilege of carrying on. We have our Club Leader, Miss N. G. Levy, with her big heart and her big brain, ready after sixteen years of experience to do even better work for the Club people she loves so well. Even though for the moment we have no Club home, no Congregational centre of our own, we are receiving endless kindness and hospitality from our neighbours. I do now and then feel numb with pain and overwhelmed by our present difficulties, but I know that these moments are due to weakness and weariness. I remind myself that our young people are ready to share the burdens which are now resting on our tired shoulders. These young people are full of love and faith. Moreover, they are determined that our Club shall revive, and shall always express their highest conception of Judaism. So I would conclude with the words of Matthew Arnold:

> Then, in such hour of need
> Of your fainting, dispirited race,
> Ye, like angels, appear,
> Radiant with ardour divine!
> Beacons of hope, ye appear!
> Languor is not in your heart,
> Weakness is not in your word,
> Weariness not on your brow,
> Ye alight in our van; at your voice,

Panic, despair, flee away.
Ye move through the ranks, recall
The stragglers, refresh the outworn,
Praise, re-inspire the brave!
Order, courage, return.
Eyes rekindling, and prayers
Follow your steps as ye go.
Ye fill up the gaps in our files,
Strengthen the wavering line,
Stablish, continue our march,
On, to the bound of the waste,
On, to the City of God.[2]

                                        Private Collection,
                                      Hannah Feldman, London

[1] Whitefields Tabernacle, the London church where Lily Montagu held religious services for the two weeks following the destruction of the West Central Club, Settlement and Synagogue. Among the services held there was the memorial service referred to in this Club Letter. According to Lily Montagu, over five hundred people were in attendance, including Club leaders, members and friends. For the following year and a half, the work of the West Central Club was carried on in the building used by Whitefields for their Day Nursery (Montagu, *My Club and I*, London, 1954, pp. 136 and 145).

[2] From Arnold's poem, "Rugby Chapel."

CLUB LETTER NO. 118

November 1949

Have you thought of the many kinds of fear there are in the world? You yourself probably entertain some without always being conscious of their presence, and certainly you are not given to analyse them. But it is rather helpful every now and then to examine the motives which govern our actions and see if they should be cherished or controlled or altogether banished.

There is a fear of our doing something which is not expected of our set and so making ourselves conspicuous and perhaps even ridiculous. This, I think, is not a bad sort of fear. After all, with the progress of civilisation we can assume that our conventions are fairly sound, and it is better not to break away from them so long as our conformity does not involve the sacrifice of principle. There is a danger that certain conventions are mistaken for binding principles and too much attention can be paid to them. If you respect your need for sleep and even on holiday refuse to turn night into day, you need not be ashamed even though you act differently from your companions. You need not smoke more cigarettes than you can afford because the others do. You can wear clothes that <u>you</u> prefer even though you may be considered on that account old-fashioned; you can be careful about your language while your companions think a few swear words exalt your manhood or womanhood.

A more serious aspect of present day life affects girls particularly, for it engenders a fear which often leads to foolish conduct and eventually to real misery. The girl is afraid of not marrying. When I entered into social service we found girls most anxious to get married in order to escape the unhappiness of workshop life. Wages were so miserably small that a girl could not possibly save for "later on." She was employed only for a time, for it was assumed as certain that she <u>would</u> marry and so there was no suggestion that she should look upon her work as a career in which she should be as efficient as possible. But today the outlook is quite different. A girl commands a high wage if she is efficient whether in sewing, domestic or clerical work or salesmanship. She need not be afraid of facing her future in the field of industry, but the dread of loneliness does overwhelm her with some morbid feelings. Nothing I can say can satisfactorily remove this fear, and there is no doubt that a happy married life is the best and most natural for every woman - and man too, as a matter of fact. But it is worse for girls to remain unmarried for loneliness is necessarily intensified by the circumstances of their lives. But a healthy minded girl does not allow herself to be worried or discouraged. She determines that she will face the world bravely whatever happens, and she realises that while marriage holds the best to be expected from life, a self-respecting independence is second best, while marriage for the sake of marriage without love or good companionship is nothing less than hell on earth. She will not then be a victim to fear; she will not degrade herself by running after any man; she will not make herself contemptible by disregarding the claims of her own personality in order to attract attention from a man for whom she has no particular regard. She determines to uphold the sanctity of sex relations.

Today our fears are not limited to the circumstances of any particular section. The whole world is full of fears for these are shared by men and women of all conditions. Sometimes we think that we are the victims of a kind of doom which we know not how to avert. Something terrible is going to happen. There is little security anywhere. Dreaded unemployment stalks towards us and we seem unable to conquer the monster; society is on the verge of bankruptcy, we are told; war is inevitable since the powers of destruction are in the hands of certain nations and they will certainly want in time to kill those they hate, since killing seems the only way to free themselves of evil-doers. Disasters of all kinds seem to follow one another in quick succession, and we can only contemplate them in utter powerlessness.

Politicians and social reformers and even so-called religious leaders advertise their remedies in shrieking voices, and then they quarrel with one another, for unconsciously they know that the problems are too difficult for them to tackle adequately. Reforms - political, social and religious - are <u>feared</u> because people are afraid that their own feeble line of security is menaced, for their particular followers are being led into new channels away from themselves. They are baffled by their own loneliness and fear.

I suggest to you that as Jews and Jewesses we must somehow or other raise ourselves out of this life of fear. Don't you know people who directly an illness is mentioned feel that they themselves have some of the symptoms; others who are full of superstitions and little self-deceptions because they want to escape troubles which <u>are</u> <u>said</u> to lead to fatal illness or sudden death?

We are getting ourselves into such an unhealthy state that even our enjoyment of life is threatened. We are, friends, I think out of focus. Elijah, when he stood alone under the juniper tree, conscious of a great spiritual triumph but also conscious of his personal weakness and loneliness, heard within him a still small voice. And this voice came from God and told him to go forward and carry on with his own work and be unafraid. This faith in the God within, part of the spirit of righteousness, urges us to test life anew. Instead of dwelling on the source of our fears however real and legitimate these may seem, we should, I think, shift the field of observation. The girl who can think of nothing except getting married should try to improve the powers of her own personality so that she has better qualities for her passage through life, even though it be a solitary passage. The social and political fears lessen if we can persuade ourselves that peace can only come through righteousness. We must turn towards the Lord and make Him the centre of life. If we fear the Lord - which means reverence for perfect love, truth, beauty, goodness, - these will cast out all fears. Many illnesses <u>are</u> infectious, and so are all forms of faith if held with sincerity and enthusiasm. The few true believers - whatever their race or creed - can combat and overcome the utter helplessness which creates devastating fear. Their number <u>must</u> increase since they alone hold the key to the Courage which can equip us for true service, and the faith which alone can banish fear. Since the role of righteousness observed throughout the ages is seen to triumph in the history of the past, so it must have dominion in the future. We must by our own small contributions increase the reality of this righteousness. Then we can go forward rejoicing in life which is in its essence good because it comes from God. "Now therefore let the fear of the Lord be upon you; take heed and do it, for there is no iniquity with the Lord our God."[1] "O House of Israel, trust ye in the Lord!"[2]

Private Collection,
Hannah Feldman, London

[1] 2 Chronicles 19:7.

[2] Presumably a paraphrase of Psalm 115:10 which reads: "O House of Aaron, trust ye in the Lord."

CLUB LETTER NO. 154

May 1953

DIAMOND JUBILEE: 1893-1953
OF THE
WEST CENTRAL JEWISH CLUB

How can we best adjust ourselves to our Jubilee celebrations? My sister and I would like you to know how deeply grateful we are to you all for the love you are showing us. There are moments when we feel a trifle embarrassed and overwhelmed and would rather like to hurry into a secret place of refuge till May 16th and May 17th have passed. You say that this is a festival of recognition, but such festivals are usually celebrated <u>after</u> the central figures have disappeared out of sight and the reality of their characteristics can no longer obstruct the idealism so generously given. No, my friends, we do not feel worthy of all the lovely things you say about us - but, we are deeply touched by the tenderness in which you deal with us, ignoring our failings and weaknesses and exalting any good quality we possess. We feel very grateful to God for allowing us to live and to work even after our Jubilee. Of course, we miss our dear friend Constance Lewis, who played such an important part in the Red Lodge Trio.[1]

Sixty years ago, it was not the fashion in our set for girls to work, but our parents were workers and we were brought up by them to regard social service as a necessary part of the daily routine. We, in a small way, helped several organisations by personal service, but we had no training. We absorbed the spirit in which our parents worked, loving simplicity and sincerity, and disliking show of any kind.

When we began Club work and became friends with our members, our own lives became absorbingly interesting. We saw vast possibilities unfolding themselves. Our Club became affiliated to the London Club Union, and I enjoyed exchanging ideas with the Hon. Maud Stanley, the Pioneer Club leader.

At first, we had our Club superintendent, but gradually, we found a rota of friends who were responsible for the Club every evening in the week. You can imagine that as I spent more and more time with my girls, they taught me much about the realities of life. I found out how they wanted to spend their leisure, how attracted they were by study, how they loved art and music, if only they had the chance of hearing and seeing what cultured people and artists had to give them.

The only differences I had with my dear Mother were based on the belief that we would overwork ourselves. I began to visit the homes of my girls, and to win the friendship of their parents. I kept records of the lives of our members, and, every holiday, I summarised these records and viewed the character and tendencies of our members and their hopes and aspirations as far as these could be revealed to me. My father begged me to refrain from bending over these Club books hour after hour, and to give more time to enjoy myself. I was convinced that my records would be invaluable to my successors, and I had to persist.

All the records were destroyed in 1941 in our tragedy. But the Club goes on.

My friends, I can assure you that my sister and I valued education and friendship above all else. We tried to share what we possessed with those who had been denied our opportunities. That was the beginning of our Club sixty years ago. We tried to give opportunity for every kind of sociability and recreation. But the process was a very long one. Your mothers and grandmothers remember the annual fortnightly holiday to Littlehampton, when each member had to present a health certificate for fitness before being allowed to go. The strict hour for gate closing was nine p.m. Coach excursions provided bliss and rapture, and sitting next to the partner of your choice was all important, even if the arrangement involved a meeting lasting half the previous night. It was considered a privilege to join in morning prayers, and religious discussions in the evening; the learning of hand-work in the garden was a source of immense happiness; the picking up of strange acquaintances was one of the deadliest sins - there is a long distance between such holidays and the present trips abroad with all modern amenities but the Club feeling is to be traced throughout the different holidays distinguishing and making the holidays of all kinds memorable.

Sixty years of Club life. When we consider what has counted most in these years to my sister and myself, I would make three headings: (1) The friends we have made.

Through close contact with our members, we have made thousands of friends and these are scattered all over the world, and it is not unusual to be rung up on the telephone and to be asked - "I was a member thirty or forty years ago - can I come and see you." We have delightful contacts with our "old girls" in tubes and buses and while walking in the streets. But we have also some hundreds of friends with whom we have kept in regular touch, especially through our Married Members' Guild and through correspondence. No member has ever been regarded by us as an individual unit - we learned to know her as a member of a family. We cared for her whole life, her home, her education, her occupation and her religion. So, these friendships were not superficial. The members gave us love and loyalty, and the power to face our Club problems and to rejoice in our small successes. But, there were also the special friends, who grew up in the Club and became our colleagues. This brings me to our second great blessing. We have had such immense happiness from seeing the children grown up in the Club become <u>our</u> <u>colleagues</u> and take responsible positions in the Club and Settlement administration.

First, of course, there is our great-hearted, big-brained Miss N[ellie] G. Levy, who twenty-eight years ago undertook the Club Leadership. Miss D[ora] Isaacs whole-heartedly took up the Settlement work while assisting in the Club. They gave us the relief we needed to enable us to develop other work for which we were responsible, but they and the other worker friends never for an instant allowed us to feel "unwanted" in the Club.

The devotion of a large band of special helpers among our members, each one of whom was deeply appreciated by my sister and myself, but too numerous to mention by name makes it possible for us to feel that our work as founders will not be forgotten. They as "our children" have given us new ideas and interpreted anew many old ones. They have achieved the difficult task of carrying on our work, developing it in every direction, and transforming our Club from a Girls' Club into a Mixed Club.

Miss Levy herself holds an important position in the Club world and brings her West Central experience to assist many wider organisations. Everywhere her work is acclaimed and her opinion respected.

During our long years of service we have had a few colleagues who did not serve their apprenticeship <u>in</u> the

Club, and these, also, have enriched our lives. There is Miss Lazarus, who gives selfless devotion; Miss King, who although retired, is always ready to express to us her personal friendship and her Club interest.[2] We still have Miss Poxon and Mr. Harding, who have shown our young people how to express the beautiful in sculpture and handwork.[3] All these friends and colleagues and others to whom we are grateful have immeasurably increased our personal happiness in Club work and we thank God for their loyalty and courage.

The Club and Settlement have - and this is the biggest blessing of all - given us <u>the opportunity to express our faith</u> in our work. We believe, as you know, in a living Judaism in harmony with modern life. It has been our privilege to offer you this presentment of Judaism, but, of course, we have never interfered with the belief of those who sincerely follow the Orthodox observance of our ancestral religion. But, when I accepted Liberal Judaism, I was shown how to permeate our way of life with a reflection of God's attributes. The God idea could be brought into our daily life, in spite of our limitations, weaknesses and imperfections. Some of you became interested in Judaism and we studied together and prayed together until we became strong enough with the help of residents in the West Central district, to form a Liberal Congregation. Now, after the passage of twenty-five years, we are about to build our own Synagogue, and the special inner group of our Club will join in this magnificent and holy task.

To those who were not prepared to accept the Liberal Jewish presentment of Judaism, with all its manifestations, we were, nevertheless, able to formulate a religious message. For all forms of Judaism express the Unity of God and enjoin their followers to seek God at all times. So we have been allowed, to a certain degree, to build our Club life on the foundation of our faith and motivate all our activities with the God idea. We rejoice today that our Club spirit is one of mutual service, great happiness, sincere peace and aspiration, friendship and faith.

Today, while we are recording the blessings we have received in abundance, we are conscious of our many mistakes and failures. We know full well that if we had been better we could have done much better.

We remember, too, our friends times of great sorrow and disappointment, and especially the terrible war years and the destruction of our beautiful Club building in Alfred Place in 1941, which caused the death of twenty-seven Club friends. We are about to withdraw from much of our Club work, and we leave you burdened with a great responsibility. When our premises in Charlotte Street were condemned, we had no choice but to take the large building which you, in your affection, called Montagu House. We could not have faced the financial responsibility which this venture involves had it not been for our complete confidence in our young people, who came forward and offered to carry our burdens. Apart from the financial needs, we leave it to you with confidence and hope to carry on the spirit of the West Central and to value the Club always as expressing the best in Judaism. Will you see to it that the members continue to enjoy themselves thoroughly and that their pleasures leave behind no vain regrets? Let the members work for a high standard in all branches of education; cultivate always loyal friendship. Know that the Club is yours and you must ensure its future by your own efforts and sacrifices. Let it always be a house of prayer.

We ask God to bless each one of you and your leader. May He help you to make our Jubilee the starting post for splendid developments in the Club as you advance in your personal lives. So it will grow in power and usefulness and increase and "with God be the rest."

> Private Collection,
> Hannah Feldman, London

[1] Lily Montagu, Marian Montagu and their close friend, Constance P. Lewis, were dubbed "The Red Lodge Trio," referring to the home at Palace Court (nicknamed The Red Lodge) that they shared together for over thirty years. For a greater description of Constance Lewis' involvement in the Club, see Lily Montagu's *My Club and I* (London, 1954), p. 66 ff.

[2] Margaret King, who in her tribute to the West Central wrote: "When I first knew the West Central Club in 1919 it was as an opportunity to work freely and happily with young people in the fields of literature and English . . . Happy adventure in singing and acting together, the clash of mind with mind in discussion, the demands on willing service made by a living, democratic community provided true education, in the days when the state's provision was scanty indeed." (See *The West Central Story and its Founders*, a pamphlet put together by Nellie G. Levy, probably in 1968 though no publication date is given).

[3] Ethel Poxon and George Harding. Their tributes to the West Central Club can also be found in *The West Central Story and its Founders*.

VII. RELIGIOUS ORGANIZER

INTRODUCTION

The founding of the Jewish Religious Union in February, 1902, marked Lily Montagu's formal entrance into the Anglo-Jewish community as a religious organizer. Though she herself saw the West Central Girls' Club as religiously-based, it was the J.R.U.--conceived, organized, and large supervised by Lily Montagu--through which her genius for religious organization was firmly established. Montagu's desire to form the J.R.U. as an association committed to the revitalization of Anglo-Jewry's religious life stemmed from the conviction that she had been called to do so. It was her vocation, she felt, to create an organization of Orthodox, Reform and Liberal Jews, "sympathetic" to the belief that the community's religious life needed to be revivified through whatever means possible. The name of the organization: The Jewish Religious Union, signified the group's commitment to Judaism, religious faith and the unity of the Anglo-Jewish community.

The first four documents included in this chapter detail the important role that Lily Montagu played in the founding of the J.R.U. The first, a letter sent out on March 24, 1899 to over a dozen prominent members of the community, most of whom were relatives or friends, attempted to ascertain whether they acknowledged, as she did, the legitimacy of Liberal Judaism. The letter, apparently written at the encouragement of N. S. Joseph, a member of the Orthodox New West End Synagogue and a close friend of the Montagu family, followed the publication of her essay, "The Spiritual Possibilities of Judaism," later identified by Lily Montagu as that which led to the creation of the Liberal Jewish movement in England. Though Montagu failed to record either the names of those who responded to her letter or the kinds of answers that she received, the responses apparently convinced her that there was a significant number of Jews who shared her liberal religious convictions. Subsequently, in November, 1901, she sent out a second letter, asking those interested in helping "to strengthen the religious life" in their midst to communicate with her. Among those to whom this letter, as well as the first, was sent, was Claude Montefiore, the man that Lily Montagu hoped would agree to become the Union's leader.

The "First Meeting of [the] J.R.U." to which Lily Montagu refers in her paper dated November, 1901, was a preliminary gathering of ten men and women asked by Montagu to formally express their "willingness to associate together" through an organization which would work towards adapting Judaism "to the progressive needs of . . . [their] . . . contemporaries." According to the J.R.U. Minute Book, all of those present supported her plan and agreed to form an initial leadership committee on which they would serve. The members of the committee were: Lily Montagu; Claude Montefiore; Oswald Simon (a self-professed Liberal Jew who somewhat earlier had initiated, though unsuccessfully, his own efforts at communal religious reform); Henrietta Franklin (Lily's eldest sister); Morris Joseph (minister of the Reform West London Synagogue and leader of the so-called Hampstead group, a short-lived association that similarly tried to revivify the community's religious life); Albert Jessel (an honorary officer of the Orthodox United Synagogue and cousin to Lily

Montagu); N. S. Joseph; and Isidore Spielman (President of the Jewish Historical Society, an ex-warden of the New West End Synagogue and, like Jessel, Lily Montagu's cousin).

By the time formal elections were held, two weeks later, Lily Montagu had convinced Montefiore to become the association's President, with she, Albert Jessel and Simeon Singer serving as Vice-Presidents of what, by the third meeting, had become identified as the Jewish Religious Union. A circular letter stating the objects of the Union was sent to over one hundred British Jews and several new individuals joined the leadership committee. At the Union's first official meeting, held on February 16, 1902 at the home of Lily's sister, Henrietta, a proposal by Lily Montagu that "this meeting sympathizes with the objects of the Jewish Religious Union and will endeavor to secure their fulfilment" was unanimously carried. From that time on, Montefiore became the group's official leader. Yet it was Lily Montagu who insured its continued existence by assuming responsibility for its major activities and daily affairs.

In her address, "What I Owe to the Synagogue," given at a reception in October of 1950 (and included here), she describes at some length her role in the founding and organizational development of the J.R.U. Focusing on her work as Organizing Secretary (though by 1938, following Montefiore's death, she became its President), she alludes to the early propaganda meetings that she led and the constituent synagogues that she helped establish. She also refers to the World Union for Progressive Judaism, conceived by Montagu as an organization that would unite Liberal Jews throughout the world in their "struggle against materialism."

Lily Montagu arrived at this conception in 1925 if not earlier. In her sermon, "Unfinished Man," delivered in

June of that year, she expressed the belief that the creation of an international Jewish Religious Union would significantly strengthen the Liberal Jewish "cause." By October 1, 1925, the J.R.U. approved Montagu's formal suggestion that such an organization be established and supported her efforts to convene its first conference during the following year. From 1926 until 1959, the headquarters of the World Union were located in Lily Montagu's own home, with Montagu taking responsibility for many, at times most, and during the Second World War, all of the Union's activities. Serving as its Honorary Secretary and later as its President, she took care of its correspondence, helped issue a number of publications, arranged and often led its meetings, assisted in creating Liberal Jewish congregations throughout the world, and organized a number of World Union "sections" in an effort to broaden its work and widen its appeal.

The sermon included at the end of this chapter: "Peace, Peace, Where There Is No Peace," represents one of Lily Montagu's few organizational ideas that met with only limited success. A pacifist most of her life, Montagu sought to inaugurate, within the World Union, a special Sabbath dedicated to the Jewish ideal of peace. While celebrated for many years (though even then sporadically), most World Union leaders apparently failed to share Montagu's enthusiasm for what she hoped would be an annual event. This sermon is included not as a symbol of Lily Montagu's organizational failures but as an example of the kinds of activities that mattered to her most. Though the primary concerns of many other World Union leaders may have included the raising of money and the creating of new and bigger congregations, Montagu's major concern remained the spiritual one of bringing World Union members to an understanding and appreciation of the moral teachings of God.

PRIVATE

12 Kensington Palace Gardens W
March 24th 1899

Dear [   ]¹

Since the publication of my article on the "Spiritual Possibilities of Judaism" in the January number of the <u>Jewish Quarterly Review</u>, I have become convinced of the necessity of formulating a programme in which prominence should be given to such vital elements of Judaism as are consistent with Truth and with modern standards of morality.

Having reason to believe that you are in sympathy with the opinions expressed in my article, I venture to ask you to put in writing your own views on certain important questions which are subjoined, and which I am simultaneously submitting to about 12 friends who sympathise with my objects.²

I. What are the vital principles of the old Judaism that must be preserved in the new?

II. If these "vital principles" do not include belief in the miraculous Divine Revelation heretofore accepted, what is the Authority on which we are to rely in judging of right and wrong?

III. What forms and ceremonies should be retained on account of their historical or ethical or sanitary value? (Special reference to the seventh day Sabbath and to festivals commemorating alleged miraculous events.)

IV. What is to be the special function of the Jew under the new Judaism?

These preliminary questions are designed to elicit only the outline of a programme. It is therefore desirable to answer them without considering for the moment the practicability of carrying out the programme in the near future.

>Yours sincerely,
>Lily H. Montagu

>Private Collection,
>Eric Conrad, London

[1] The following is a carbon copy of the letter sent out to Mr. [Philip] Hartog (1864-1947), Lecturer in Chemistry at Manchester University, who delivered a sermon at the J.R.U. services in January of 1903 on "Science and Religion." He was related to Lily Montagu through marriage.

[2] A handwritten draft, by Lily Montagu, reveals that this letter was sent to the following people: Mrs. Ernest Franklin, Mrs. N. L. Cohen, Miss S. D'Avigdor, Miss N. Myer, Mr. N. S. Joseph, Mr. C. G. Montefiore, Mr. I. Abrahams, Mr. C. (?) Simon, Dr. Schorstein, Mr. Laurie Magnus, Mr. I. Spielman, and Mr. Israel Gollanz. Since Philip Hartog is not on this list, one may assume that this letter was sent to more than twelve people. In addition, the reference to "C. Simon" may either be a mistaken reference to "O[swald] Simon," who was involved in the J.R.U. from the beginning, or a conflation of two names—C[harles] Singer and O[swald] Simon, both of whom were early J.R.U. members.

PRIVATE AND CONFIDENTIAL

>12 Kensington Palace Gardens W
>November 1901

I venture to address this letter to those of the Jewish Faith who feel with me that the moment has come for us to try to strengthen the religious life in our midst.

The belief has forced itself upon me that if we care sufficiently for Judaism to desire its continued existence we must reformulate our creed and express more clearly the claims which it justifiably may make upon our action and our lives. The advancing secular life which is familiar and dear to us must be linked with, and illuminated by the faith handed down to us by our forefathers.

If we continue to adopt a "laissez faire" policy in the conduct of our lives, and remain uninfluenced by any definite religious doctrine, and indifferent to the religious needs of aspirations of those who are allied to us by the ties of blood or common fellowship, our Brotherhood must slowly cease to exist as an effective force in the development of humanity. If instead we endeavour by associated labour reverently to reconstruct the fabric of our faith upon its groundwork of simplicity and truth we shall, I think, be able to testify to its beauty, increase to power and influence and secure its continuance as a factor in the cause of righteousness.

We cannot fairly demand from our children loyalty to a high moral ideal unless by subjecting them to the influence of some religious system we have trained them to live consciously in the Presence of God. For the sake of our children, then, we must vitalise our system until it produces this consciousness which is the predominant aim in all forms of religious belief.

Moreover the enjoyment of the treasures of education places an undeniable obligation upon us.

We must by the devotion of mind to the service of religion prove that enlightenment and piety bear supplementary and not antagonistic relations to one another.

When once we have reformulated our creed and strengthened its relation to life, we shall be better equipped to take part in the grim warfare raging around us, the strife between truth, beauty and goodness on the one hand, and on the other, indifference, materialism and sensuality.

I would ask those who sympathise with the proposed work of reconstruction to communicate with me, and I will endeavour to arrange a meeting - when the nature of our undertaking and various methods for its accomplishment may be discussed.

Yours faithfully,
Lily H. Montagu

Private Collection,
Eric Conrad, London

PAPER READ AT FIRST MEETING OF J.R.U. CONFERENCE INVITED TO START MOVEMENT

November 23, 1901

I should like to put before you what I deem to be the object of this little Conference. I feel that there is in our midst a number of men and women whose lives are influenced by religious aspiration, whose Judaism makes a definite claim on their every day conduct and I desire with your help to bring these people together in order that they may accomplish an important piece of work - They must become articulate. A certain proportion of our community regard piety as synonymous with obedience to a religious system which has been hallowed by the devotion of our Fathers - so long as this hallowed obedience can influence every phase of conduct so long does it promote righteousness and therefore deserves our homage.

But since this system cannot help the large number of men and women who, almost in spite of themselves, have been influenced by the forces of Anglicisation, Education and emancipation; who refuse to hold as divine that which they believe to be the creation of the human intelligence, some effort is needed to adapt the ancient faith to the progressive needs of our contemporaries. We must make this effort. If once we admit the principle that man is called upon to <u>think</u> before he has a right to observe - the principle which is a corollary of the ancient Jewish doctrine of personal responsibility - we are false to the charge which our Father has laid upon us if we do not try to adapt our religion to the necessity of our daily lives. By our inertia we encourage the existence of that class of Jews who have ceased to recognise religious obligations, and have replaced them by devotion to self aggrandisement; to whom the joys of self-sacrifice are unreal and must be replaced by the pleasures of worldly advancement. Then again, our inertia is responsible for the defection of some men and women whose allegiance is essential to the development of our mission - They lead, let us admit, useful and religious lives, but they recognise no distinctly Jewish influence by which they may be led to the consciousness of God. Their interest in us is barely sentimental and we are soon obliged to mourn a loss we have made no effort to avert.

We have to ask ourselves today: "Is there enough inspiring force in Judaism to make its continuance desirable?" If we answer in the affirmative we have to show what the force is and how our lives can be subjected to its influence.

As I believe in the continued possibilities of Judaism as a missionary religion; as I do homage to its essential and peculiar doctrines - the proper conception of life and nature, the indivisibility of morality and religion, the idea of individual responsibility and the sanctification of one day in seven, I am desirous of strengthening the consciousness of Judaism in our midst. The following methods suggest themselves to me.

As the habit of worship can militate against the degrading tendencies of our age, for by the effort of aspiration we can achieve self conquest, I would ask you to approve and to assist in organising children's services in London and the provinces. This is not a difficult piece of work. Four such services are already established and two more in process of organisation. But our missionary work must not end there. The immediate future of our brotherhood is with the young men and women whose interest in Judaism needs to be stimulated. For them I would ask you to help to institute services - Many of us feel that the Synagogue service excepting for its antiquarian interest does not have any real influence on our lives. We cannot however hope for any change while we can only talk vaguely of potential worshippers. If, however, we can establish and conduct effective services outside the Synagogues we shall be justified in claiming attention from the authorities. Instead of saying to them: "Look at the people who never attend divine worship. Why don't you try to reach them?" We shall say: "Look at the people who do attend and are influenced by the services which we have organized - we demand the Synagogue's hospitality for them." I would suggest that we commence very quietly with one service conducted by a properly qualified leader upon the lines which we feel to be best adapted to our needs. At the same time I would recommend that we try to arrange lectures on definitely religious subjects in order that we may create an atmosphere which may stimulate the desire for services.

One of the many practical difficulties which occur[s] to me is that we can't find leaders and lecturers until we have formulated our conception of Judaism, until we have become so far articulate that we know what we want to learn

– and to observe [ ]. For this reason I would suggest that we try to embody in literary form our ideas of a working religion which is distinctly Jewish in its origin, methods and aspirations. Would it not be possible to ask the best men and women among us to assist in this work which might supply the link necessary to bind our faith to our daily lives? I would treat of such problems as of ceremonials, the presentment of our Religion to the uneducated, the Jewish conception of the existence of sin, a future life etc. etc. Of course no writer could pretend to formulate a creed which would be acceptable to his neighbours but I contend that writers selected by an association of the kind we are considering would probably have the power of evolving thoughts which would be based on such broad principles that they could at least <u>suggest</u> definite religious conceptions to the rest of the community. It appears to me that our <u>indefinite</u> condition threatens our existence as a Brotherhood for it justifies every form of disloyalty.

A manifesto of this kind would help us to define our own faith and so make transmission possible. Mr. [Isidore] Spielman will ask you to consider the desirability of attempting the three forms of work which I have suggested and the methods by which they may be initiated. I should merely like to add that in this work I only desire to show my devotion to Judaism by making other people prove theirs by association. I have no qualifications which would fit me for a more important place in any religious movement. The fact that men and women of every religion are going through a phase of agnosticism offers to me no consolation whatever. If it is true that other religious lights are burning low then surely the moment has come for ours to shine forth and to shew the imperishable nature of its flame. I hope before we separate today we may express our willingness to associate together and particularly do I hope that every man and woman who joins us will do so as [a] form of service - in a spirit of prayer. Thus and thus only can we hope to eliminate from our efforts the elements of rivalry, selfishness, and vanity which would prove destructive to them.

handwritten draft
Conrad collection

WHAT I OWE TO THE SYNAGOGUE

Reception: October 18th 1950

Thanks.

I should like to tell you some part of what I owe to the Liberal Jewish movement, especially as it is expressed in this Synagogue.[1] You must forgive me if I am somewhat autobiographical, but since you have been good enough to invite me this evening as your guest, I think you may want to know a little more about this person whom you are honouring in such a generous way.

When at the beginning of this century, my article on: "The Spiritual Possibilities of Judaism" appeared in the Jewish Quarterly Review, and through the encouragement of my friend and teacher, Dr. Montefiore, I followed it up with questions to the leaders of the community, I learned from the response that it was to be my privilege to help to organise a movement which should gather together the believers in a Judaism which was not static, but which had to grow to meet the spiritual needs of the day.

I came from a home in which Judaism was a reality. I was one of ten children, and we all were taught to order our lives around our religious observances. Our parents did that. My father's public and private life was directly influenced by his interest in Judaism as he conceived it. The accomplishment of his work, his form of entertainment, his personal sacrifices, expressed his faith. My mother supported the same conceptions, but recognised that in the set of Jewish society in which we moved, we were in the minority. My father saw all around him the lax Jews, and considered them dead leaves which would drop off, and the faithful would remain and pass on true religion to the next generations.

I began to worry about the so called dead leaves. Through the children's services held at the New West End Synagogue, I saw how the children of these same people responded to a different presentment of Judaism and rekindled the interest of their parents.

Dr. Montefiore was prepared to stand by my side, as he said, and naturally he became our leader. He and Dr. Israel Abrahams and others helped us through their scholarship and deep personal faith. After the first meeting in February 1902, in the house of my sister, Mrs. Franklin, that sister who from the beginning right up to the present day has helped me with her kindness and sympathy to find the right values in our work and to bring others to the same understanding, we organised the Jewish Religious Union for the Advancement of Liberal Judaism.[2]

I saw all around me how men and women were dropping Judaism because it seemed out of date and did not belong to their lives, and I had been shown by Dr. Montefiore that they had not understood the meaning of their inheritance. They must be called back. The J.R.U. was formed, and we, a handful of men and women, faced and survived the abuse and unkindness of those who thought that we were causing schism when we started Sabbath afternoon services in the Wharncliffe Rooms. My father and other Jewish leaders regarded our efforts at the beginning with benevolent tolerance. So long as we did not interfere with the times of the existing services, we could not do much harm, and might draw in some of the waverers who never attended real services. Moreover, a Jewish movement initiated by a woman could not be of serious importance anyhow.

But people flocked to the services, and gradually it became necessary to explain through a manifesto the meaning of our presentment, how it was derived from the teaching of the prophets and that it was in harmony with the best thought of the age.

I am not going to tell the rest of the story in detail. I will only dwell on the highlights.

The J.R.U. existed for ten years before our Rabbi[3] came. I cannot tell you how often during that period we had solemn meetings to discuss the possibility of going on or the advisability of giving up for the time being. At one moment we thought of joining the Reform Synagogue, but we found that we should have to compromise; our presentment of Judaism would be sacrificed to convenience. By then our great following had dispersed after the fascinating novelty of our services had passed. The Orthodox lay leaders who had helped us at the beginning to arrange supplementary services found their official consciences no longer allowed them to support us. They must forget their personal predilections. We had found it necessary to establish a Synagogue and were worshipping regularly in the small building in Hill Street. Worse and worse, we were looking for our own cemetery and so would, in competition with themselves, soon be able to offer the most acceptable amenities to a large section of Orthodox supporters. Even the generously minded Orthodox Rabbis who had already risked much by cooperating with us withdrew, one by one.

The all-important truth was forcing itself upon our consciousness, that we could not work on a system of compromise and achieve anything worthwhile. During the supremely interesting task of establishing our Synagogue as a symbol of our faith, we had been obliged to decide on the essentials and to discard the unessentials. Such methods would have to be followed now and henceforth.

Then Dr. Montefiore went to the U.S.A. and in consequence of his visit, we were able in 1911 to give our call to Dr. Mattuck. He came to a very small group; he showed us how we could develop and fructify, and, friends, here you are today.

What do I owe to this Synagogue, I as a humble individual?

First, there has been the splendid leadership of Dr. Montefiore with his loving sympathy, his great personal goodness, his scholarship and faith. Then Dr. Mattuck, with his great power of reasoning and brilliant estimate of the worth of human life and thought - his magnetic personality. Then there have been the other leaders and the wonderfully happy companionship with them and my colleagues as a whole. I think now of Mr. Lionel Jacob, Mr. Lindo Henry, Mr. H. R. Lewis, [   ], Mr. Duparc and many others.[4] The Synagogue has formed a glowing background to my life.

We had our adventures. For many years I was Organising Secretary of the J.R.U., during which time we formed our branches. I should like, if you had the patience to listen to me, to tell you how each one came into being in the various parts of London and in the provinces. The history in each case was so different and so interesting. Their dependence at the beginning had to be checked, and as their independence asserted itself, they brought great spiritual strength to our movement. "Don't dissipate your strength," said our dear President. "Consolidate what you have got." This wise advice gradually gave way to the need for spreading our message. Groups were hungry for spiritual food. We had to share our treasures. Today, the Union, far better organised than in my time, is still obliged to act on the call of groups who want to become, not branches any more, but constituents of a Union with a proper constitution, which knows that funds must be continuously and systematically sought. In the old days we worked on a less practical basis, and collected funds in a somewhat jerky manner when the urge to do so could not be ignored. And somehow the help came. The propaganda methods I know were most reprehensible. We are much wiser now. For example, one of our present flourishing Congregations held its first propaganda meeting in the house of a friend. One or two people appeared and our host, a very ardent young man, ran up and down the street to see if he could find anybody. He reappeared his eyes sparkling with a Christopher Columbus look bringing in a couple who if I remember rightly were sincere adherents of an Orthodox Synagogue.

I owe to the Synagogue and its spiritual leaders the help and stimulus of our services, and the opportunities for learning about Judaism. I need the weekly observance and the facilities for study which the Synagogue offers, and I rejoice in them. In the future, the outward features of these services will in all probability change. They may become more aesthetic in character, less conventional and changed in many other ways, but as they stand now, they certainly suit me and attract me. The festivals as they come round are a source of stimulus and joy. I feel the deepest sympathy for my friends who spend the Day of Atonement in the hope that they may be well over it. For myself, I thank God every year that I can join with the crowd in experiencing His presence through the aid of our prayer book and the addresses of our Ministers who help us to push open the doors leading to God.

Yes, I have learned that [   ] guidance is always attainable, but the effort to obtain it must be made by us. We have to work with God and for God in the creation of His Kingdom.

Through the desire to share with others what had been given to me, I asked Dr. Montefiore and Dr. Mattuck to help me to start the World Union For Progressive Judaism. I knew that in every country there were Jews who would join us in our struggle against materialism. There were splendid Liberal organisations much older than ours in Germany and in America. Some of their leaders had already helped us to establish our English Union. Now the time had come for us to work together and to found new congregations in different parts of the world and to strengthen existing ones till we became a great spiritual creative force with world responsibilities.

So we began this international religious work in 1926 through my belonging to this Synagogue and working under our leaders, and under Dr. Mattuck's guidance I have carried on for 25 joyous years.

I had always wished that I could be a Minister.[5] There was a time when for that reason, and that reason alone, I wished I had been a man. For many years, in spite of one or more timid suggestions from our colleagues, the thought of a woman reading or preaching was considered altogether improper. I even remember our dear Dr. Israel Abrahams saying to me on the Eve of a Day of Atonement Service when an important reader had been taken ill: "Why on earth are you not a man?" And we both had to agree that evidently God had not planned that I should take part in leading a service.

In 1915,[6] Dr. Mattuck recommended that I should preach at the L.J.S. That recommendation coming from our leader and probably just at the right moment received almost unanimous approval even from those who a few years earlier thought my appearance on the Synagogue pulpit would have been dangerous. That day in June 1915 on which I spoke on "Kinship with God" was a day of supreme happiness to me. Of course, I wished I could study and be a real Rabbi. If I had gone to Dr. Mattuck then and asked him if he thought I might become a Rabbi, he might have said: "Well, there is nothing really against it," and being a very sagacious man, he would have added: "Don't you think it would be better for you to qualify as a dressmaker?" But I was twenty years too old anyway.

In 1928, I dared to found a Congregation in the West Central district in connection with my Club and Settlement. Those members who formed the nucleus have remained faithful, though after 22 years the Congregation is an independent organisation most of whose members have no connection with the Club. Here I have had the opportunity I longed for in a lay capacity, and my work was recognised when in November 1944, I with a group of others was officially inducted as Lay Minister. I don't know whether the other Lay Ministers felt the same exalted joy over this appointment as I did, but my glow has not cooled off even yet. It is maintained by the conference of Ministers to which I am privileged to belong.

I have done a good deal of social work in my time, and in this work my Synagogue has given me the inspiration I needed. I worked for many years with the Women's Industrial Council and the National Union of Women's [sic?] Workers, as it was then called, and the Anti-Sweating League and the Clubs Industrial Organisation, and I was guided by the teaching that every human being and every small group of people however weak and apparently unimportant had their own dignity and claim to self-fulfilment. With the help of Mrs. Arnold Glover as co-founder and Miss Nellie Levy as secretary, we started the National Organisation of Girls Clubs which has now grown into the magnificent National Council of Girls Clubs and Mixed Clubs, much patronised by royalty and serving masses of young people. From the beginning we felt that since we were certain that the work was necessary, we must give all our poor best and God would make the work bear fruit.

As a Magistrate, especially in the Juvenile Court,[7] I know through my Judaism that since every child was made in God's image, not one could be lost; all could be made to live a happy and useful life, at one with God, if we the responsible people could make society fit for the work of redemption.

Most of my life has been given to the West Central Club and Settlement. I have had the joy of seeing Liberal Judaism at work. Though we have representatives of all kinds of Judaism in the Club, we never force our particular brand; but we teach it by our method of work. Because our Club Leader, Miss Nellie Levy, and our colleagues in the Settlement, Miss [Olga] Lazarus and Miss [Dora] Isaacs, have grown up under the influence of our Synagogue, they have established a strong bracing religious atmosphere. Most of our young people do not attend services, but they have religion in the Club. I doubt whether we should have had much to share with our Club and Settlement friends if we had not had our living Judaism. Club work means sharing the best we know.

About twenty years ago we started a Children's Home and have had much help from our various Synagogues. The children are taught Liberal Judaism.

Preceding and during the war years I worked among German and Austrian refugees and revived many old friendships under new and sad conditions and made many valuable new [   ]. God showed us how to use spiritual strength and the New Liberal Jewish Congregation emerged.

Friends, I am getting old, and I may never have an opportunity again of telling you what I expect for the future of our movement. So you must give me a few more minutes.

I should like, however, to pause for a moment to say that I have had a wonderfully happy life. I share my home with my sister Marian who promotes all my interests and gives me wise and loving guidance. We think and feel together and she loves the Synagogue as much as I do. I have in Miss Lewis a friend who helps to make our home, and who understands the place of Synagogue in our lives. I have a secretary, Miss Jessie Levy, whose mind can comprehend the intricacies of the World Union, and who can carry out the detailed work of my own Congregation. I have my dreams and hopes. One day there will be a West Central Liberal Jewish Synagogue. We have the site, and the months and years go by, and the Ministry of Works keeps busy while it has much to do in refusing our license.

One day, friends, this mother Synagogue of ours and our Union, and the World Union for Progressive Judaism will get nearer to self-fulfilment. Of course, this implies that they will fulfil their main purpose as conceived at present, and then cultivate new hopes and new methods, fresh ideals, for the world is in its making. We have each one of us to be conscious that as members of a Liberal Union we stand for the Liberal presentment of Judaism. It is a definite belief, and while the majority of Jews are alienated from our Synagogue, not always through apathy, but also because the Synagogue to which their fathers were attached has no appeal for them, we have got to show forth by our conduct and by our words that Liberal Judaism is something real in our lives and can transform the lives of all who like ourselves humbly seek truth and love from God. We have to change our own sense of irresponsibility. It is not sufficient that you like our services well enough to attend occasionally, that you are attracted by the social and cultural activities, that our school is useful for your children. You have to understand and transmit the message of Liberal Judaism.

This Union was called into existence to serve the whole community and through the community the whole of mankind. I believe the time will come when all Liberal Jews will recognise the claims of groups in every part of the world. So they will become World Union conscious, and give the material and moral support necessary for the development of our work.

I would urge you to beware of the popular cry - Uniformity. We have a different presentment of Judaism from that of our fellow Jews. We respect every sincere believer. We desire to work with them in all Jewish activities. But we do not want to share their belief. We believe in ours and think in time they will accept it for we hold it to be true. It is different and we thank God for the difference and do not want to spoil our work by an easy-going unthinking tolerance or compromise. Our movement in its early stages was nearly wrecked by compromise. A few years ago we tried to unite all sections of the community in combating the a-religion of Jews by explaining the basic principles which we had in common. We had interesting meetings. We were polite to one another, but we did no good and had to disband. Our message was lost in a sea of amiable vagueness. We must be definite. We must offer our own good tidings to the world. We have accepted our charge. We must try to fulfil it.

It is only thus I think that we can save the drifting away from Judaism by large numbers of Jews that is going on today. They don't want labels, they say. They want freedom of thought. They don't object to intermarriage if it means happiness for the people concerned. I say we have no right to drift or to approve others drifting. That sort of happiness cannot compare with the joy of service to which we are called. Of course, we are free, but it must be the freedom to worship God and do His work, not the freedom to forsake the truth which is our inheritance and to which we must give life by our own devotion. We have to find God anew for ourselves, and we shall find Him to be the God of our father.

I thank you for having listened to me for so long, and for all your kindness to me tonight.

> Archives, Liberal
> Jewish Synagogue, London

[1] Presumably, the Liberal Jewish Synagogue.

[2] In fact, however, the Jewish Religious Union did not declare itself to be an organization specifically committed to the "advancement of Liberal Judaism" until 1909. For a discussion of why this was so, see my Lily Montagu and the Advancement of Liberal Judaism (Lewiston [N.Y.], 1983), Chapter VIII.

[3] Israel Mattuck.

[4] See Annotated List of Proper Names.

[5] There is no evidence to support this claim. Indeed, Lily Montagu opposed early suggestions that women serve as preachers for the J.R.U. It was only with the later support of Israel Mattuck that Montagu gained the confidence to become a religious leader.

⁶See note 2, following text of "Address, Germany, 1930," p. 170.

⁷From 192C-48.

⁸The word here is possibly "links." The "l" is clear as are the "k" and "s" at the end. The two letters in between cannot be ascertained.

UNFINISHED MAN

June 13th, 1925

In Liberal Judaism we stress the thought that Man is unfinished - that in partnership with God, he may, from generation to generation grow in spiritual stature - that with every achievement, at which he arrives, the vision of something greater and better is revealed to him. This conception inflamed my imagination when I was still young, and even today I feel its very great magnetism. I think it <u>must</u> attract all "young" spirits of every age and justify their feeling of youth. We don't want to feel finished - a finished being is no longer alive. So long as we live, we have to contribute to the creation of the world. God has given us our life for this purpose. As little children we asked God, in our prayers, to "make use of us." Today we sing "Creation's Lord, we give Thee thanks that this Thy world is incomplete. Beyond the present sin and shame, wrongs, bitter, cruel, scorching blight, we see the beckoning vision flame, the blessed kingdom of the right.' The externalities in which our faith finds expression, alter from age to age, to fit its changing form - so we progress in science, art and industry and in religious observances. We grope our way along the path of life - God's command encouraging us all the time as it rolls down the ages. "Be thou perfect [   ]." Any rigidity in the expression of our faith spells death.

And yet, in the wonderful ordering of human life, there need be no feeling of instability, of unrest. The religious man is saved from that, inasmuch as he communes with his changeless God. A few weeks ago, while I was considering this subject, I heard Mr. Mattuck give a most helpful sermon upon one aspect of it. He spoke on God's law and man's morals, and showed the intimate relation which must exist between them. He spoke of our need for an absolute standard by which we might correct our own sense of values. He compared our desire for self-expression, considered as an end in itself, with our desire for self-realisation through service. Cynics would tell us that, since our knowledge of the absolute standard is necessarily so very slight, we have no right to assume spiritual progress. But the believer is unperturbed since he knows himself merely as a humble seeker. That humility gives him his religious sense. But in the face of doubt itself he <u>dares</u> to believe - that if he flings himself on God - God Himself will clear his mortal vision and help him to discern the path of progress.

We of this generation, who cannot altogether escape the Pagan cult of modernity for its own sake, have got to strive with all the intensity of which our being is capable, to cleanse our vision in the light of God. It is so easy to vindicate any pleasant point of view by saying that it reveals progress. We want so badly to resist any form of compulsion - we want our individuality to be free and untrammeled; so we may seek to exalt moral licence by calling it freedom; so we may flout the claims of our family, our class, our country, our brotherhood and affirm that we are seeking the complete life for ourselves, and that no other considerations can be allowed to hinder our research. Here we are up against the biggest of life's problems - the one which every man and woman has sooner or later to face. We have to add a little something to the creation of the world or we shall have missed our purpose in life. How can we be sure that the something which we bring - as individuals and as groups, is made of good material? The term "religious exercise" is no longer popular, but I do really believe that the practice alone can help us whatever name we venture to apply to it. We want to get into touch with God - through prayer and through aspiration. Our very desire to attach ourselves, in a sense, gives us the power. Do you remember a beautiful poem (of Longfellow) which tells of a young novice who escapes from the nunnery to serve God in the great world outside?[1] She returns after many years fearing that she will not be re-admitted. She finds that her absence was not even noticed, for in her place, an angel was fulfilling all her tasks and growing into the woman the young girl desired to be. She had thought her environment antagonistic and had turned away from it to seek something better. But all the time she wanted only to serve. She came back to find that God Himself had set her in a large place. The place had really not changed but it could no longer crush her by its limitations for she was sharing it with God now, and it stretched out towards infinity. Yes, the secret would seem to be that we must try to discipline ourselves under the ideal of Truth and Love and Justice, Beauty and Purity. If we [are] aiming towards something which clashes with these conceptions we must draw back. If the minute something which we are bringing to the spiritual treasury of our generation is in harmony with this ideal, surely we may, yes indeed we must, persevere.

May I plead with you to test your own, and as far as you can, other people's ideals by these tests? Will you for example have patience with me, when I venture to say that in my view, the man or woman who speaks or writes or thinks of the next war without a sense of degradation is an irreligious person? Will you understand that I judge this because I believe, as we all do, in the God of Love, Who rules by law and not violence. For me that faith is expressed and only expressed in the active pursuit of the peace ideal - and not only that - but in the active repudiation of the war ideal. And if you sympathise with me in theory but dislike the application of the theory, will you forgive me for suggesting that, in the light of religion we must not set any limits to the possibilities of the human capacity for righteousness? We must trample on expediency and in its place exalt goodness, justice, holiness, indeed all the attributes of God.

A short time ago, a keen thinker and zealous worker gave an address here on the immigrant Jew. He described the formative influences which in his own home helped to make the foreign Jew what he is. He also described his natural gifts, his intelligence and power of endurance, his industry and his devotion to his family. But the lecturer was not blind to the fact that the immigrant's sense of truth is warped and his sense of social obligation has genera[ted] to yield to the gratification of the personal ideal. In the case of the immigrant Jew, it does not need much imagination to see that it is hard for a man who has had to fight hateful injustice and cruelty all his life, by means of his wits - it is hard I say for such a man to idealise society and his own relation to it, or even to believe in the existence of an absolute standard ofrighteousness and truth, which has an undeniable claim on his individual life. But it is not only the immigrant Jew who tests his life's values by expediency. Surely it is not only he, who is not ashamed to put his conduct in different compartments and label some practical and some religious? It is not only he, who is truthful, honourable, just and faithful when it is advantageous, or at any rate, quite <u>safe</u> to be any of these things? Is it too pessimistic to say that a great section of the population today do not consciously consult absolute standards at all? Their instincts are naturally good, partly perhaps because their forbears <u>did</u> discipline themselves under the conception of perfect right, as far as this conception can be understood by imperfect human minds. Of course we can excuse ourselves if we act brutally or dishonourably without knowing anything about God's law of mercy and justice. But we cannot so easily excuse ourselves if knowing this law - and accepting its claims - we set it aside, ignoring it because we find it in our way.

It seems to me that we ought to seek our mission today in proclaiming once again the lessons implied in the Shema, the manifesto of our Brotherhood. In that declaration we formulate our belief in a Universal Omnipresent God, to Whom we must bind ourselves with the bonds of love. This love must be an integral part of our being and express itself in all our human relations. We Liberals go further and say that all our outward religious observances are valued, <u>if</u> or <u>because</u> they strengthen the bonds which bind man to God. They are not ends in themselves but they are useful or useless if they can serve the one great end of religion - the union of man with God. We deplore the religious indifference, in our community; the fact, and it is a fact, that Judaism has over vast sections of our people no claim beyond some unethical racial claim. What can we do to combat this indifference, this apathy? We can do nothing it seems to me, unless we <u>can</u> persuade men and women by example, even more than by precept, that they are not Jews unless they do believe in the absolute standard and try to harmonise their lives with this ideal. Of course we must fall short perpetually but it does make a difference to our attitude if we admit and are influenced by the divine standard. It is only thus that we shall get rid of this miserable juggling with truth which is so popular - this cheap morality, tested by the rule of expediency.

Today we are continually hearing, from people who would be startled if their loyalty to Judaism were suspected - that they felt obliged to perpetrate some little deceit - tell some business or social lie - outwit some objectionable acquaintance. They know their conduct was wrong, but, after all, other people would not have done better. The justification for conduct lies then more in the approval of some of our contemporaries, troubled by religious standards, than in the demands of our God. Do we not ignore what the Lord requires of us while we are so busy in trying to please our fellow-men?

And if we <u>do</u> tighten the bonds of religion, if we <u>do</u> stiffen its demands our lives will not for that reason become sombre and gloomy.

Think of the sense of protection which comes from feeling ourselves encircled by the everlasting arms of God! Think of the joy and enthusiasm, the stimulus and hope which are kindled in our hearts if we know ourselves walking humbly with God - helping Him in the creation of that which is good. Bernard Shaw makes his hero Caesar ally himself with his gods in the creation of new life - turn away from the old and degenerate world, whose trust is in brute force and materialism to the founding of the kingdom which shall endure for ever. And Caesar was a pagan!

The task which I suggest to you is immensely difficult. It needs the best courage and the strongest faith - but it is undoubtedly the task of the Jewish Religious Union of which this Synagogue is the most important branch. In the work of restoring religion to the Jews, and through them of strengthening the influence of the God-idea throughout the world, might we not find great encouragement if we could join with all the other progressive Jewish religious forces in all parts of the world? Even as an international J.R.U. we should tremble before the stupendous greatness of the work before us - But the establishment of such an international force would in itself surely be infinitely valuable. Here certainly, the Theistic Zionist and anti-zionist [could] stand on the same platform and work for the same ends. We should find scope and opportunity for all the propaganda work of which we are capable - scattered in the different countries, united by devotion to the same ideal, we could put up a not unworthy defence against the only dangers of which we have every reason to be mortally afraid - the dangers of indifference and materialism. At this moment, friends, I feel that these dangers are terribly near and hideously threatening. They are made terribly and hideously powerful because of the destructive elements they contain within themselves. They are strengthened from without by that section of anti-semites, who can claim intelligence and some degree of idealism - who, mistaken though they certainly are in their methods, are working for a not unworthy end, in so far as they wish to destroy the disintegrating forces which menace civilisation. If our race, from being a kingdom of priests degenerates into a company of materialists, then they in their fanatic zeal are prepared to destroy us body and soul before we have time to frustrate that which we value most in life.

I ask you to consider the idea of creating an international Jewish Religious Union which shall reveal in their dogma and in their lives the progressive teaching of our faith, for one day before long we may ask our J.R.U. how far we are ready to carry it out. The big Union (of which I am thinking) shall gather together all the spiritual conceptions which are being formulated all over the world, through the inspiration of Judaism. These conceptions, limited and altogether imperfect as they must necessarily be, shall be handed to the generations which shall come after us, together with the consoling hope that "what we choose is what we are, and what we love we yet shall be. The goal may ever shine afar. The will to win it makes us free."

Forgive me if I seem arrogant for daring to put forward in a personal unofficial way a scheme so bold, so vast in scope, so tremendous in possibility. Surely the service of the Highest demands nothing less - surely we dare not limit its development to what we ourselves can do or expect others to do?

Surely as Jews, we are to hitch our waggons to a star and, as Jews, we dare do nothing less.

Archives, Liberal
Jewish Synagogue, London

[1] She is probably referring to his poem "Evangeline."

PEACE, PEACE WHERE THERE IS NO PEACE[1]

Peace Sabbath, L.J.S.,
April 19, 1947

You are called together by the World Union for Progressive Judaism for a Peace Service. This Union exists to make Judaism a strong, vital influence in the lives of our Progressive Congregations throughout the world.

Today, we are trying to dedicate our hearts and minds to the creation of peace, and to combat in a spiritual sense those tendencies which are militating against the achievement of our goal. Some people have hesitated to attend one of these special peace services, because they say there is so little peace in the world. What is the use, they ask, in lauding peace in its various aspects while in nearly every corner of the world there is conflict between individuals, classes, races and nations? I say to you that this is the most potent reason for associating Judaism with the peace idea. It would seem to be the best way to make us live by our faith. Abiding peace is essential if we are to live.

We who are Jews believe in the connection of daily life with our religious ideal. We have to unite faith and practice. We the people of the Shema, who repeat our manifesto at all our services, believe in the Unity of God as revealed in the brotherhood of man. "Mercy and truth are met together, righteousness and peace have kissed one another." (Psalm 85, V.10) "Great Peace have they who love thy law." (Psalm 119, V.165) Here we have the connection between Jewish faith and Jewish practice, the introduction of the God idea into every day life.

We must seek the causes of strife and try to eliminate them. By surrendering ourselves to the guidance of God, we shall create the conditions in which peace will be possible for all men. These tasks involve spiritual and moral considerations which are immensely difficult and complicated and require endless effort. "If" says Dr. Bidder, "our minds are great enough now and our ideals are wise enough, the best men among us may set a new order in the world, which will give it peace, trebling the value of every man's work, and the time for happiness and the speed of discovery and the value of life." This year, next year, in a hundred years, this will be attained. Peace will not be won by conquest or obliteration; it must be invented and constructed and maintained by endless effort, such as is given to the perfection of war. This endless effort can only be stimulated by the challenge of religion; these complicated problems can only be clarified by the light of religion.

The peace conceptions which we are considering have universal application. We are not concerned with the relations between one country and another, nor with treaties which they have made. On the spiritual plane you will find that peace knows no boundaries or artificial limitations. Some of you are thinking that the peace ideal may have a religious basis, but nevertheless, more strife has been created in the name of religion than by any other single cause. In reply, may I suggest that these struggles are caused by lack of real religion. People who quarrel under the banner of religion do not know that their banner is in shreds. Real religion is woven of love, righteousness, justice, peace, and includes the qualities of kindness and understanding. It is presented by those who because they are in touch with God reverence human personality created in His image.

It is often stated that the ideal of human brotherhood was first formulated by the founder of Christianity, that it was he who first preached love and goodwill among all men. No, friends, this is not so. The conception of peace and brotherhood was realised long before the Christian era. When Abraham went forth from his father's house to spread the conception of God's unity in the land of strangers, he felt that through that teaching all mankind would be blessed. The Oneness of God expresses itself in the oneness of men, and in the sanctification of the whole of life. Abraham was the founder of our religion, and from him generation by generation we have been called upon to testify to the fundamental doctrine of God's Unity. Abraham became the friend of God and as such showed gentleness and friendliness towards his nephew Lot, allowing him to settle on the most desirable land while he himself took the less good, in the knowledge that every corner of the earth can be illuminated by the spirit of God.

Carry your thoughts back to a spot in the wilderness where a young man lay with a stone for his pillow. To him in his restless sleep, the sleep of a guilty man, was shown a ladder leading up to God, upon which angels, or as we would say, angelic thoughts ascended and descended. Through that man the whole world was to be blessed. He became a Prince of God, and you and I and all our fellow Jews are that man's descendants. This legend reveals our possible contact with God, our essential faith in the sanctification of ordinary everyday life.

Moses gave us the laws by which Jewish life could be welded together. He showed the connection between spiritual life and human every day practice. He revealed truth as he conceived it, and applied it to all human activities and experiences. He established the kinship between God and man. "Thou shalt be holy, for I the Lord thy God am holy." He applied his spiritual faith to the creation of better health and social and educational conditions. He was no pacifist, but the leader of a warring nation who evolved the ideal of peace as portrayed with unsurpassable beauty by the Hebrew prophets. All nations must live in harmony with one another; indeed, all created beings, even the animals must be able to live together without fear - the wolf and the lamb shall lie down together. Man's talents must be directed to the service and not to the destruction of mankind. The sword must be beaten into the ploughshare.

How can that conception have a realistic bearing on the matter since men and women quarrel without remission? We need weapons, if not for aggression, then for defence. It is possible, because God demands it. He will accept no form of worship by which men seek to cover their lack of unity in life. I could multiply instances from Jewish history and the Bible where, through their religion, men and women were [   ] to seek peace and practice it. But instead, I would ask you to consider now your own responsibility for world peace, you who proclaim yourselves Jews. How can you contribute to its attainment in the name of your religion? As Jews you have a wonderful inheritance of fortitude and the power of forgiveness. Throughout the generations Jews have been hurt and vilified, but they are ready to rise up again as soon as their tormentors cease from their persecution. Ever since the days of Adam and Eve, the Jews have been able to turn their back on the garden of Eden, and travel on in the name of God. When they can find peace in all countries, the world itself will be at peace. Their destinies are interwoven.

How far are you responsible for the failure which in spite of promises and spoken aspirations is depressing us so fearfully at present? Who are our enemies? Have you any? People whom you don't trust or whom you thoroughly dislike. Perhaps they belong to a section against whose characteristics you have always had a prejudice. What can you do about it, you who speak so bitterly about the hatred and prejudices of others? We cannot say we love everybody, even though the Bible tells us to do so. We can even justify our dislike by reminding ourselves of the unlovable and awkward qualities of our neighbours. May I suggest that as we dedicate ourselves today, we ask God to show us how to understand our neighbour and try to give him the opportunity he needs for self-development. He is probably thwarted, and therefore, his point of view is objectionable. Half the world is disagreeable through frustration. Go forth radiating life.

Here I would venture to make a suggestion which is both practical and spiritual. Make a resolution today to work for peace by the instrument of prayer and the effect of prayer on your life. Pray to God every day that peace may come to all men and all countries through the establishment of justice in the world. Some of you may have lost the habit of morning and evening prayers, but I would beg of you to start again quite simply. At the end of the day, lift up in your prayer anyone you have wronged or slighted during the day, or who have wronged or slighted you. Hold them for a moment in God's presence, as it were, until the light that comes from Him and the love which is in Him, folds about both you and them. Let all malice and bitterness and sense of hostility fade from your heart. Pray also for those in positions of great responsibility, for all who have the task of creating relations between the nations, for those who mould public opinion, for the teachers. And persevere in this praying. Do not give it up after a week or two because you see no results. More things are wrought by prayer than this world dreams of. God is waiting for us to do our share that together we may establish peace and truth in the earth.

At this drab period in the history of the world, our suffering is rendered unnecessarily acute because we have so little faith in one another. We don't believe in the goodness of life, we don't trust our fellow men; we don't expect a better time; so we have ceased to work for it. We speak disparagingly about m[a]n's spiritual development.

It is beginning to mean less and less to us. We say with a shrug, what can we expect of human nature? I suggest to you that this point of view is thoroughly unJewish, indeed thoroughly atheistic. God has given us our personality and placed perfectibility in our nature since He has made us in His image. Above all, he seeks our cooperation in the great work of peace, and until we do cooperate with Him, there will be no peace. George Eliot makes Stradivarius say:

> If my hand slacks,
> I should rob God, since He is fullest good,
> Leaving a blank behind instead of violins.
> He could not make Antonio Stradivari's violins
> Without Antonio.[2]

Leslie Weatherhead adds to this: "We can see how true this is by considering for a moment the alternative. If God can and will do things for man which man can do for himself, then it would be a far easier solution to life to leave Him to do it. Why send for a doctor and use his skill? If God wants to heal a person surely He can do it. Why pray for another? If God wants to comfort him surely He can do it. Why take our message across the seas and lose some of our best men and women by tropical disease? Surely if God wants to evangelise the world He can do it. Why go and comfort the broken-hearted when God can do it? We see the fallacy at once. God cannot do it. And when it is not done, people suffer because of that fundamental reason that God, to educate His race, stands by, refusing to interfere even though His restraint means suffering for His children."[3]

Consider yourselves as English men and women upon whom your country depends if she is to exalt herself in righteousness. We have got into the habit of using words without realising their implication. Talking of democracy does not make us democratic. The word cannot make the change in our outlook; we have to change our minds and hearts. It is not easy. We must use our intelligence and make some sacrifices of time and ease. We rejoice in popular franchise. What trouble do we take about using our vote? We like to speak of world citizenship. We have facilities to discover the truth about other countries. Instead, there is a tendency merely to laud them passionately at the expense of our own, and then praise ourselves for being so broadminded. How many of us belong to the United Nations Association and attend its local meetings? Are the young people of today going to repeat the sins we committed which caused the downfall of the League of Nations? We criticised but failed to support the peace methods. You think, and I hope rightly, that you know much better. How are you supporting the United Nations Organisation? All sections of the country must cooperate if a better life is to be secured. Class division and conflict cannot help us. Some of you think that labour is responsible for all that is evil today. Others with no less heat denounce the capitalists. What is the use of this hot air? By your respect for the opinions of others - I don't care for the word tolerance, it gives a suggestion of patronage - you will speed the possibility of universal peace.

Most sections in the country hold that peace can only be fully achieved if all men and women are freed from the fear that homes and food are unobtainable for them. Yet we have still to ask the least fortunate to show patience as they advance towards their equitable state of freedom, for society can only move slowly if she is to be saved from fresh disaster.

> Still in thy right hand carry gentle peace
> To silence envious tongues; be just and fear not,
> Let all the ends thou aimst at be thy country's, thy
>   God's and truth's.
>
>   (Shakespeare)[4]

Under the leadership of Mr. [Israel] Gollancz, you are soon going to discuss practical problems. Don't conclude that my point of view is merely visionary. We must all be visionaries if our practical work is to be effective. We must believe in our Judaism, for that promises the ultimate triumph of righteousness, and peace can only be evolved through righteousness. We say we will not have any more war. If we are to prevent it, we must cease to doubt the other fellow without even understanding him. That is our first responsibility. Then we must believe in peace, and that faith is only possible because God is.

In conclusion, I ask you to think of our fellow Jews in the United States of America, South America, Australia, South Africa, India, Palestine, France, Holland and Great Britain who are celebrating this festival with us, and together ask God to renew our faith in Him and our desire to serve His cause. Then indeed there will be an important group of people who as an essential part of their religion believe in the power of the spirit and therefore will earn the right to say - Peace, peace; for there will be peace.

                                                   Amen.

                                    Archives, Liberal
                                    Jewish Synagogue, London

[1] The title of this sermon is presumably a paraphrase of Jeremiah 6:14 and 8:11: "Peace, peace, when there is no peace."

[2] From Eliot's poem "Stradivarius," frequently quoted by Lily Montagu.

³For a development of this idea, see Weatherhead's Psychology, Religion and Healing (London, 1951).

⁴From Henry VIII, Act 3, Scene 2, lines 445-448.

VIII. RELIGIOUS LEADER

INTRODUCTION

As early as the 1890s, Lily Montagu began to assume a role of religious leadership within the Anglo-Jewish community. At the invitation of Simeon Singer, she led brief worship services for children at the New West End Synagogue (continuing to do so until 1909) and at the West Central Jewish Girls' Club, regularly conducted evening prayer. She also conducted Sabbath and Holy Day services which, by 1913, gained recognition as a separate section of the J.R.U. However, it wasn't until 1918, when she began to preach at the Liberal Jewish Synagogue, and even more so, until the late 1920s when she became lay minister of the newly established West Central Liberal Jewish Congregation that Lily Montagu truly emerged as a religious leader.

The first sermon included in this chapter, delivered at the Reform Temple in Berlin in August, 1928 (the same year in which the West Central Congregation was formally created) stands out as the first sermon given by a woman from a pulpit in Germany. Delivered, in German, during the worship service held in conjunction with the World Union for Progressive Judaism's first International Conference, it testifies to Lily Montagu's recognition as a religious leader even within the World Union. Yet it was in England that Montagu formally assumed a religious leadership role.

By the end of 1943, Israel Mattuck proposed to the J.R.U.'s Executive Committee that qualified lay people be certified to act as ministers were fully trained rabbis not available. Though this recommendation, approved by the

Committee and the J.R.U. Council, was precipitated by the shortage of rabbis that the war-time situation had created, the J.R.U. continued to train lay ministers even after the war had ended. Qualifications for induction included some knowledge of Hebrew, Bible and the principles of Liberal Judaism as well as evidence of the ability to preach and to supervise religious classes. Positions were to be available both to men and women and with the exception of witnessing conversions, lay ministers were entitled to assume all rabbinic functions.

Lily Montagu was formally inducted at the first such ceremony held in November of 1944. One of a handful of inductees, she was asked to speak on her colleagues' behalf, she said because of her age but perhaps too because of her prominence. In her address, she describes religious leadership as a vocation, emerging out of a sense of contact with the living God. Having been called to bring others to the reality that "Judaism is strong enough and wide enough to inspire them and their children forever," she urges her fellow lay ministers to rededicate themselves to their work and to the revivified faith of their fathers.

The texts that follow this address testify to the variety of activities in which Lily Montagu, as a lay minister, was engaged. Included here is a service she apparently created for the blessing of a baby, a memorial address she gave at a home service in memory of her sister, Florence Waley, and an outline of a marriage ceremony that she performed. Included too are prayers written by Montagu, the first, part of a special Service of National Prayer, dated May 24, 1940, the remainder, examples of private prayers that she incorporated into public worship.

Club Letter 111 describes Lily Montagu's 1948 lecture tour of the United States, one of several such tours taken during her lifetime. It reveals the recognition that

Montagu was afforded as a religious organizer and leader even ouside of England. While on tour, she preached in eight synagogues, gave numerous addresses on behalf of the World Union, and spoke on a variety of topics to different groups of people. "Everywhere," she confided, "we discussed the power of personal religion." Her main interest in coming to the United States, it seems, lay not in generating organizational growth, even for the World Union, but in awakening within her listeners a spirit of devotion which she enjoined them to spread throughout the world by individual and collective effort.

Finally, in "Strengthen the Things That Remain," a sermon delivered on the occasion of her eightieth birthday, Lily Montagu clearly discusses the relationship between vision and vocation. Beginning with the faith of her ancestors and her own call to bear witness to God's reality, she describes her assumption of religious leadership as part of God's "special purpose." It is because "I have felt God very near to me," she writes, that "I have been able to work for Judaism." Thanking her congregation for their friendship, faith and loyalty, she reiterates her resolve to revitalize the world by spreading "true religion."

FOR REFORM-SYNAGOGUE, BERLIN[1]

August, 1928

It is a great honour for me to be allowed to speak before this distinguished assembly at the present time, when we are all gathered together to consider the spiritual possibilities of Judaism.

You have told me that you will forgive my many linguistic shortcomings, and I hope you will further make every allowance for an untrained preacher who would find it difficult to address so great an assembly, even in her own tongue.

You are present here as representing an organised religious community, but surely you feel with me that the relation of the individual soul to his God must always be in the foreground [of our thought]. The Psalmist brings to us his message as does the Prophet and the Priest. The relation between the universal man and his God is of such a holy nature that we do not often attempt to deal with it from the pulpit. And yet it is exactly this aspect of religion that is of supreme importance, and we have to consider how we can bring it home to ourselves and which way we want to demonstrate it to those for whom we are a leader. We, with all of our limitations, our hopes and our aims, seek to approach the perfect, infinite God. Without wanting to penetrate into the holy of holies of our co-religionists, we must strive to lead them to this communion with God [as well].

This morning, I want to examine only two aspects of this subject. I would emphasize that personal religion has a definite relation to organised religion and that personal religion must be given attention as it tends to become weakened and eventually ineffective. By "organised religion" I mean the external expression, the public observance by the religious community of the teachings of our faith. We know that it is the fashion today to decry organised religion. It is enough, we are told, for each person to lead a good life: outward observance is of little importance. It is conduct which matters supremely. "Why should a man attend services when he can lead a good life without doing so?" And who, in having this opinion, thinks himself thoroughly modern and we who think differently, old-fashioned. Let us examine the question more closely: Judaism is our religion, and we all want to lead a Jewish life.

The [organised] religious community to which we belong influences our opinions and gives our religion its characteristics: indeed, it makes it possible for it to exist.

As the great theologian, Baron von Hügel, said: Nobody would enjoy the sense of bounding health, racing along some dune on a balmy spring morning, without having eaten a good breakfast beforehand. There is a connection between the lump of camphor in our drawer and the odor which the camphor gives. Religious customs[2] are, in religion, the camphor and the breakfast, and the detached believers would have no camphor scent, no bounding liberty, had there not been from ancient times these concrete, heavy, primitive[3] things. There are certain things that we get out of organised religion which give our personal religion nourishment, but we should not get the influence of the past by a mechanical process; we must strive to make this assimilation ourselves.

If God, as we believe, is the God of life, then we must seek to harmonise our lives with His. The task is a difficult one. If God were not the moving force of all life but static, the approach would be less difficult. God demands partnership from us. We must move forward with Him in the creation of joy and righteousness. On account of modern inquiry, which we have no desire to ignore, our conception of God has somewhat changed. Yet modified or elaborated as it may be, the teaching of our ancestors that God is not only immanent in all things but is also outside of them since they cannot contain His perfection, urges us to seek direct communion with God at all times.

Our fathers taught that righteousness leads to God. If ours is to be a Jewish life, it is not enough to say that theoretically we believe in righteousness, truth, love and beauty. We must actually express these beliefs in our life.

Our fathers laid stress on irreproachable conduct, and it is that emphasis of theirs that directs our thoughts into activity today. It is because of the teaching of God's Unity which has been transmitted to us that we feel that all of life must be consecrated--body, mind and soul, because the Creator is One and indivisible and expresses Himself in His creation.

The conception of the immanence of God, derived from faith in His Unity, has grown stronger with the advance of modern thought. We believe in one moving force through which we and all the universe are created. God is manifested in us and in all our doings.

It is from the past that we have received the doctrine that sin separates us from God, but that we can turn at any moment from our evil doing and by our own efforts again come into contact with the spirit of goodness, which is God. We believe in the oneness of humanity, as all people are children of God. We believe that the spirit that comes from the eternal God is eternal, and that nothing can loosen this tie. We believe that we are a Brotherhood scattered over all of the world, but united and kept alive for the specific purpose of spreading belief in the One God, and this belief is expressed in all of the doctrines that we have inherited.

Now I suggest that these beliefs colour our personal religion. They come to us in the first place through the study of our Bible and our history. But we must work on this inheritance before it can be of any real value to us. As Goethe said, we must "earn it to possess it." It must come to life through the activity of our own spirit. It must be adjusted to the needs of modern thought and modern life. [This process can be greatly facilitated through the observance of] Sabbaths and Holy Days [which] give us the opportunity to commune with God in fellowship. Moreover, the teachings contained in our ceremonials emphasise [the importance of] leading a good life. If they did not do this, they would be completely worthless. There would be no value in worship services and symbols did they not, preserved in their Purity and Beauty, serve as aids to right living.

Personal religion can thus be influenced and nourished through public worship,[4] but this result cannot automatically be achieved. An organised religion is made up of fractions of personal religion and each person must make his own contribution to the spiritual possessions which will form the inheritance for succeeding ages. Organised religion is a necessary background. I repeat, while we are children, our parents fit our lives into this background, but as we grow older, we once again adapt this background for ourselves. And yet there are numbers of people who say that they do not want organised religion.

What happens? I think this happens, and I say it with a full sense of responsibility: in nine out of ten cases, or in ninety-nine cases out of a hundred, ordinary people lose their sense of consecration. They lose their interest in prayer. They lose the consolation and stimulus of religion. They become indifferent and callous, and worship their own whims and fancies, their own material advancement. Of course there are rare souls who still lead the most intensely spiritual lives without any organised help whatever, and I have allowed for them in the one in ten. But I think they are really so rare that they should not be counted as more than one in a hundred.

I also freely admit that there are a number of average people who without any allegiance to the fellowship of Jews retain something of the religious side of life, even while they lose most of it. We would ask ourselves whether we dare say that we or those whom we wish to influence, belong to the class of exceptional souls who can do without any prop whatever. We ask, further, whether we would care to possess or to transmit a feeble, attenuated faith which lacks the blessing of virility which a living Judaism gives.

Now the second problem I want to suggest to you is: what can personal religion, which I prize as the most precious of all things, do for us? We must admit that there is a difference between a life touched by infinity and a life limited by that which is perceived by the senses by facts provable by the human mind. We want the unprovable, we want love, truth and beauty, and we can only find these on the spiritual plane. Personal religion can give us a standard of being. If we can admit nothing better outside ourselves, we do not bother to struggle for the best. Religion urges us to fight evil as contrary to the Divine Law. It urges us to combat abject misery, sin and disease because God is. In His name we can work, as we believe in co-operation with Him, since through Him goodness must ultimately prevail. Personal religion can give us a reason for trying to find a purpose in life. It gives us hope in moments of despair. Since we can actually come in contact with the God of Love, we cannot doubt the existence of love. Religion can consecrate happiness and intensify it. It can give consolation in times of sorrow. It can lift our lives out of dull monotony and give them a touch of poetry and romance. It can combat loneliness and give us increased dignity and self respect. It gives special beauty to family life and also to friendship. It can, in short, make life worthwhile.

Now friends, if we want personal religion I would urge in all sincerity that we must not cut ourselves adrift from organised religion; if we do, we lose the best nourishment we can obtain. Organised religion has a part in the evolution of personal religion. It is the material upon which personal religion is grafted, but the process of grafting must be individual. Every human soul must, through thought, prayer, and study,[5] cultivate his own religion to suit himself. We Jews produce, each for himself, from the stock of Judaism, a living variety of the Jewish religion. We must work out and apply the doctrines which we receive from the past. We can find help if we seek it through prayer, by getting into contact with God. We must study and read, and we must not grudge the time that this study demands. We must try to acquire a religious view of life, to think as well as to pray. We have to ask ourselves whether each situation in which we find ourselves is right, if it is in harmony with Judaism. We have to ask ourselves whether the social conditions under which we live are based on righteousness, whether the pleasures we follow are good, whether our moods are worth bothering about, or whether they are unworthy. We must ask ourselves: are we living as if we were conscious of the presence of God and are we expressing every day something of His love? We must be sure that the books we read or write elevate our life's worth and that our friends have the same endeavour. We must know whether our relations with those whom we employ or with our employers are right, whether our work is honest, whether we are furthering the spiritual interest of our country, and whether we are working for the cause of international peace.

We have to answer all of these questions for ourselves. And many of us have also in our small, inadequate way to seek to persuade others to desire personal religion for themselves. I would venture to suggest that the only hope that we may influence others lies in the strength of our personal religion. If that is real and effective, it may here and there be our lovely privilege to kindle with the light of our enthusiasm some other wavering, seeking soul. Personal religion produces personality. We can only feed our bodies without it, but not the whole being, and personality, which is the whole being, depends on the evolution of religion [to make it strong and effective].[6]

It follows that if we want to live completely, we must have a care to bring our lives into touch with the Divine. In this union we may find the strength that we are seeking; for our eyes will be given the power of true vision. Perhaps too, the hope of immortality comes to us when the spirit finds itself in contact with God through religion, with God, with whom there is no death. Indeed, it was through communion with God that the idea of eternity first came to be felt in the human heart and each of us can attain personal beliefs through prayer and meditation. Then we shall feel that if we love, we can live forever; then we shall know that the search for truth calls us to a service which must endure forever. Thank God that we men and women are allowed the experience of love and the search after truth. Thank God that the only finality is in Himself.

---

[1] Translated from the German by Ellen Umansky, with reference to Lily Montagu's early English draft on which this sermon obviously was based. Major discrepancies between the German and English translations are noted.

[2] The English version says "the institutional" instead of religious customs.

³Though the German explicitly says "primitive," in the English draft Lily Montagu wrote "clumsy."

⁴In the earlier, English draft she wrote "organised religion" instead of "public worship."

⁵The English draft says "practice" instead of "study."

⁶The bracketed words appear in the English draft, but not in the final, German version. They are added here for the sake of clarity.

SERVICE OF INDUCTION FOR LAY MINISTERS
OF THE JEWISH RELIGIOUS UNION

Liberal Jewish Synagogue
November 19, 1944

It is my privilege, due to my age, to speak on behalf of my colleagues and myself.

I thank you, Dr. Mattuck, for the beautiful service which has meant so much to us all, and for the words of hope and encouragement you have addressed to us.

We have all, as you have pointed out, been leading Congregations for some time. We have recognised our privileges and been very thankful for them, even though we were deeply conscious of our inadequcy. We have achieved a little because of the love and confidence which our congregations have give to us in such fill measure. We are grateful for that trust; it has been among our most precious possessions. But we know we have lacked scholarship and the insight and experience which a Rabbi possesses through his training and the opportunities which come from whole time service, which of course has been denied to us. We have acted each according to his capacity, to the best of his ability, and we dare to say that, like you and our other Rabbis, we have experienced the sense of vocation. We could not have done anything as leaders if we had not thought that God was with us, using our imperfect service, and since it was directed towards Him, we were being helped by Him. For myself, and I feel sure my colleagues feel as I do, the experience has been one of great joy. The trust - the holy trust - has been stimulating and helpful.

When I was young, I wished I could believe in reincarnation, because I wanted to come back as a man for the sole purpose of serving as Rabbi of a Liberal Congregation. Today, I am satisfied to be a Lay Minister.

After what you have said, Dr. Mattuck, we feel more desirous than ever to do better. We have discovered for ourselves, and your words have confirmed our conviction that Ministers of religion, lay or ordained, must share every human interest in order that all their congregants should be able to count on their sympathy. Our vision must be wide enough, moreover, to convince our congregants that we are in our humble and very faulty way trying to serve not merely their Synagogue and ours, but the whole of humanity, and they give us the platform for the great service which contains infinite possibilities. We pray to God that we may be more worthy of the privilege.

As Liberal Jews, leading Liberal Jewish Congregations, we are deeply conscious of the fact that our religion is not watered down Orthodoxy, but that we have a constructive religion, a positive message. We think that our form of Judaism is proving itself the Judaism of the future. Our people must assimilate it and live by its teaching. It is the religion taught us by the Hebrew prophets, the religion which is interpreted in life, which progresses from age to age.

If through this ceremony today, we can induce young men and women to join the ranks of Lay Ministers because they want to share our privileges and joys, for they must know these are many, we shall have done something very useful. We need young people who feel as we do the sense of vocation and are eager to spread the message of a living Judaism. We want them to come and qualify for the Lay Ministry, and perhaps in time through their zeal, enthusiasm and hard work, they will feel ready and inclined to work for a Rabbinical diploma.

May I, Dr. Mattuck, thank you again for the help and encouragement you have given us today and during our years of service under your leadership. Whenever we have come to you, we have been helped. You have shown us that no difficulty is insurmountable if we honestly surrender ourselves to the service of God. You have helped us through your keen intellect to unravel some of our thoughts when they have become confused. You have always stimulated us to further effort, and we are deeply thankful, to hear you say today that we have been of a little use to you and our cause.

We should also like to thank Mr. Edgar, Dr. Brasch and Rabbi Kokotek for their unvarying sympathy and encouragement and the practical help they have always been ready to give us. We acknowledge also that without the loyal cooperation of our Officers and Councils, we could not have achieved any good results.

I think our dear Dr. Montefiore, whose influence is always amongst us, would have been pleased to know of this service of induction. He always impressed upon us the need to intensify and extend the work of each of our Congregations. He encouraged us as leaders to give attention to our people whenever they wanted to come to us, and to serve them as well as possible, the interesting ones and those others whom he would have called 'poor blessings.' He urged us to take trouble about our work, to prepare our sermons carefully, and to realise that our very best could never be quite good enough for the Congregations we were trying to lead.

In conclusion, I should like to read a few of the words I wrote as a young girl nearly fifty years ago, in the article which stimulated the formation of the Jewish Religious Union.

If we examine our Judaism with a trusting spirit, we find that it contains the germs of life; we find that its abiding essence is simplicity and truth. At present our thinkers are oppressed by the religious lethargy from which our age is just emerging . . . Let us dare to speak with courage to our brothers and sisters, and to our sons and daughters; let us bid them not hesitate in their search after the divine, because they use data and methods not already tried by their ancestors. Judaism is strong enough and wide enough to inspire them and their children for ever; let us ask them to make progressive demands upon it. Let us tell them indeed that they can only be Jews and Jewesses if they do live up to the ideals of truth and morality expounded by the best teachers of their age.[1]

So today we rededicate ourselves to our work, believing we are trying to live according to the faith of our fathers when we feel ourselves in contact with our God who is unconditioned by time, Who is all-loving and omniscent - God, the Eternal.

Archives, Liberal
Jewish Synagogue, London

[1] From her essay, "The Spiritual Possibilities of Judaism today." <u>Jewish Quarterly Review</u> 11 (January, 1899): 216-231.

SERVICE FOR THE BLESSING OF A BABY

[No date]

I love the Lord, because He hath heard my voice and my supplications. Because He hath inclined His ear unto me, therefore will I call upon Him as long as I live. The cords of death compassed me, and the pains of Sheol get hold upon me: I found trouble and sorrow. Then I called upon the name of the Lord; O Lord, I beseech thee, deliver my soul.

Gracious is the Lord, and righteous; yes, our God is merciful. The Lord preserveth the simple, I was brought low and he saved me. Return unto thy rest, O my soul, for the Lord hath dealt beautifully with thee. For Thou hast delivered my soul from death, mine eyes from tears, and my feet from failing.

I will walk before the Lord in the land of the living. What shall I render unto the Lord for all His benefits towards me? I will offer to Thee the sacrifice of thanksgiving, and will call upon the name of the Lord.

Blessed art Thou, O Lord our God, King of the universe, who bestowest mercies upon thy children.

Blessed art Thou, O Lord our God, King of the Universe, who hast kept us in life, preserved us and enabled us to attain to this occasion.[1]

Lo, children are an heritage of the Lord; and the fruit of the body is His reward.

There is none holy as the Lord; for there is none besides Thee, neither is there any rock like our God.

The Mother Will Say

My God, I turn unto Thee with a deeply grateful heart, for the deliverence which Thou hast wrought for me. By thy help, I have come through a time of great trial, through pain and weakness, unto strength. Thou art our guardian.

Thou enrichest our life with many gifts. Humbly we behold Thy goodness in the gift of children for which we offer the fullest thanks of our hearts. And I beseech Thee, my God, help me and my husband to be worthy of the blessing Thou hast given us in this child, and to show our gratitude to Thee by unwearying efforts to lead him in the way of righteousness and holiness. Teach us so to guide and instruct him that he shall grow up to be loyal to Judaism and a worthy member of the Jewish community.

Minister

Dear God and Father, we entreat Thy fatherly love for this child. May he learn more and more, as he is more able to know, that Thou art ever near him, growing up in Thy presence as in the sunshine, and keeping the sense of it all the days of his life. Open his eyes to see the beauty and wonder of the world about him, so that there may be a perpetual spring of freshness in his heart. Still more, let him learn to love the goodness that is in man and woman. We do not ask that he shall be spared the trials and troubles which no human being may escape. But we humbly beg for him a strength that shall increase with his years, and courage to face and subdue all evil. Grant him above all a loving heart that he may live to do thy will in faithfulness. Cause him whose name shall be [   ][2] to attain unto virtue and knowledge, and to be a blessing. Bless him with long life.

The Shema might be recited.
Priestly Benediction.

Archives, Liberal
Jewish Synagogue, London

[1] Accompanying these two blessings are their Hebrew translations, which Lily Montagu presumably cut out from some book or pamphlet and taped to the page.

²This service was used in the blessing of Raymond Sion David Barda.

[MEMORIAL] ADDRESS GIVEN AT THE HOME SERVICE IN MEMORY OF FLORRY WALEY

January 9th, 1944

AT THE RED LODGE, 51, PALACE COURT W2

Thou shalt show me the path of life. In Thy presence is fulness of joy. At Thy right hand are pleasures for evermore.

They who walk in darkness shall see a great light. They who dwell in the shadow of death, upon them shall the light shine.

Why then, do we mourn?

My dear friend Mr. Montefiore gave some explanation, and I will read you a passage from one of his sermons, on the aspects of Judaism. Here he explains that although we recognise that our dear ones have gone to a better and higher life, we are sad when we remember that we shall not see them again on earth, with all their little peculiarities, which made them so dear to us. These little characteristics might not be good enough for the heavenly life, but they mean a good deal to us who loved them on earth.

I stand as one of the mourners, and I am so glad to be standing among friends. We mourn for Florry Waley and she was my sister, so I feel her going with particular acuteness. We all experience a sense of loss. She was one of a band of six sisters, and her going makes the first break in that band.

She was thoroughly unselfish. Her life had much sorrow as well as a great deal of joy. We think of her energy and her honesty of purpose, and her devotion to duty. She was thoroughly upright and never allowed any quibbling in the work that she had to do. Nothing was second best.

She had a great deal of responsibility in dealing with the education of her children. She was a most loving wife and Mother. I am not however going into these relations. Three of the children are here to testify, and they know and God knows.

We are sorry that Sig is away, but we are sure that he is thinking of us, and he was a good son to my dear sister. How she rejoiced too in her grandchildren!

She did social service all her life, and was specially interested in the establishment of the Jewish Reading Room, situated in the East end. She worked very hard for the Jewish Creshe, and helped to further some educational work among professional people but most of us here know her as a social worker, as treasurer of our Club and Settlement. She was scrupulous in the performance of her duties, and gave meticulous care to every detail. She tried hard to make us a little more business like, and spent many hours in putting some small thing right if it happened to have gone wrong in the financial part of our work.

How she rejoiced in the Jubilee offerings, which might make the "Dream Club" of the future possible. During the sad war years while she was at Woodstock, she made herself loved by her neighbour and gave her service in several branches of work. This we realise from the tribute we have received since the time of her passing.

We mourn for Florry as our sister, Mother, friend and worker. As for her, she did not want to leave. She wanted to see peace and to return to London, and her many interests.

In recent years she shared our holidays, and we were always amazed at her energy. She had such a good memory, and I know that time when we were in Switzerland, she was able to recall the actual names of the places she visited when on her honeymoon with her husband, and she wanted to visit these places as far as her energy would allow. She always enjoyed views, and on holidays looked to have a good view from her window. The distance meant so much to her.

Shall we think of her now, knowing more of love and righteousness because she is nearer to God with whom there is no death? Let us think of her giving and receiving love which is without end, and let us thank God for her life.

Archives, Liberal
Jewish Synagogue, London

OUTLINE - WEDDING CEREMONY[1]

Marriage @ L.J.S.
Sunday, 16th December 1945

Importance of the day.

Keynote - home.

All the sadness in your heart, connected with the past.

You long for the presence of dear ones, and they are not here.

The friends around you cannot make up for those who are absent, but they can bring, as I hope they do, warmth, joy and sympathy.

The friendship of God.

He is so near that as we call upon Him we feel His love reflected in our hearts.

You are about to establish a home.

May I remind you that a Jewish home must be full of peace and aspiration.

Through your companionship you will create your own happiness, and I know enough of you to be aware of your desire for service.

You will have your opportunities to spread the happiness which is in your home, and to make it felt in your little world outside.

Let us join in prayer.

> Archives, Liberal
> Jewish Synagogue, London

[1] For wedding of Elfreida Boehm and Rupert Guterman.

SERVICE OF NATIONAL PRAYER

> Brighton and West Central:
> May 26, 1940

We have come together to obey a call to prayer, because our beloved Sovereign[1] commanded us to regard today as a day of national prayer.[2] Of course - . But what does a day of national prayer really signify? It means, doesn't it, that we as a nation are up against a very real and extremely serious danger, that we are using our mental and physical resources to the utmost, and having done that, we realise that we have not done enough.

As individuals, we know how ready we are to pray when we are in trouble; we turn to God as children go to a loving father. We want security; we want to feel ourselves in His everlasting arms, to take comfort, to collect courage. There is something of the same feeling in our hearts today. We need comfort; we do want to renew our courage; we do want to feel the security of God's loving-kindness towards us. We are terribly anxious about many of our relations and friends. When casualties are reported, these are no longer numbers to us - they represent our own nearest and dearest. We are even to a certain extent worried about our own lives. So we do ask for protection for our beloved, and the power to cast out selfishness and fear from our own hearts. We ask for increased faith in God's love and mercy.

We know that in these times of crises, there is a spirit of adventure and uncertainty produced by the circumstances of the moment. There is a factor in our lives over which we have no control; which indeed is beyond human control altogether. So we come to God. It is because of this element of adventure and risk that our Prime Minister[3] has called this age a sublime age as well as a terrible and dangerous age, in which to live.

Friends, I think the importance of this day will be, in a great measure, lost for us, if we merely unite in prayer for our own safety, the safety of our families and the victory of our country. Of course, it would be absurd to deny that we do passionately and devoutly want these things. If our country were to be conquered, our life would be lost in darkness. Truth, faith, love, righteousness, all would survive, but who can say <u>by</u> <u>whom</u> they would be expressed. Our personal hopes would all be extinguished, because freedom would, for the time being, be lost. We must pray for the triumph of our cause today, and if we add our personal prayers, we believe that we can do so without sin in the sight of God. I believe such prayers are efficacious, because they give us new courage and illumination for the furthering of our purposes, which though barbarous in themselves are directed towards the creation of universal good. We are fighting for freedom and justice and righteousness, and so we are fighting for God. As we pray, we realise God's love and we <u>know</u> that He did not mock us when He gave us the power to love. These boys who are snatched from us must fulfil their lives. Our sorrow and sacrifice and loss are real and overwhelming, but the young lives go to God and we leave them in the light of His light. So we may pray with confidence and hope.

But I say to you that our service today is for a wider and deeper purpose than to offer prayer for personal or national safety, or even for the victory of the allies. We want to realise our own responsibility for war and pledge ourselves to work for an enduring peace as soon as this nightmare is passed. We must lay the foundations for this enduring peace even now. It is not by the methods of war that good will ultimately be evolved. It is too wasteful and destructive a method. It breeds hatred, fear and suspicion between men. It weakens our moral restraint. It produced heroism, but is also sacrifices other human potentiality by robbing us of some of the best young life in our midst. Today, we have to pray for courage and determination to drive out evil from out midst, to frustrate violence through violence. There is no other choice. But, at the same time, we must dedicate ourselves, if we allowed to live, to build up a new Europe on the foundations of justice, love and righteousness. We must try to cast hatred out of our hearts. We were told when the war began that we were not trying to destroy the German people, but only the poisonous doctrine of Nazism. Now that passions are running high, and we are tortured and frightened by the actions of our ruthless enemy, it is difficult to keep our purposes clear. The primitive man, who survives in all of us, is inclined to say: We must give back to the enemy what we get from him. We must not spare him any of the abominations he inflicts on us. We must teach him by the only method he understands, the method of unscrupulous vioelnce, of unlimited cruelty. But friends, I venture to suggest that in so far as we accept Hitler's ruthlessness and imitate it in our desire for revenge, we show ourselves defeated by him. We have bowed before his authority. We must be stern in order to live, but in God's name let us exalt the honour of our country untarnished by human passions, and not degraded by human fears.

Let us pray on this day of national prayer for the revitalisation of our ideals. In the face of the common enemy, we are throwing away all class barriers, and are showing ourselves capable of working as a united people, who are able to put the interests of the whole nation before that of any individual member or group of members. Let us pray that we may be able to preserve this unity even when life becomes normal again, and uphold a new struggle against poverty, ignorance and crime. In this new Europe, there must be positive faith in righteousness and justice. There must be the desire to yield sovereign power for the sake of world peace. There must be the aim so to spiritualise the ideal of patriotism as to bring us back to the teaching of Isaiah, and transform ourselves into a servant people, called to the highest service of God through the service of humanity.

We ask in our anxiety and disappointment why God allows the spirit of evil to triumph. Why does He not interfere to stop the misery and cruelty? Why does He let the innocent suffer? In the light of God's light, as we pray, it comes to us that God sets before men the possibility to combat evil and to exalt goodness, a blessing and a curse, and He says: Choose thou. If God were to act for us, he would have to withdraw the gift of freedom. He has left to us the work of creating good on earth and rejecting evil. He works through law and refuses to intoduce the miracle which would rob us of our confidence and even of our freedom. We have faith in the changeless God, <u>because</u> He rules by law and never withdraws Himself; nor does He make spasmodic revelations. He is there all the time in the midst of the universe, ready to assist us if only we desire Him with our whole hearts and souls. Seek the Lord at all times. Call upon Him while he is near. Let the wicked forsake his sin, and the unrighteous man his thoughts, and let them return to the Lord.

Let us on this day attach ourselves more strongly to God. Let us in prayer realise our kinship. We have the privilege of working for God and with God in the creation of good. Let us become conscious of ourselves created in the image of God.

We pray today with all the members of the nation, to whatever creed they belong. They all cry to the God of the universe. They all desire to receive light on their way. They all are seeking to establish righteousness and justice and aiding peace.

As the Jewish group, we wish to become more Jewish, more alive to the call of God. We want to contribute to the spiritual treasury of the world our specific Jewish teaching. We have something good to say on the sanctity of human life, and on the brotherhood of man. We have been taught that we must be free in order to serve the Highest. We would pass on that teaching and express it with our whole lives. We believe that something of the Spirit of God lives in every man so that he cannot be annihilated. God has put eternity in his heart. So, as we pray, we believe we have 'forever' in which to live and work. With God there is no death.

But we must begin our service at once - today- and use our intelligence and our highest feeling in the serivce of our God. Let us raise our idea of citizenship, and never allow ourselves to sink into indifference or denial. Let us make every effort to realise ourselves fully so as to serve our God more adequately. Though conscious of our weaknesses and imperfections, we throw ourselves on God and listen with all our being to His words whispered in our hearts.

Rest in the Lord. Wait patiently for Him, and He will give you your heart's desire.

Be still and know that I am God.

Because God is, righteousness <u>must</u> triumph. The sadness will last only for the night; joy will come in the morning. There can be no despair or finality.

Be still and know that I am God.

Amen.

Archives, Liberal
Jewish Synagogue, London

[1] George VI.

[2] The day of prayer (May 26, 1940) was the day on which the British Government ordered the evacuation of their expeditionary force from Belgium, as the collapse of Belgium (invaded by Germany two weeks earlier) seemed immanent.

[3] Winston Churchill, who had become Prime Minister on May 10 following the resignation of Neville Chamberlain.

PRAYERS BY L.H.M.

PRAYER FOR THE NEW YEAR

[No date]

Almighty Father,

We thank Thee for having brought us together on this sacred day of rejoicing and high resolve. Let us feel Thy nearness.

As we peer into the New Year, we are faced with deep mystery. What is to happen to each one of us and to our Congregation, we ask? We pray to Thee that we may have no fear, except the fear of disobeying Thy law of righteousness, of withholding love from our fellow beings, the fear of being slack in our work for peace. Oh God, renew our strength and guide us on the way of life.

Our God, we remember especially today the charge given to us by our parents, by those who have passed out of our sight, or by our mothers and fathers who are happily with us today, to seek to build up Thy Kingdom by our faith in Judaism by which we live. Our Father, give us the courage to go forward in hope and steadfastness.

Amen.

PRAYER FOR SERVICE

September 27th, 1941

Almighty Father,

On this Sabbath of Repentance, we, thy children, come unto Thee, sure of Thy nearness, and seeking to renew our hope. We recall the mistakes and disappointments and sorrows of the year that is past, and also its challenge to us to renew our faith and serve Thee with our whole hearts and souls. Oh God, help us to do better and to be better. Teach us to serve, so that we may bring nearer the day when oppression will be overthrown, and the life of the world will be founded on justice and good will.

We think today especially of the children in our midst. Let them enjoy in peace the fulness of life, the realisation of joy, and the revelation of beauty.

We think of the sufferers of all nations and pray that through recognising the reality of Thy presence, we shall all be quickly let out of darkness to light, from doubt to faith, from mistrust to lasting confidence.

Amen.

SPECIAL PRAYER

Youth Service:
April 11th, 1942

Almighty Father,

In these times of difficulty and sadness, we, thy children, would speak our hearts to Thee. We long for the time of peace, based on sincere foundations of justice and of truth. We believe in the possibilities of brotherhood of people putting the interest of the general number before their own personal desires. Since they can attain this condition of thoughtfulness through Judaism, we humbly ask Thee to make thyself more fully realised in our midst. Strengthen our purpose to combat misery, ignorance and sin, and thus show forth our devotion to Thee. In spite of our weaknesses, let us be of use working with Thee in the creation of righteousness and the spread of love.

Renew our hope, quicken our faith, and let us walk with steadfastness in the way of life.

Amen.

ATONEMENT PRAYER

[No Date]

Almighty Father,

We thank Thee for the opportunities this day gives unto us - opportunities of thought and prayer, for self-examination and self-dedication. We humbly ask Thee to help us to feel Thy presence in our midst renewing our hope and our faith.

At this sacred moment, we remember our failings. Against Thee, Thee only have we sinned, but Thou art our Father and knowing our weakness dost guide us to better achievement, if only we surrender ourselves to Thee. Let us then overcome the evil which separates thee from us. May we hear Thy charge to be faithful to the religion of our Fathers. Give us the courage to obey, even if obedience means sacrifice and suffering.

Give us renewed joy, Oh Lord, by endowing us with the power to overcome fear and to create happiness for those we love and for the stranger within our gates. Let us ever seek to serve Thee by serving one another in sincerity and truth, and so bring nearer the time of peace and happiness for all humanity.

Oh God, we thank Thee for life. Let us use it in Thy service.

Amen.

PRAYER FOR CHANUKAH

December 5, 1942

Our Father,

On this festival, we remember with gratitude the heroes of the past, and we give thanks also for the brave men and women of today. Our Father, do Thou let us also serve Thee according to the measure of our strength.

We would try to keep pure and holy the faith for which our fathers struggled and suffered, and through which they triumphed. We know that in some lands people are made to suffer terribly, and even little children are not allowed to be happy. Show us how when we are old enough, we may be of some little use in making the world a little more loving and more just. Let us begin at once to prepare by being gentler and kinder to everybody we meet.

It is sometimes difficult, O Lord, to fight against wrongdoing, to speak the whole truth, to be industrious and earnest in our work, and unselfish and good tempered in our play. Again and again, we try, and again and again we make mistakes. Help us to be faithful, loving and forgiving, and to do what is right even when the right path seems for the moment difficult and uncomfortable.

Give us courage, O Lord, to bear sickness, sorrow and pain whenever they may come to us, courage to try faithfully and hopefully to seek peace and joy for those who are unhappy, to remember Thee at all times, and to call upon Thy name.

Amen.

BRIGHTON 21ST ANNIVERSARY

May 27, 1956

Almighty Father,

We thank Thee for bringing us together on this happy occasion to speak our word to Thee. Our hearts are full of gratitude for having enabled us to worship as a Congregation during the last 21 years. We have come to this

Synagogue in time of joy and in times of sorrow and felt Thy presence in our midst.

We have received fine leadership from men dedicated to work with Thee and for Thee. We think especially in affection and gratitude of our present leader who has worked steadfastly and courageously. We would remember all those who helped to found our Congregation and who subsequently strove for its welfare, and who are no longer with us.

We think also of those who whether as officers or teachers or musicians or as ardent congregants are inspired by the desire to serve our Congregation, and through such service to help the House of Israel, and indeed the whole of mankind.

We turn, O God, to look at the future, and in a humble spirit, we dedicate ourselves anew to Thee. We would ask Thee to bless the children in our midst, so that they may grow up as witnesses of Thy reality. We ask Thee to bless all who worship here, now and in the years to come, so that they may seek and find Thee in this Sanctuary, and may carry from it the inspiration of a living Jewish faith which will express itself in mutual good will and friendliness, in the search after truth, in the practice of justice, in the effort towards righteousness, in reverence for beauty, in work for peace and in the giving of love.

Thus may we approach a little nearer unto Thee in humble and joyful service, O Thou who are the Father of all, the Creator of the Universe. We bless and praise Thy glorious name.

Amen.

RELIGIOUS LEADER   355

[No date]

Our God and Father,
   We thank Thee for letting us come together on this Sabbath morning to speak our word to Thee, our word of gratitude and of supplication.
   Some of us have travelled from far countries so that in fellowship we may consecrate with our prayers this great [World Union] Conference. At this moment, through feeling near to Thee, we feel near to one another in thought and aspiration.
   Let us take the opportunity given to us today and in the days that are to come of seeking truth from Thee, of strengthening our faith, of discovering evidence of Thy love within our souls, and of experiencing friendship and mutual regard for our fellow seekers.
   Oh God, let us leave this holy sanctuary more deeply conscious than ever before of the desire which should fill our hearts to dedicate ourselves to the work which the Conference will imitate. Inspired by the devotion of the past, and by our own communion with Thee in worship, let us make Judaism live for ourselves, our children and indeed for all mankind.
   As we surrender ourselves here and now to Thy guidance, let us in joy and peace and good fellowship witness to the reality of thy holy, loving eternal presence.

                                                        Amen.

PRAYER FOR PEACE CELEBRATION

[No date]

Almighty Father,

As we unite with the Jews of all nations in the search for peace, we humbly ask Thee to make Thyself known to us. Help our country to overcome any desire for self aggrandisement and the fear that other people or nations may us. Let the spirit of understanding and cooperation inspire us. We would dedicate ourselves here and now to the achievement of freedom for ourselves and for the whole of humanity. As witnesses to the reality of Thy being, we would try in our imperfect human way to further the cause of righteousness and justice and truth and let these lead us to abiding peace. We would remove the feeling of hatred and the desire for vengeance from our hearts and recognise one another as Thy children. We thank Thee for life; let us use it in Thy service.

Amen.

SPECIAL PRAYER FOR SERVICE OF INTERCESSION

[No date]

We would speak to Thee, our Father, while our hearts are oppressed with a deep sense of sorrow. Our co-religionists are being treated with unspeakable cruelty, from which death itself is a deliverance. We suffer with and for them, but we are unable to help. We cry unto Thee, How long, Oh Lord, how long? We know that our enemies cannot affect the Jewish spirit, and we ask Thee to give us the courage to be faithful to Judaism, and to do honour to the martyrs among our people by being true to the faith for which they are dying, and to express it in our lives.

In all our afflictions, Thou art afflicted, Oh God of love and peace. We humbly ask Thee to speed the time of abiding peace and may we be among those who will be allowed to work with Thee and for Thee in the deliverance of humanity from oppression and fear. Only in that deliverance can our brotherhood find their salvation.

Amen.

A PRAYER FOR THE UNITED NATIONS

[No date]

Gracious God, who art the Father of all people from everlasting to everlasting; suffer us not to turn aside from Thy guidance in the troublous times that afflict us. Look with compassion upon Thy warring children. Impel us, we pray, to build bridges of understanding across age-old hatreds and seething strife.

Grant renewed strength and insight, O God, to all who seek world peace through the United Nations. Bless those international servants who have dedicated themselves to work in council halls and on far flung missions, that the curse of war shall not again scourge the human race. Spur us to further the efforts of the United Nations to feed the hungry, to clothe the naked, to heal the sick, to teach Thy children everywhere how to live a more abundant life.

Strike from the hearts of us and of all people, we beseech Thee, fear and self-righteousness and pride. Direct us in our own beloved and mighty land to have mercy and to walk humbly before Thee. Show Thy children, while there is yet time, how to live together in hope and peace all their days.

Amen.

Archives, Liberal
Jewish Synagogue, London

CLUB LETTER NO. 111

February 1949

I have already spoken to so many groups about our visit to America (I was accompanied by Miss Marian [Montagu] and Miss Jessie Levy, the Secretary of the World Union for Progressive Judaism), that I hesitate before using a monthly letter for the same purpose. But I have been asked by so many members to write on our visit, that I feel compelled to do so; and I will try to deal with some aspects which may be new to you.

You have all heard that our outward as well as our return voyage was very rough; but happily we were very little inconvenienced. On both boats, the "Parthia", the smaller boat, as well as the "Queen Mary" which is vast in every way, we were impressed by the wonderful organisation. The stewards and staff were responsible for providing the elaborate meals and the smooth running of the library and entertainments as well as having regard to the domestic comfort of every individual passenger. They acted with perfect precision and there seemed no hitch anywhere, and apart from the wonderful discipline which made the smooth organisation possible, there was an element of care and kindness especially noticeable on the smaller boat, which we greatly appreciated. But a strange fact was that, apart from the ship's officers who had special tables in the dining room and conducted the Sunday morning service, we did not see the crew who, under orders, guided the ship safely through troubled waters and to whom, therefore, we were most indebted. Is not that what happens in every day life, the people who do most for us in securing our safe progress through life are generally unrecognised? Think of the people at the docks who unload our food, those who work the transport and the lighting and heating systems, and hundreds of others! We only pay attention to all these essential workers when through a strike or suchlike they cease to function. But this is a depression. We arrived in New York on Sunday evening, November 7th, the passage having taken eight days.

We were the guests of the National Federation of Temple Sisterhoods, and our programme was carefully prepared for us. In this way we visited besides New York, Boston and Cincinnati, Chicago and Philadelphia. I was a delegate of the World Union for Progressive Judaism and in that capacity took part in the conference at Boston of the Union of American Hebrew Congregations to celebrate their 75th anniversary, and of the National Federation of Temple Sisterhoods, attended altogether by 1,500 delegates. These are affiliated organisations, the Union comprising 300 Liberal Synagogues and the Federation having 70,000 members, and include also the National Federation of Temple Youth who held several meetings. On one occasion I was privileged to speak about the World Union, and tried to interest my audience in Judaism as expressed in many lands. I spoke of the dearth of Synagogue buildings in our country and roused sympathy among those who worship in magnificent

Temples with large rooms for social gatherings, for libraries, and schools. I gave the history of the great Progressive Jewish communities in South Africa, Australia, and South America which were all created by the efforts of individual men and women who believed deeply in their faith and were unafraid of the necessity to overcome great difficulties. I told them of the small groups decimated by persecution accompanying the horrors of war. Above all, I pleaded for the congregations in Palestine, Holland, France, India, Uruguay, and other places from which the young people drift into materialism because we cannot give them the form of Judaism they need, as we lack the leaders and material to support a religious revival. The subject arrested the attention of my audience, and I was much moved by the response which I received. For example, when I afterwards attended the Executive Board of the National Federation of Temple Sisterhoods of which I am an honorary member, the Sisterhoods pledged themselves to work for Progressive Judaism in many lands and no longer to be satisfied with the limited interests with which they had so far been concerned.

In connection with a huge meeting on the succeeding day, Dr. [Leo] Baeck addressed the assembly and stressed the great need for personal sacrifice if Judaism was to remain a living influence in our midst. We must give the best of ourselves, our Jewish conscience, to humanity. He described the challenge offered to the two great centres in the U.S.A. and in Palestine to sustain Jewish life throughout the world.

From Boston we went to Cincinnati and stayed in the home of a matriarch of the Jewish religious type.[1] She is 86 years of age but still very active. She is filled with passion for art especially when it portrays subjects of

Jewish interest, ancient illuminated Jewish books, liturgical objects of all kinds, lovely portraits of Jewish leaders, including members of her own family. She is well known throughout the city, and had no difficulty in gathering together to meet us for tea a party of over one hundred people interested in Judaism. In memory of her late husband she caused to be built a magnificent gymnasium in connection with the Hebrew Union College where young men are trained for the Liberal Jewish ministry and women also as teachers. A few Christian students learn Hebrew here and some branches of Jewish theology. We were invited to the midday service in the College after we had toured the splendid library and were much impressed. The students conducted the service. In the evening I addressed the young people and was invited to their common room afterwards and held an informal discussion in a group which reminded us of our Club discussions, especially as the main theme was "How can we best overcome the apathy of young people."

We went from Cincinnati to Chicago where, as in all the other cities we visited, we were shown some of its beautiful features. Chicago is one of the cities on Lake Michigan, and I cannot tell you how beautiful are the parks in which are the great buildings overlooking the lake. These include two fine Universities and the Temple of the Bahai Community who profess to draw the best from all religions and to worship in accordance with this idea.

I had the opportunity to preach in Chicago on Friday evening, on Saturday morning, and on Sunday morning to very large congregations, and we were invariably invited to the homes of the Rabbis and introduced to the leading congregations of their Temples. Everywhere I found the most efficient administration and success in attracting vast numbers to the Temples. As in our London Liberal Congregations the Rabbis are interested in all social questions and are the real leaders of the community. I recognised, as do the Rabbis and lay leaders of the Congregations, that personal religion must be strengthened if the Jews in America are not to lose themselves in the magnificence of the Temples and in the attraction which vast congregations give through their numerical power. Something more vital is needed.

It was my privilege to preach in eight Temples while I was in the U.S.A. and to address groups of many kinds, including Women's Societies and young people's groups. Everywhere we discussed the power of personal religion, and I was able also to dwell on the great potentialities of our World Union.

From Chicago we went to Philadelphia. Before we left Chicago Rabbi Smoller who is the Director of the Chicago Federation of Reform Synagogues and interested in all the Progressive congregations in the city, took us for a drive in those parts of the city where the less prosperous live. We saw the quarters of the coloured people who are overcrowded. They are free to live where they wish in this city, but they prefer mainly to segregate themselves. Although happily they attend the Universities and take part in the civic and social life, I fear they are generally conscious of the prejudice which exists against them. We visited the Jewish market place and saw the small homes and the Jewish people's institute with its fine theatre, library, and gymnasium. We also saw the Italian quarter and certain streets where the derelicts of all communities, representatives of all social classses, mainly the victims of intemperance, have herded themselves together. In Chicago as well as in the other great cities we were sorry to find that the average Jewish man and woman regard politics as outside their responsibility. In one city particularly, we were told on all sides that the mayor and his colleagues were notoriously corrupt, but nobody seemed to feel that his religion should impel him to clear up his local government.

From Chicago we went to Philadelphia where Rabbi [David] Wice, the American Director of the World Union, invited us to his beautiful home, and arranged for us to visit Independence House where the Declaration of Independence was signed, and which houses the great Independence Bell which is beautifully inscribed with the affirmations of faith in liberty. We also saw the people's art school founded by a Jew, and including a Temple containing the symbols of all the great religions, among them a Sefer Torah. I preached and addressed several meetings in Philadelphia and was particularly pleased with a children's congregation. The children, dressed in little robes, conducted the Service; one small boy officiated beautifully at the Kiddush ceremony and showed a proper personal interest in the contents of the Kiddush cup.

From Philadelphia we went to New York where I was able to address a large assembly of women in the assembly room of Temple Emanuel, the largest Temple in the world, and once more had an encouraging response. We had the joy of meeting the members of the Montagu Club in New York[2] at a reception given by one of the Ex-Presidents of the National Federation of Temple Sisterhoods. That meeting expressed friendship in its most beautiful form. The years tolled away and we discovered anew that neither time nor the Atlantic Ocean can separate real friends. A non-member of the Club said it was a "religious" meeting, and that description was not related primarily to the little prayer

I gave by request as I always give after Club affairs, nor was it in any way marred by the joyous, most hilarious character of the gathering. God was in our midst; He had gathered us together.

> Private Collection,
> Hannah Feldman, London

[1] Presumably, Mrs. J. Walter Frieberg

[2] A social organization of past West Central members, inaugurated by Lily Montagu on a visit to New York in 1930. The Club existed for many years, meeting at members' homes, and frequently sending gifts of money as donations to the West Central Club or Synagogue.

STRENGTHEN THE THINGS THAT REMAIN

January 2nd, 1954

SERVICE OF THANKSGIVING FOR LILY MONTAGU'S 80TH BIRTHDAY, LIBERAL JEWISH SYNAGOGUE

I always find the story of Jacob's Ladder, set between heaven and earth, one of the most moving in the Bible. Jacob was guilty of one of the most miserable offences possible to man. For the sake of self-advancement, he had taken advantage of the weakness of his father, the being to whom he owed most in the world, and he had deceived him. He was now full of fear mingled with deep remorse.

He feared the punishment of God, and the vengeance of his brother. He was conscious of painful insecurity, for he knew not what was in store for him. Then in his sleep, which came to him in spite of his fears, because he was young and physically strong, he had the revelation of God's love. The angels, which we may regard as embodied thoughts of love, descended towards him, and aspirations, again embodied as angels, went up to God. He was no longer alone in the struggle for righteousness in which he must engage if he was to have peace of mind, for righteousness and peace are closely connected. The thoughts from God began to influence him. He found that he could cast out his fears and go forward to serve God by being a blessing to all men. After all his meanness and wickedness, he found that God still loved him, and by contact with God he could strengthen his desire to be good, after his sin and his remorse.

We have all of us known disappointment. Perhaps we thought we were settled on a new course of life; perhaps we thought the amenities of our lives were to be increased, possibly by better accommodation or a somewhat larger income, or by some special kindness which had come to us and to which we believed we were entitled. Suddenly everything toppled and we asked ourselves whether life had any meaning for us any longer. Then the wonderful thought came to us to strengthen what remains, and if we are accustomed to communion with God in prayer, we believe that the encouragement comes from God Himself. We must strengthen that which remains of value in our lives after we have fully realised our disappointment. We still possess courage and hope, and perhaps we see a new door opening, even though it seemed that all doors were permanently closed.

I am afraid I am going to be rather autobiograhical in this address, and you must forgive me. You know my age, and I have an idea that you must think that my interest should be weakening in all that remains, for the time must be short. But, friends, this is not so. When my dear parents passed away I felt that my life was just broken and could never be mended again. But I did manage to turn to what remained, and to you, who are mostly some decades younger than I, and who have also endured severe losses, I suggest to you that we should, in the midst of our sorrow, when it comes to us, count up what is left and strengthen it.

My parents left me with an example of unbounded energy. No time could be wasted with impunity, whether by unpunctuality or by procrastination. They had laboured so hard to enforce the strict observance of Judaism in our home in order to enable us to carry on in faith. I believed I could strengthen this legacy of faith by expressing the guiding principles of religious life in new forms suitable to the age in which we live. My parents gave us, by their complete fidelity to their spiritual inheritance, a vision of the essential in life which I was to try to strengthen. They left with us a passion for social service, the material means by which we could live a balanced life of respect for human personality, a love for art and literature, and a steadfast loyalty to friends and family. Above all, they left us with faith in the eternity of love and their own lasting interest in our welfare. These remained and these could be strengthened and life made what it has been, the source of great happiness. May I recommend this attitude towards life after a severe loss. Let us strengthen what remains.

Many of us are inclined to look at the world through dark spectacles. We see the faults of humanity so clearly. Men and women are drifting from bad to worse, and the depressing atheistic words are spoken: "What can you expect from the world today?" We can expect everything, of course, that is good, even though life around us may possess some grim features. Nobody can deny that man is made in God's image, that God has given him a part of His own divine spirit. So we must look for the loveliness in humanity while not ignoring its less good tendencies.

Our moral code may be weakening, but we have still the power to apply, if we will, religion to everyday conduct, and so we can give the necessary authority for moral life. Morality and religion have become separated, but they have not been annihilated. Chaos has resulted because they have been parted. Now this is surely a hopeful challenge. We must begin to exalt the power of religion in its relation to the moral grit which still remains in every man, although it may be so deeply covered that it can hardly be recognised. The good makes the right appeal. The good inclination re-appears, even though we have not yet got rid of the evil inclination, in spite of long centuries of civilisation. If we are to try to combat the bad inclination, as did our fathers, we have once more to re-establish the authority of religion, and we must do this through sincerity and conviction.

One of the evils most often deplored today is the broken home with its dire influences on the children reared in that home. Can we do a little something about it by reintroducing the power of Judaism into the married state? It has been somewhat forgotten. Let us start with the first step.

We see that as a matter of convenience, the number of secular marriages before the Registrar is increasing. Such marriages appear desirable even to those who believe in God. I do not for a moment advocate, as the Israeli government does, that there should be no civil marriages, that all must be religious. Such a policy appears to me profane in its insincerity. But if the God, in whom the young people profess to believe, can be realised as present when invoked at a marriage ceremony, I cannot help thinking that this attitude of mind must increase the solemn and binding nature of the vows that are uttered.

This brings me to ask you to consider our religious work as a whole. You are all interested in the work you, as Jews, have to do in the cause of Judaism. You agree that it is not enough to come to Synagogue more or less regularly, and to be satisfied with our form of service and to go home and criticise or appreciate the sermon, and to give at your family table the reasons for our small attendances, if they are small. There is work to be done to spread the religious faith among the mass of unaffiliated Jews and indeed among the general community.

Once more, I must crave your indulgence for giving you some thoughts derived from my personal experience. I have known times when religious observance was thoroughly popular in our community. It was part of my work among young people to advise them to take an interest in Sabbath services and in consecrating the Sabbath Eve by family prayers. There was a time when this branch of my work had a fair response and we even formed a guild which attracted good numbers of those who valued the Friday evening observance in the home.

All this has changed. The young people do not value institutional religion, and the Sabbath Eve, if it is noticed at all is considered by the majority - there is still a minority of the faithful - as the best evening for going out. But friends, it is for us to strengthen what is left. Probably we have not been convincing enough when we have tried to show that our institutions were preserved as vehicles for moral teaching which is needed today quite as much as yesterday. We find many unaffiliated Jews, but we hardly ever find young people who profess atheism as did the youth of the last generation. There remains among them a real longing for some spiritual help, some security that a better world will come into being. If they can be convinced that the establishment of this world will be the work of God who invites their cooperation, and they will work on the foundations He has laid, there is hope that Judaism will revive.

Again the love of home and family has not diminished. If such love can be consecrated anew by Sabbath Eve celebrations, the well-being of our children may be greatly assisted. If these celebrations can, under modern conditions, not be revived at home, the family unit may be sanctified in the Synagogue on the Sabbath Eve. There is so much to do if we are to bring Judaism into everyday life, and we must start immediately or we shall be too late.

The majority of Jews in this country are, we must confess, Jews only by the accident of birth, except perhaps for three days in the year. But this, at least, is what remains to us and we must strengthen the influence of these days by some kind of following up from the Synagogue into the home and business places, dancing rooms and concert halls. If, as I have asserted, there does remain to us a conscious, or even a subconscious desire for God, the hour has struck for us to gather together whenever we can and to strengthen our precious possession. It can and will find expression. We must dare to face the possibility that a new Judaism will appear, perhaps unlike the old Judaism in form, but, nevertheless, real, sincere and powerful for good.

Since we belong to the community of Liberal Jews who have strengthened for themselves their ancestral faith through study and research, we hold that our Judaism contains eternal truth. We cannot think that it will disappear. New forms and new symbols may be used to sustain and develop the spiritual life of the changing generations, but life in its essence has been given us for ever. We say to ourselves: "Adonai Lee velow erow." The Lord is with me. I shall not fear.

I have been able to work for Judaism because throughout my life I have felt God very near to me, and I have believed that He had a special purpose for me to accomplish. On this important anniversary, I must look forward. God has renewed my strength which I can still use humbly and gratefully in His cause. But I know that my powers will fail before long, although I shall continue as long as I can to strengthen what remains. What then? If I can by that time have strengthened what has so lavishly been given me during these twenty-five years of our Congregational life - your loyalty, your friendship and your faith - then you will feel the strength to go forward without me, clinging to and working for all that is worth preserving in Judaism and feeling that the best is yet to be.[1]

Archives, Liberal
Jewish Synagogue, London

[1] Here again, Lily Montagu uses the words of Robert Browning to express her own thoughts. "The best is yet to be," a line she frequently quoted, is from his poem "Rabbi Ben Ezra."

APPENDIX

INTRODUCTION

The following documents should be of interest to scholars pursuing further study of Lily Montagu's life and work. The first, a letter written to her older brother, Louis, executor of their father's will, testifies to the hostility which Samuel Montagu felt towards Liberal Judaism and more particularly, towards Lily Montagu's involvement on its behalf. Lily Montagu's letter alludes to the stipulation in her father's will that she and Marian be provided with a generous stipend on which to live with the proviso that no inherited funds be used to advance the Liberal Jewish cause. While Lily's offer to refuse her father's legacy was apparently rejected (perhaps her mother and/or her sisters convinced her that it was in her best interest to maintain her generous albeit restricted inheritance), it underscores Montagu's personal commitment to the religious faith by which she lived.

The four letters that follow may never have been read. They were written by Lily Montagu in September 1919, September 1939, December 1939, and June 1940, and placed in envelopes indicating that they were to be opened only after her death. With the exception of the last, these letters were not typed and seem to have been quickly written. While in each case, I have tried to decipher as much of the text as possible, there are several words, particularly names, that I have been unable to identify. Scholars wishing to examine the original texts should refer to my microfilmed collection of Lily Montagu's sermons, letters, and addresses, deposited at the American Jewish Archives in Cincinnati. Though it is unclear why the 1919 letter was written (perhaps the recent death of her mother made Lily Montagu more conscious of her own mortality), the last three were written at the beginning of the Second World War, a time of great insecurity not just in England but in Europe as a whole.

In writing these letters, Montagu followed the example of her parents. During their lifetimes, both wrote letters to be opened after their deaths (also included in my microfilm collection). Again, it is not clear whether these letters were ever read. The Montagu letters reveal the centrality of Liberal Judaism in Lily Montagu's life, identify a number of individuals about whom she cared as well as organizations to which she devoted great effort, and describe those personal possessions that she found most precious. When necessary, I have added, in brackets, a brief description of individuals mentioned (since those appearing only in the appendix are not included in my annotated list). Lily Montagu's relationship with most of these individuals, however, is clearly explained in the texts themselves.

Finally, I have included an outline of Montagu's sermon, "Seeking and Finding," dated January 19, 1963. It is significant for two reasons. First, it is illustrative of the kinds of outlines from which Montagu preached later in her life. As her eyesight began to fail, she gave sermons from "headings" rather than from written texts. Though for a while, she alternated between written texts and "headings," by June of 1962 (as she confided to Bernard Hooker, Rabbi of the North London Progressive Synagogue, in a letter dated June 18 of that year), she was forced to rely on headings alone. Second, "Seeking and Finding" may well have been Lily Montagu's last sermon, had she been

APPENDIX   373

able to deliver it. According to her nephew, Eric Conrad*, it was on Friday evening, January 18, that Lily Montagu fell while climbing a flight of stairs in her home (having previously been downstairs in her library). Lapsing into a coma, she died four days later--exactly one month after celebrating her eighty-ninth birthday. The outline from which "Seeking and Finding" was to be delivered underscores those religious concerns that remained central to Lily Montagu's thought. Included here, as elsewhere, are the relationship between faith and conduct, the importance of opening oneself up to the Divine presence, and the possibility of finding God through prayer.

*in a personal interview at his home in London, July 20, 1977.

CONFIDENTIAL

12 Kensington Palace Gardens W
March 8th, 1911

Dear Louis,

I am sorry to bother you with a long letter but it is unavoidable. I hope you and Gladys[1] are having a nice time. As you are away, you do not realise the pain we are enduring here through the awful publicity of the will in all its details. Our Holy of Holies is being dragged into public - and torn about. We are regarded as types of unfilial duty. Until 3 years ago, my relations with Father were unalloyed - and Marian till the end was his companion and secretary. Of course I have no remorse, and if my time were given me again, I could not act differently - happily, one does not know the pain beforehand. I know Father never foresaw this notoriety; if he had, he would not have acted thus, he would left a letter for ourselves. He never denounced me in public - it was part of his orientation to shield me tenderly from notoriety.

I have never been happy in taking his money because, in spite of all your kind arguments, two facts tormented me:

1. If he had wished me to be relieved of anxiety the work to which I have devoted the last 16 years of my life . . . would not have [been] ignored . . .
2. If it were merely his money, I might not give it to religious causes - you could not say I might not give money from other sources you say "no money gifts at all" - that makes your reading incorrect. Father objected to my taking a prominent part in this work - He knew my private life was not in discordance with his views, but he wished to curtail my power of usefulness in a primitive sense, knowing it was all I cared about. There never was a more loving Father. Therefore he cared enough for his principles to hurt - I am glad he cared so much. That caring, though its expression was so woefully mistaken, I think has helped the world and will live long after differences between liberalism and orthodoxy have vanished. I hope I have inherited a little of that caring, and I am called to put it into the form of a sacrifice.

Now neither you nor I foresaw that the people - with a small and big "I" would believe that I am taking the £300. I have had letters from simple honest good people sympathising - the ordinary "man in the street" who unlike yourself, has not read his own desires into the causes to save me pain - believe that I have to make a financial sacrifice. I am not going to degrade my Father's memory and humiliate myself and insult our cause by standing on public platforms and proclaiming "Father only believed in the power of money in religion - so long as I don't give money, I can enjoy all the things I care for out of his legacy - He did not recognise my influence apart from money." Neither could I remain silent, and act a fraud. Father's daughter must be honest. He wanted her to be happy, and she is going to be - she can't be if she has no peace. I don't know if you understand our relations to our girls[2] - we stand in an exalted position of which we are unworthy. To many we stand for conscience and standard. They have seen the will - and its awful clauses. It goes without saying that they tacitly believe that we have made the sacrifice. Their love and respect has been built up with years - would you wish us to lose that and so spoil all the labour of the past? The girls understand that there is a clear difference in faith. Don't you see if we translate that into terms of money in order to get what we want - we do more harm to them than we have ever done good? Would you exchange Stuart's[3] confidence in you - it may be idealised - for anything in the world? Unmarried women don't lose the mother yearning and aspirations. Now we know full that in a certain direction our power of usefulness will be narrowed. It will be hard to readjust life - but that sacrifice will be as nothing to the alternative I have described. Outside Father's small legacy, we shall be free - we shall be honourable - and so bring honour to his memory instead of the disgrace which comes from even apparent shuffling.

 I am telling my second secretary that she must go after Easter - my brothers will pay my debts till then. I have speculated a little - but my eyes had not been opened. My family will help me to pay for my own secretary and the expenses of her work stationery, etc. through the Club. Beyond that, we will continue to struggle as we have in the past - through our own fault, for Father would have helped if he had been made to understand. One favour I ask - don't let us worry with more explanations and discussion - Mother is worried enough. Help us to convince her that we shall be happy without money. The poor darling has had enough to bear - we ought all to unite in tender care of her.

       Your loving sister,
        (signed) Lily H. Montagu.

I need not write to you separately as Lily has shown me this letter and I agree with all she says. We are sending copies to all the brothers and sisters.
       Yours
        (signed) Marian.

         Private Collection,
         Eric Conrad, London

[1] Louis' wife.

[2] i.e., the members of the West Central Jewish Girl's Club.

[3] Louis' eldest son.

HANDWRITTEN LETTER, TO BE OPENED AFTER HER DEATH

           September 2, 1919

I declare to the world that I die as I have lived, devoted to the teaching of Liberal Judaism and believing that in furthering its cause, however feebly, yet to the best of my ability, I have continued the work so nobly begun by my dear parents. Like them, I have tried to bear witness to the truth as I conceived it.

Liberal Judaism as a living faith has been the main inspiration of my life and work.

Although through misunderstanding I have not been able to assist the Jewish Religion Union (the body who in England are responsible for the advancement of Liberal Judaism) by material gifts, it has been my highest privilege to devote to its service the best work of which I was capable. I ask all those who are in sympathy with my aims and ideals to give to the J.R.U. work and money so far as they are able.

This is the kind of memorial which I should prefer above all others if any kind of memorial is desired by my friends.

I trust that my brothers may make it possible for my dear sister, colleague and friend Marian Montagu and my friend Constance P. Lewis to carry on the work of our Club and district so far as seems right to them.

I leave £10.0.0 to each of my married sisters and to each of my brothers and £5.0.0 to each of my sisters-in-law and brothers-in-law as a symbol of my affection in order that they should buy some personal gift in memory of me.

I leave £5.0.0 to each of my nephews and nieces and in addition £50 to my nephew and godson Philip d'Arcy Hart. I leave £50 to my friend and secretary Vera Robinson and also my named enamel pendant. And ask her to accept these as symbols of affection and deep gratitude.

I leave in affection and confidence £20 to each of the 10 representative members of the W.C. Girls Club Committee who are on the committee at the time of my death and also to Miss E. Bloom, Miss R. Cohen, Miss M. Pyser, [who, like E. Bloom, later served as Honorary Secretary of the Club's Married Member's Guild] Sister Pauline Levy and £10.0.0 to Miss Mathilda Smyte.

I leave such money as is necessary under my sister Marian's direction to maintain Mary Bonin [a member of the Girls' Club] during her training for the singing profession and so fulfil my promise to her, and also to maintain Maurice Isaacs during his training for the navy. I ask my sister Marian to use all small loans which are due and will be paid to her for me as loans to other needy people irrespective of class or faith.

I leave £25.0.0 to my friend and colleague Olga Lazarus as a small mark of affection and deep appreciation and in hope that she may still carry on some part of our work; also my copy of the <u>Synoptic Gospels</u> by C. G. Montefiore also my collection of George Eliot; £10.0.0 to my assistant secretary Miss Stonestreet, £10.0.0 to my kind colleague Miss M. Davis and leave £5.0.0 to Miss R. Ward.

I leave in affection and deep gratitude £10.0.0 to my dear friend and teacher Mr. C. G. Montefiore to spend in any way he may think fit in memory of our long and happy friendship and my copy of Robert Browning's poems, Max Muller's <u>Thoughts on Religion</u>, and Mazzini's <u>Duties of Man</u>. Also £5.0.0 to each of my colleagues Mr. A. Lindo Henry, Mr. Lionel Jacob, Dr. Israel Abrahams, Mr. Max Herz, Mr. Arthur Joseph, Mr. Arthur Levine, Mr. H. R. Lewis, Mr. [   ] P. Jacobs in grateful appreciation of their unfailing sympathy courtesy and encouragement.

I leave £5.0.0 to my friend and colleague Mrs. Arnold Glover in gratitude and appreciation.

I leave £2.0.0 to Miss Emily [   ] and Miss [   ] Green of the National Council of Women as a small token of gratitude and in order that they may each buy some small remembrances of me. I leave £5.0.0 to Rabbi Mattuck in order that he should buy some small remembrance of me as a token of friendship and great regard.

I leave £10.0.0 to each of my friends and colleagues Miss R. Delgado [Honorary Treasurer of the Club], Miss M. Stateham (?), Miss D[   ], Mrs. W. Elkin, as tokens of affection and deep appreciation.

I leave in affection and gratitude £2.0.0 to each of the workers in the W.C. Club not heretofore mentioned including our New Solicitor and our Dentist and to the workers in the N[ational] O[rganisation] [of] G[irls] C[lubs] office who whether voluntarily or professionally have worked with me for more than 2 years in order that they may buy some small personal present in memory of me.

I leave in affection and gratitude £5.0.0 to my friend J. dePass[?] so that she may use it in her work and my copy of Truth in Religion by C. G. Montefiore.

I leave in affection £5 to each of my friends Jane Canor, Alice Joseph, Gertrude Miller, Mrs. G. E. Nathan, Mrs. Arthur Levine, Mrs. Alfred Eichholz, Miss E. Canz [   ] A. M. Bishop, Mrs. George Godwin, J. Ramsey Macdonald, Sir Matthew Nathan and my dear old tutor Thomas Oldfield.

I leave £5.0.0 to Jeannie Smith, Annie Marsch (?), Mary Macdonald, Miss Julie Knoth (?) and [   ] March to whom I owe so much for their unswaying kindness to me.

I leave £10.0.0 to the Women's International League and to the National Council of Women.

I should like all the rest of my money divided in the following proportion: 2/5 to the West Central Girls Club, 1/5 to the Emily Harris Home, 1/5 to the National Organisation of Girls Clubs, 1/10 to the Green Lady Hostel Littlehampton and 1/10 to the Tilford Road Clinic. I leave my [   ] beads to my sister Mrs. Ernest Franklin and my copy of the Bible for Home Reading and 3 other special books she may select.

I leave my etching left me by Mrs. N. L. Cohen to my sister Florry Waley together with 3 books she may select.

I leave any 3 books (which she may select) and my portraits of Mother and Father as young people and Emerson's works to my sister, Ethel d'Arcy Hart.

I leave all my other books and personal possessions ms.s. etc. including the possessions left to me by my dear Mother and not yet realised to be used or disposed of by my sister Marian Montagu and my friend Constance P. Lewis at their absolute discretion. I should like Marian to keep my J.R.U. prayerbook with the illuminated dedication and my special copy of <u>Liberal Judaism and Hellenism</u> with the letter it contains and my water portrait of Mr. Montefiore and [   ] and my [CLL?] sonnets given to me by Simeon Singer. I should like C. P. Lewis to have my [   ] biography of Margaret Macdonald and my little book of life and death.

I make these two beloved friends my sole executors of the whole of my will and know that they have helped me all through my working life they will know best how to help me now.

Should I however survive them I leave to my nephews and nieces including the children of Mr. J. Ramsey McDonald to make what selection of my personal possessions they think fit and the rest to be used or disposed of for the benefit of the W.C. Girls Club and its members.

I leave my share of the Red Lodge to my Sister Marian Montagu.

I plead with all those who work among girls to <u>give</u> themselves unreservedly consulting their own personal aspirations upon deciding the legitimate scope of their labours. After 25 years service, my apprenticeship is only just complete but I have found joy and infinite hope in my work. I leave to my many friends and colleagues whom I have been unable to mention for material benefit a share of the happiness I found in work which is the expression of religious conviction. Believing as I do, in the eternity of life and love, I hope still to assist in the progress of the work which will go from strength to strength changing outwardly with changed conditions but based on sympathy with the individual in giving him the opportunity for self development and social service.

Archives, Liberal
Jewish Synagogue, London

SHORT PAPER WITH OUTLINE OF WHAT I WANT DONE WITH REGARD TO MY WORK IF I PASS AWAY

September 1, 1939

I am sitting at Club and waiting for car.

I want to say that I have been very happy and my life seemed still full of possibilities re[garding] work and I shall be very sorry if I am called away but if I am, I believe I shall be able to work for the Causes [?] from the other side.

I feel most of all my parting from my most beloved sister Marian. I think we shall join one another somewhere and somehow because we love each other so dearly and God could not have given us the power to love like this if it was not a love which should go on forever.

I hope to be with my dear beloved Mother and Father and C. G. M[ontefiore]. Give my special love to E[dyth] Stonestreet of 5 Otis Street, Milton, Mass, U.S.A. Her friendship has meant ever so much to me. I love and admire her and hope that she and her husband and child will realise all that is good. My dear Constance has been wonderful to me always. Her love and devotion have contributed much to my happiness. She will come to me and till she does O[lga] L[azarus] will help[?] her and she will go on being kind to people and forgetting [?] herself.

I love all my sisters most specially [?] and wish I could help [?] them. I have always been very busy and so have not seen them as much as I should have liked but our love has been very real and they have known they could count on me when they particularly needed me.

Re Work and Work Friends   Sept. 2nd

If we have war my work - that which I care for most will stop and if I am spared I shall be too old probably to be any good. But I am talking of "if I go" - The very problem is a nuisance. I am leaving all I can to the work but I don't think I shall have anything to leave. Our house will be needed to pay the Flower Co. over draft [?]. That little business meant so much to us. It was a real excitement. My girls were [?] deeply interested. If even on a small scale you can [help] people run a business and live by it you are contributing something worthwhile.

But I am sorry we have not lived to see the co. flourishing. We have a good traveller and splendid workers and with time it should be a real success.

O. Lazarus is just a marvel as a woman and a worker. But I really don't see our settlement going on when we are gone. My secretary Miss Paynter has done marvels. She will always find work. The district has changed so much that perhaps it will not matter so much and O. L[azarus] will do wonderful work anywhere. She is a religious woman.

Our Club is under the leadership of Nellie [Levy] to whom I owe so much. She is a fine character and wonderful leader and friend. She will keep going until she is too old for club work and then the Club will not be [   ]. I believe it has affected [?] a great deal and I could not begin telling of the multitude of girls whom I love and

APPENDIX 383

revere. But it is about the World Union and the JRU that I worry. Since my dear friend C. G. M[ontefiore] went nobody living understood what these mean to me. My secretary Jessie [Levy] has an idea and she will carry on if she has the chance[?]. She is absolutely reliable and has a fine delicate personality. But the W.U. must have money and someone to push all the time. If it has two field secretaries and money for propaganda, it will be a force in Judaism. The J.R.U. needs [   ] leaders to work under Dr. Mattuck. Then it too has a wonderful future. I want to give up my court work this year anyhow being too old in the eyes of the world. It has been a huge [?] interest. I should like to ask all who love me to help in keeping up the World Union and JRU. I can't see how the W[est] C[entral] [Congregation] will carry on permanently without a minister. Perhaps there could be one for S. London and W[est] C[entral].

Dr. [Rudolph] Brasch will go far I think with N. London. I have been very happy in connection with S. London work and am only sorry I could not help more. In every part of my work I have hosts of dearly beloved friends. I pray to God to bless them all and I thank them. Let them go forward with the work of express[ing] Judaism in all they do.

Archives, Liberal
Jewish Synagogue, London

December, 1939
I am writing this letter as a supplementary document to my will dated and in consultation with my beloved sister Marian with whom I work in the closest possible sympathy. Life being so precarious in the present time we feel that

we must consider in close detail the picture of the activities for which we have for many years been responsible. We are aware that the funds available for maintaining these activities will after our death be very meagre indeed; they have always been inadequate. But we have been very rich in friends. And we rely upon them to make some of our wishes at any rate possible of realisation. Naturally they can do no more than their best.

West Central Day Settlement. Since the foundation of this Settlement it has we think done very valuable work. But we recognise how greatly the district has changed. The Settlement does no longer satisfy one of the primary conditions for fully[?] successful working, i.e., serving the neighborhood. In a large measure our associates come [from] a distance. The upkeep of the building is very difficult. The work which provides opportunity for daily consultation and much visiting requires whole time voluntary service which after our death we do not think will be easily found owing to the severe economic pressure prevailing in modern time. The work has been a source of the greatest happiness to my sister and myself and we have made many close attachments with many of our associates. Even if the building cannot be maintained we hope that the work of our devoted and most able colleagues will be utilised. Miss O[lga] Lazarus after more than 25 years service has through her experience and sympathy made herself invaluable to large numbers of our associates. Through her health work and general services as district worker her services are of such great value that she should be utilised. Miss [Madeleine] Simonis is an admirable organiser of child welfare. Miss [Winifred] Paynter is a splendid settlement organiser. The employment bureau initiated by Miss [Constance] Lewis is as needed in these days of labour exchanges but in every settlement the shred(?) of kindness and understanding our industrial problems is needed and these Miss Lewis has in full measure. We are troubled on account of our tenants. The W. C. Club which is a flourishing organisation brilliantly managed by the Club Leader, Miss N. G. Levy. In these days it matters not whether a club serves the neighbourhood or if its members come from a distance. It is all important that there should be a live and well attended Club and the West Central managed as it is by its ex members [   ] is extraordinarily[?] useful. Its future does not in any way depend on our presence. But if its locale is no longer available an obvious loss will be felt by our community as the Club covers a multitude of useful activities. A solution could only be found if the Club itself could be [   ] so that it might continue to use the premises at 31 Alfred Place and be responsible not only for its present evening activities but also for the Day work at present under the aegis of the Settlement. The W. Central Flower Co. is also housed at the Settlement. Starting as it did as a philanthropic effort it is now a business proposition employing a number of people. It owes its existence in a large measure to my sister. It has gone through a dark period but under the management of Miss L. Fersht[?] it shows now very good promise and expressing as it does a fine spirit of cooperation we believe it should prove a valuable social experiment.

As organising secretary of the J.R.U. and subsequently president I have done much work for the organisation which has served as an inspiring background for all my work. The results have grown out of my work mainly carried on at my office in Alfred Place. One of the constituents of the J.R.U. is the W. C. Liberal Congregation of which I am chairman and lay leader.

I am frankly anxious about its future when I am gone. My friend-secretary Miss J[essie] Levy is able to uphold its organisation as Hon. Sec. and she indicates the surest[?] of affection and consideration which I think essential to the well being of a Congregation. Our membership, though small, is active and interested. Our services are well attended. The influence of the congregation has spread far beyond its membership but as our work is mainly voluntary I have great fears that it cannot be kept up unless the J.R.U. itself can supply the leader. The congregation is self supporting - with its fair size and school, its hall (in the Settlement - once again a generous landlord), its burial arrangements - so long as it has an other[?] minister whether a lay leader or a professional.

The World Union has its offices also at Alfred Place - and like all other activities with which I am connected it cannot afford to live[?] for its founders. But it is the biggest adventure of my life and the one fraught with the greatest possibilities. It was started in order to serve as a wedge against the growing religious apathy and the materialism of the age. Under [?] the inspiring presidency of Mr. C. G. Montefiore and with him Rabbi Mattuck as chairman the start was possible and its work has developed - we have the vision today of a strong international organisation but after 14 years its probation[?] period is not yet fulfilled.

My dear secretary Miss J. Levy shares the vision. She has the qualifications necessary for an organisation[?]. She is methodical, businesslike, very tactful and possesses the [   ] of sympathy and [   ] to a marked degree. She can continue to work if her professional services can be retained and she knows the personnel[?] of our constituents in every country if not personally still by correspondence. The life of the W[orld] U[nion] will be

APPENDIX 387

safe under the present leadership with Miss Levy as secretary but it needs to be upheld by the financial help of those interested in the future of Judaism.

The N[athan] House* has been well started by my sister and myself. While Miss L[yman?] remains matron and it maintains its present advisory committee I see no reason why it should not continue usefully after the war.

New premises must be found in London and the premises of Bethune Rd. disposed of but it is a House of unique characteristics and should have the support of the community. Perhaps it will do this more easily when we have gone.

My Juvenile Court work has been of absorbing interest to me and been much assisted by my secretary. I intended to retire after the war giving the work to younger women[?] for whom it is probably more suitable. I am grateful to all my colleagues for their help and understanding and especially to our learned clerk Mr. B[   ].

I have enumerated the chief activities of my present life. I have intentionally not dwelt on the numerous writings and addresses which I produce regularly nor on the home worship service which I hope will not altogether disappear. Other people will carry on - hopefully in different ways and with greater success.

If as I hope (on selfish grounds) my sister will survive me she could always give information about what I did and what I tried to do - my dear friend Miss C. P. Lewis may also help - my secretary and our Club leader - both the Misses Levy - understand the working of all our schemes[?] and the areas for which we are labouring.

---

*see June, 1940 letter.

I am only writing this letter for those whom it closely concerns and with whom I feel bound to share my hopes and aims[?] and upon whom I rely for their continual work.

I should merely like to thank all my colleagues, the officers of the Settlement and Club and Childrens Home[?] the workers of the F[lower] G[uild], the members of our congregation, the workers of the J.R.U. and W[orld] U[nion] for their friendship and loyal cooperation. They have contributed largely to the great happiness of my life and to its very limited usefulness.

> Archives, Liberal
> Jewish Synagogue, London

> June 15th, 1940

I propose in the light of present insecurity to lay down a few suggestions as to the carrying on of my work if I should no longer be available. I write without any kind of foreboding but just from an objective point of view. I have been extremely happy in my work and shall be sorry to lay it down. But I have a firm belief that what is valuable in the work will survive and that I may possibly be privileged still to help in the life of the Beyond.

My beloved sister Marian will assist those who carry on with all her wisdom and devotion should she survive me. We have worked together and thought together and although I have had the laurels nothing could have been achieved without her loving stimulus and unfailing cooperation.

Constance Lewis has not had the physical strength to do much outside work in recent months but she by her love and sympathy has contributed greatly towards the essential background of Home.

The financial aspect of my work has never been very satisfactory and I fear that my personal finances have become very much worse through war conditions. I trust that if there is any money available which would naturally and legally be reabsorbed in the family estate, the family would see fit in the first place to make the future of my work as secure as possible and that my colleagues who have given me devoted service should be treated as fairly as possible.

My sister and I have recently realised all the stock that was available in order not to cause our family more trouble than is necessary, but this makes our own resources very small.

I appeal nevertheless to my family - who will recognise my desires from the statements in my will - to help as far as they can. They know that we have not spent money in a self-indulgent manner and that during my lifetime I have not made many appeals to them for financial help.

I will now enumerate the branches of work with which I have been closely identified apart from my Magisterial duties which have been of great interest to me but which make no claim on me when I can no longer fulfil them. Also of course my subscriptions to Court and Social Organisations and hospitals lapse.

Maud Nathan Home*. I see no reason why this small Home should not continue to function usefully under its present committee. We owe a great deal, our success indeed, to our Matron. We have subscribed - my sister and I between us fifty pounds a year - The financial position

---

*named in memory of Lily Montagu's cousin, an early J.R.U. sympathizer and sister of Mrs. L. B. Schlesinger, third President of the West Central Club.

of the Home tends to improve with good management. If a good contribution could be given to enable the Home to receive as heretofore the most deserving children regardless of their capacity to pay the future usefulness of the Home would be assured. It has achieved great usefulness through its happy atmosphere and seems to fill a real need in the community.

The West Central Girls Club is now a Central rather than a local club. I hope I may live to see its jubilee. It has worked for 47 years from very small beginnings. Thanks to the leadership of Miss N. Levy who has worked with magnificent devotion it is doing remarkably fine work as an educational and recreational centre. The religious influence direct and indirect is strong. Its chief value lies I think in the personal relations between leader and members, and its democratic management. It offers to working women opportunities for social service and they have risen splendidly to these opportunities. They include some of the finest people I have known in any class of life - the most devoted, especially H[annah] Feldman, D[ora] Isaacs, Lyddie Tasch but there are many others. We have been wonderfully fortunate in our LCC teachers especially Miss [Margaret] King and Miss [Ethel] Poxon and Miss Arbdur and Madame Zoond. To these and their colleagues to our splendid club workers - men and women - I offer my most grateful thanks and my deepest appreciation. I have every expectation that in their hands the Club led by Miss Levy has still a fine future. The financial side gives anxiety on account of the Central and expensive situation and the heavy expenses which are inevitable. The Members shoulder this responsibility as far as they can. We have had a wonderful treasurer in Mrs. Waley. We can only hope that some method of subsidising will be found. I have masses of letters from Members which express the love and devotion of

APPENDIX 391

the girls. I have destroyed a still larger number. The records in the Club files and reports give some idea of the extent of our work but the most important records are in the lives and characters of the members. They have enriched my life immeasurably and I am very grateful.

W. C. Settlement has been a Day Settlement since 1919. We have done some useful work through district visiting and later as a visiting centre for the homes of our Members in many districts. The visiting has been less for purposes of relief than for mutual understanding which has led to the unraveling of personal problems. Health work of all kinds and childrens work have been accomplished chiefly through the splendid initiative and work of Miss O[lga] Lazarus. In recent years Miss Simonis has been an admirable children's worker. The war conditions have made much visiting impossible but our people have approached us, calling by appointment and on their own account. Since the refugee problems have arisen we have done all we could working with all existing organisations and stimulating personal relations which originated in the World Union and found expression in the new liberal Association of the J.R.U.

The Settlement Sec. Miss W[inifred] Paynter has done admirable work for the Refugees and in all our other activities. Our case papers are at the Club and kept as carefully as possible. On financial and personal gounds I do not see how the Settlement can survive us. The district having changed so much I feel that the need for the Settlement tends to disappear. I hope many years of useful work are before my splendid colleagues and I wish I could relieve Miss Lazarus particularly from financial anxiety. Also I am anxious about the future welfare of the Club which is so greatly dependent for its premises and background on the Settlement. I have been too much absorbed in my work to have very close relations with other organisations excepting the Hospitals and health organisations but I hope that a way will be found for using our premises for the <u>district</u> in the daytime leaving the evenings for the use of the Club. If money were available the building would be very useful for social service but we have never been able to get any considerable help from the Jewish community, it always being supposed we could pay for the upkeep of the building as well as all individual cases.

<u>W. Central Flower Co</u>. I have been Chairman and am deeply interested in this venture which has been of use to a large number of girls and women. It owes its success in a great measure to the enthusiasm and patience of my dear sister Marian who is Treasurer of the Company. Had it not been for war conditions we should have paid off the overdraft but this is now a heavy responsibility to meet for which the bank has first claim on the sale of our house. We have very skilled workers and a first class Manager in Miss Fersht[?] who has always been a loyal friend. The Company has given an opportunity to workers to carry on a self managing business under happy conditions. Their material advancement would have been greater had it not been for war conditions but the hours were short, the Jewish workers got an opportunity to keep their religion and we were good tenants for the Settlement. The work was technically good and artistic and compared to other firms our times of slackness were few.

<u>JEWISH RELIGIOUS UNION</u>. This organisation founded through the assistance of my dear friend and leader Mr. Montefiore in 1901 and establishing the Liberal Synagogue in 1911 has been the supreme interest of my life and has inspired all my other activities. Until Mr. Montefiore's death he and I worked together very closely and in warm sympathy. I miss his help more and more. In June 1939 I

APPENDIX   393

was made President in succession to Mr. Montefiore. Thanks
to the leadership of Dr. Mattuck the synagogues in the
Union are of outstanding importance in the community
especially the L.J.S. It has been a joy and privilege to
me to work on its Council and to assist in the services as
occasional lay Preacher and Reader since 1915. I see for
this Synagogue a great future if it can retain its present
three splendid Rabbis and if its spirit can adapt itself to
the changing times. Thanks to Dr. Mattuck's vision we are
just planning a new venture in cooperation with the other
Synagogues of the Community. All institutional religion
must free itself from the fetters of buildings and organisation and give its message to the world. I hope to join a
little in the establishment of the new order when Peace is
attained but we can only do this effectively if we can
spiritualise ourselves and our co-religionists. A great
campaign is necessary. I hope I may live to see its
beginning.

The work of the <u>Society of Jews and Christians</u> is far
too small to do successful work in its present form. I am
deeply interested in its progress as also of the L.J.S. but
these in no way depend on my individual work. My Secretary
Miss J. Levy knows all about the working of the J.R.U. from
the centre and she and my friend Mr. Duparc would continue
the organisation when I am withdrawn. I am anxious about
some of our constituents - the N. London while it has
Dr. Brasch as Minister is <u>safe</u>. It will grow if only a
building can be secured. I was President for many years
but feel <u>now</u> much more assured of its success and influence
in the future as Dr. Brasch is such a deeply religious
organiser.

I am still President of the S. London and thanks to
Mr. Rich's enthusiasm and devotion it has a good future.
If the Congregation will work to multiply itself (and they

could do this) it should be possible to have its own Rabbi and become a <u>strong</u> centre. I have rejoiced in working for this Congregation which owes its life mainly to the "Rich" family.

The Brighton Congregation which I also helped to start should go well if Dr. Lemle can return to lead it; the Liverpool group can manage their own affairs and will do so if they can replace Rabbi Kleinberg with a strong leader who is determined to enlarge his congregation. The Birmingham Congregation is going through an experimental period with its new Rabbi. There should be a good future for a Congregation in the Midlands. The J.R.U. has within it the power to revitalise Judaism throughout the B. Isles. We wait for the united efforts of all liberal believers to secure funds to enable one or two travelling ministers to be appointed. With the help of such men centres could be set up in Leeds, Plymouth - indeed in all parts of the Kingdom and Judaism made a living reality. I wish I could have lived to see this dream realised. But my dear friend and secretary knows what we need and would work for its realisation if she had the opportunity. Miss J[essie] Levy too has brought our W[est] C[entral] Congregation up to its present standard of working efficiency. I should like to have lived to see a Rabbi appointed for W. C. and S. London together. Thanks to Miss Lazarus as leader and to all the other fine workers and especially to Jessie we have a lovely spirit in the congregation. Although Miss N. Levy has tried hard we have not got a large Youth Movement but our influence goes far beyond our Members. It has been a real joy to be lay minister of this W. C. Group and they have been fine and loyal and got over all their prejudices concerning a Woman Leader and with my dear sister's help we <u>have</u> achieved a little. We can never be a large group as we are not <u>local</u> and economic difficulties affect us deeply

APPENDIX   395

but we can and should live and one day have our own
Synagogue. The J.R.U. produced the World Union. I pray
that I may see the time again when an international
organisation can grow and develop. This organisation has
brought me the greatest happiness of my working life. My
dear Mr. Montefiore and Dr. Mattuck have given me all
assistance and encouragement. I have been brought into
contact with religious leaders all over the world
especially in the USA and in Germany and I thank them with
my whole heart for their goodness to me. If only men had
loved their religion enough to make sacrifices on a large
scale the W[orld] Union could have sent its representatives
to help local effort towards religion in every part of the
world. We could have worked through publications and
congregations to apply religion everywhere. But we have
been handicapped by want of money and then by the war
conditions.

I believe we have made a start. I think the idea is
<u>full</u> of infinite possibilities. If those who survive the
war will try to make the W. U. live it <u>will</u> live and
prosper greatly. Miss Levy my secretary has the knowledge
and capacity to do the organising work to which it has been
my privilege to introduce her.

I have given my activities in outline and my hopes for
their perpetuation.

I have had a busy life. My home and the hospitality
it has given have taken all the remnants of my time. I
have had no time for social intercourse or for writing. I
should have liked to see more of my friends but those I
have had have been splendidly faithful and wonderful as
helpers. Among them all I must mention my dear Miss
Stonestreet and send her a special message of love, but
they are so many, and to read more and to write a little.
But I have never been of much use as a writer so my regrets

are just personal. I should probably have been more useful if I had been able to go about more among people - But nobody can get more than a certain limited amount of activity into their lives and I have no reason to complain and every reason to be immensely thankful. My brothers and sisters, especially my sisters, are <u>all</u> very near and very dear to me. I wish I could have shared their lives more closely but they knew they could always count on my love and sympathy - and Constance whose zeal and understanding have been most precious and my beloved Marian have helped to make the Red Lodge mean much to them. I do hope and pray that some of my nieces and nephews will be a little interested in my work and help to make some parts of it live.

This paper is meant just for my immediate family and God bless and help them all.

I want to add a few more words for my dear friend Mrs. A. H. Stonestreet. She was a devoted and wonderful secretary to me but her friendship has been even more precious than her skill. I ask her - while expressing my deepest gratitude to her to see that Mr. Morgenstern and any other American members of the G[overning] Body of the World Union he and she think appropriate should see that part of this paper referring to the W[orld] Union. In case through misfortune some of my family disappears I think my dear Mrs. Stonestreet will find some surviving member to take charge of my letter and help in the carrying out of my wishes. Dr. Mattuck will I am sure do all he can and I desire that he should see this letter if he survives me. I wish I could have written separately to all my many friends but time presses and I don't think I dare spend more in writing. My friends outside and inside the Club, especially Nellie and [   ] Levy, my relatives, the friends of my girlhood and later life all know how much I

APPENDIX

love them and how deeply I am concerned in their well being. I thank them all and ask God to bless them.

June 17, 1940

Archives, Liberal
Jewish Synagogue, London

SEEKING AND FINDING

January 19th, 1963

SEEK YE THE LORD WHILE HE MAY BE FOUND.

CALL UPON HIM WHILE HE IS NEAR.

HOW DO WE SEEK THE LORD?

LET THE WICKED FORSAKE THEIR WAYS.

PRAYER.

LIFE AND RELIGION.

          Personal.
          Marriage.
          Home.
          Business.
          Recreation.
          Observation.

QUAKERS.

JEWISH WAY OF LIFE.

GOD IDEA.

PARTY IN INDUSTRIAL LIFE versus IMPROVEMENT FOR THE GOOD OF ALL.

TENDENCY TOWARDS THE KINGDOM OF GOD, versus LOVE OF POWER FOR ITS OWN SAKE.

COMMUNIST COUNTRIES.

EFFORT OF PRAYER.

> Archives, Liberal
> Jewish Synagogue, London

ANNOTATED LIST OF PROPER NAMES

ABRAHAMS, ISRAEL. 1858-1925. British author and lecturer, Reader in Talmudic and Rabbinic Literature at University of Cambridge, and co-editor, with Claude Montefiore, of the Jewish Quarterly Review from 1889-1908.

ARNOLD, MATTHEW. 1822-1888. British poet and essayist, whose works include Culture and Anarchy (1869) and Literature and Dogma (1873). It was from the latter that Lily Montagu came to view God as "a power not ourselves that makes for righteousness."

BAECK, LEO. 1873-1956. Rabbi and theologian, leader of German Reform Jewry through the Nazi era, Visiting Professor at Hebrew Union College, and elected to the Presidency of the World Union for Progressive Judaism in 1946.

BARNETT [CANON] SAMUEL AUGUSTUS. 1844-1913. English clergyman, social reformer and author. His works include Practicable Socialism (1888) and The Service of God (1897).

BRASCH, RUDOLPH. b. 1912. Rabbi and author, born in Germany, studied at the Hochschule fur die Wissenschaft des Judentums in Berlin, served as rabbi of the North London Synagogue from 1938-48 and became Chief Minister of Temple Emanuel in Sydney, Australia in 1949. He co-authored, with Lily Montagu, A Little Book of Comfort for Jewish People in Times of Sorrow (1947).

BROOKE, STOPFORD AUGUSTUS. 1832-1916. Minister and author. Born in Ireland, educated at Trinity College, Dublin, seceded from Church of England in 1880. He was the author of numerous books on English literature and theology.

BROWNING, ROBERT. 1812-1889. Well-known British poet, frequently quoted by Lily Montagu, whose understanding of "real religion" became Montagu's own, and whose sense of optimism convinced her that "the best is yet to be" (Browning's "Rabbi Ben Ezra").

BURNE-JONES, [SIR] EDWARD. 1833-1898. English painter and decorator.

CARLYLE, THOMAS. 1795-1881. British essayist and author of such works as <u>Sartor Resartus</u> (1883-84), <u>The French Revolution</u> (1837) and <u>Past and Present</u> (1843), whose "gospel of work" helped Lily Montagu forge what she believed to be a necessary connection between religious faith and social service.

CARPENTER, EDWARD. 1844-1929. British essayist and poet. His works include <u>Towards Democracy</u>, <u>Civilisation, Its Causes and Cures</u>, and <u>Days With Walt Whitman</u>.

CHAUCER, GEOFFREY. 1345?-1400. British poet, best known for his long poetical works including <u>Troylus and Cryseyde</u> and the <u>Canterbury Tales</u>.

CONSTABLE, JOHN. 1776-1837. English landscape painter.

CURWEN, [DAME] (ANNE) MAY. 1889-1973. President of the British Council for Aid to Refugees, National General Secretary of the YWCA of Great Britain from 1930-49, and Chairman of the Women's Group on Public Welfare.

DANTE, ALIGHIERI. 1265-1321. Italian author, most famous for his masterpiece, <u>The Divine Comedy</u>, completed just before his death.

DUPARC, JACK ISAAC MICHAEL. 1881-1980. Honorary Secretary of the Jewish Religious Union from 1913 to 1948 and Secretary of the Liberal Jewish Synagogue from 1913 to 1961. Worked in close contact with Lily Montagu until her death in 1963.

EDGAR, LESLIE. 1905-1984. Associate Rabbi of Liberal Jewish Synagogue, 1931-1948, Senior Rabbi, 1948-61. He served as Acting Chairman (1953) and later President, of the Union of Liberal and Progressive Synagogues, was a member of the Executive of the Council of Christians and Jews, and served as Co-Vice Chairman and later Vice-President (1962) of the World Union for Progressive Judaism.

ELIOT, GEORGE. 1819-1880. British poet, essayist and novelist, whose "religion of humanity" led Lily Montagu to believe that one serves God best by serving others.

EMERSON, RALPH WALDO. 1803-1882. American philosopher and poet, best known for his various essays on God, nature, "self-reliance," and culture.

ANNOTATED LIST   401

FILDES, [SIR] LUKE. 1844-1927. English genre and portrait
   painter.

FRANKLIN, HENRIETTA. 1866-1964. Older sister of Lily
   Montagu, founding member of the Jewish Religious Union
   and initiator of its Bible classes in 1905 and the
   Sunday School of the J.R.U.'s West Central Section in
   1915. She was active in the Parents' National
   Educational Union and the National Council of Women,
   and the author of numerous pamphlets and articles on
   education.

FROISSART, JEAN. 1337?-c. 1410. French chronicler, whose
   travel accounts, later translated into English,
   provide a generally faithful account of fourteenth
   century Europe.

GAINSBOROUGH, THOMAS. 1727-1788. British painter, best
   known for his landscapes and portraits.

GOETHE, JOHANN WOLFGANG VON. 1749-1832. German poet,
   dramatist, novelist and scientist, best known for his
   great dramatic poem, Faust.

GLOVER, MRS. ARNOLD. Co-founder, with Lily Montagu, of the
   National Organisation of Girls' Clubs, in 1910.

GOLLANCZ, [SIR] ISRAEL. 1863-1930. English Professor at
   Kings College, London, and scholar in fields of Anglo-
   Saxon and English literature. He took an active
   interest in Anglo-Jewish affairs and was instrumental
   in the founding of the British School of Archeology in
   Jerusalem in 1920.

HENRY, A. LINDO. d. 1920. First Honorary Secretary of the
   J.R.U. In the early years of the J.R.U.'s existence,
   he was responsible for choosing prayers and preachers
   for each worship service.

HUGEL, [BARON] FRIEDRICH VON. 1852-1925. Roman Catholic
   theologian and Baron of the Holy Roman Empire. Born
   in Italy, he moved to England in 1873 and founded the
   London Society for the Study of Religion. His works
   include The Mystical Element of Religion (1908),
   Eternal Life (1912) and The Reality of God (1931).

ISAACS, DORA. A member, later a teacher at the West
   Central Club and active in the National Health
   Insurance Branch of the Union of General and Municipal
   Workers formed at the Club. In 1942, she became
   Settlement Secretary to Lily Montagu. She also served

as Lily Montagu's secretary in her work with the Juvenile Courts, the Married Members' Guild of the West Central Club, and the Maud Nathan Home for Little Children.

JACOB, LIONEL. One of the first members of the J.R.U. Council, Vice-President of the Liberal Jewish Synagogue from 1914-1931 and an early Reader and Preacher at worship services held by the J.R.U.

JAMES, WILLIAM. 1842-1910. American philosopher and Professor of Philosophy at Harvard University. He was best known for his writings on psychology and religion, including The Varieties of Religious Experience, published in 1902.

JOWETT, BENJAMIN. 1817-1893. British educator, Greek scholar, translator, and theologian.

KOKOTEK, JACOB. 1911-1981. Polish-born rabbi, trained at Jewish Theological Seminary in Breslau, member of U.L.P.S. Council and European Board of World Union, Assistant Rabbi of the Liberal Jewish Synagogue from 1941-45 and later, rabbi of the Liberal Jewish congregation in Liverpool and the New Liberal Jewish Congregation, London.

LAZARUS, OLGA. d. 1962. Employed as Settlement Worker for the West Central Club from 1913-62 and active in almost all of the Club's activities, including the Club Branch of the Hospital Savings Association which she organized in 1954. In 1937, she published Liberal Judaism Its Standpoint, dedicated to her mother and Lily Montagu, the two people who she said had influenced her life the most.

LEVY, JESSIE. d. 1979. Became Lily Montagu's personal secretary in 1937, also served as secretary of the World Union and the West Central Liberal Jewish Congregation, becoming President of the Congregation after Lily Montagu's death.

LEVY, NELLIE G. Leader and Organizer of the West Central Club from 1924 through her semi-retirement in 1956. She later served as Honorary Secretary and Vice-President of the Club and helped write The West Central Story and Its Founders, chronicling the history of the Club from 1893 through 1968.

LEWIS, CONSTANCE P. d. 1952. Associated with the West Central Club from its earliest years and initiator of its Flower Guild and Employment Bureau, she shared a home with Lily and Marian Montagu at the "Red Lodge" from 1918 until her death in 1952.

LEWIS, H.R. A member of the initial Leadership Committee of the Jewish Religious Union, formed in February 1902, becoming Treasurer of the Union in 1909.

LONGFELLOW, HENRY WADSWORTH. 1807-82. American poet and author of the prose romance "Hyperion," his works include "Evangeline," "Hiawatha," and "Paul Revere's Ride."

MAETERLINK, MAURICE. 1862-1949. Belgian essayist and poetic-dramatist, and recipient of the Nobel Prize for Literature in 1911.

MARCUS AURELIUS ANTONINUS. 121-180. Roman emperor and Stoic philosopher. Author of the Meditations.

MATTUCK, ISRAEL. 1883-1954. Lithuanian born, American Reform rabbi, who served as Minister of the Liberal Jewish Synagogue from 1912-48. He was deputy President of the U.L.P.S. from 1947-54, Chairman of the Executive Committee of the World Union from 1926-54 and Co-Chairman, and later Vice-President, of the London Society of Christians and Jews.

MAZZINI, JOSEPH. 1805-1872. Italian patriot and author, who lived most of his life in London and whose works, especially The Duties of Man, inspired Lily Montagu to try to revivify the spritual life of the Anglo-Jewish community through what Mazzini identified as "associated labor."

MILLAIS, [SIR] JOHN EVERETT. 1829-1896. English painter and initiator, along with William Holman Hunt and Dante Gabriel Rossetti, of the so-called "pre-Raphaelite" movement.

MONTAGU, MARIAN. 1868-1965. Constant companion, supporter, and friend to her younger sister, Lily. Gaining recognition as co-founder of the West Central Club, she devoted her life to helping her sister advance the Liberal Jewish "cause."

MONTEFIORE, CLAUDE GOLDSMID. 1858-1938. Theologian and leader of the Liberal Jewish movement in England. A prolific writer and co-editor of the Jewish Quarterly Review, he helped convince Lily Montagu, through his books and essays, that Judaism could be a "living religion." She later convinced him to become President of the J.R.U. and of the World Union for Progressive Judaism, which he helped found with her.

MORLAND, GEORGE. 1763-1804. English genre, animal and landscape painter.

MORLEY, JOHN, first Viscount Morley of Blackburn. 1838-1923. British essayist and editor whose major works include studies of Edmund Burke, Voltaire, Rousseau, Cromwell and Gladstone.

PATERSON, [SIR] ALEXANDER. 1884-1947. British Commissioner of Prisons and Director of Convict Prisons from 1922-47, and author of Across The Bridges (1911) and Paterson on Prisons (published posthumously in 1950).

PAYNTER, WINIFRED. d. 1941. Secretary of the West Central Settlement, she died in the bombing of the Club, Settlement and Synagogue in May, 1941.

RAMSAY, ALLAN. 1686-1758. Scottish poet, whose main work, the pastoral drama "The Gentle Shepherd," was published in 1725.

ROSEBERY, ARCHIBALD PHILIP PRIMORE, fifth earl of. 1847-1929. British statesman, Foreign Secretary under Gladstone, Prime Minster of England from 1894-5 and author of several historical studies.

RUSKIN, JOHN. 1819-1900. British essayist and art critic, whose most popular work, Sesame and Lilies (1865) helped Lily Montagu establish her criteria for "great books."

SAMUEL, HERBERT LOUIS, first Viscount. 1870-1963. British statesman and philosopher. He was the first professing Jew to be a member of the British cabinet, from 1920-25 served as the First High Commissioner for Palestine, and was a member of the House of Commons and the House of Lords. He was Lily Montagu's first cousin, the son of Edwin Samuel, Samuel Montagu's eldest brother.

SCHREINER, OLIVE. 1855-1920. British novelist, born in Cape Colony and moved to England in 1881 where she published a series of novels including her most successful novel, The Story of an African Farm (published under the pseudonym "Ralph Irons").

SHAFTESBURY, ANTHONY ASHLEY COOPER, seventh Earl of. 1801-85. Philanthropist, active in several movements aimed at protecting the working classes.

SHAKESPEARE, WILLIAM. 1564-1616. English playwright and poet. Lily Montagu often quoted from his dramatic works and sonnets.

SHAW, GEORGE BERNARD. 1856-1950. Born in Dublin, moved to London in 1876, he was best known as a playwright and political essayist. Though Shaw, like Lily Montagu, was involved in the Socialist Fabian Society, it was to his plays, and not to his political and economic tracts, that Lily Montagu occasionally referred.

SIMON, [SIR] LEON. 1881-1965. British civil servant, English Zionist leader, author of several essays of Zionism and Hebrew Culture, and translator and biographer of Ahad Ha'Am.

SINGER, SIMEON. 1848-1906. Preacher, author and communal worker. He served as Minister of the (Orthodox) New West End Synagogue in London, the synagogue to which Lily Montagu belonged as a child, and was an early supporter of the Jewish Religious Union. His publications include numerous editions of the <u>Authorised Daily Prayer Book</u> and <u>Early English Versions of the Jewish Liturgy</u> (published in 1899).

SMOLLER, PHINEAS. 1903-1952. Russian born, American Reform rabbi, treasurer of the Central Conference of American Rabbis, Director of the Chicago Federation of Reform Synagogues in the 1940s and later, Director of the western region of the Union of American Hebrew Congregations in Los Angeles.

SPIELMAN(N), [SIR] ISIDORE. 1854-1925. Founder and Director of the British Board of Trade's art exhibitions, organizer of the Anglo-Jewish Historical Exhibition in 1887, President of the Jewish Historical Society of England from 1902-04, and the first Treasurer of the Jewish Religious Union.

STANLEY, MAUDE ALETHEA. 1883-1915. Founder of first British Club for Working Girls (1880) and the London Girls' Club Union (1883). Her book, <u>Clubs for Working Girls</u>, was published in 1890.

TENNYSON, ALFRED, LORD. 1809-1892. One of the most well-known poets of the nineteenth century and author of such works as "In Memorium," "Locksley Hall," "Idylls of the King," and "Enoch Arden." He was appointed poet laureate following the publication of "In Memorium" in 1850.

TOLSTOY [COUNT] LEO. 1828-1910. Russian author and one of the great European writers of the nineteenth century, whose major novels include War and Peace (1865-72) and Anna Karenina (1875-76).

WALEY, FLORENCE (FLORRY). 1867?-1944. Older sister of Lily Montagu. Secretary and Treasurer of the West Central Club, she was appointed Chairman of the Club's Finance Committee, formed in 1924.

WATTS, GEORGE FREDERIC. 1817-1904. English painter and sculptor, best known for his decorative work, portraits and allegorical paintings.

WEATHERHEAD, LESLIE DIXON. 1893-1976. Methodist minister and author of numerous books on psychology and religion, including Psychology, Religion and Healing, published in 1951.

WICE, DAVID H. b. 1908. American Reform rabbi, American Director of the World Union for Progressive Judaism from 1944-55 and later, serving as its President.

WORDSWORTH, WILLIAM. 1770-1850. British Romantic poet and poet laureate from 1843-50.

ZANGWILL, ISRAEL. 1864-1926. Anglo-Jewish novelist, essayist and playwright, whose works include Children of the Ghetto (1892). He was an active suffragist and pacifist and founder of the Jewish Territorial Organization, aimed at finding a national home for the Jewish people.

INDEX

Abrahams, Israel, 297, 301, 378
Adam and Eve, see Garden of Eden
After life, see Immortality
Anti-Sweating League, 302
Arnold, Matthew, 104, 272
Art, 23, 41-46, 47, 62, 87, 133
Assimilation, 5, 140
Atheism, 28, 196-197
Atom Bomb, 49-50, 174
Baeck, Leo, 360
Balfour Declaration, 95-96, 145-148; see also Zionism
Bar mitzvah, 218
Bible, 9, 23, 39, 57, 68, 98, 132, 204, 211, 216, 330
British Club movement, see Club movement, British
Browning, Robert, 3, 14, 21-23, 37-38, 378
Burne-Jones, Edward, 41, 44
Capital punishment, 7, 107-108
Carlyle, Thomas, 11-12, 21-23, 33-35, 38
Children, 83-84, 138-139, 143-144, 155-156, 160, 176-177, 291, 303, 339-340
Children's services, 294, 297, 325
Chosen people, Jews as, see Mission, Jewish
Circumcision, 218
Club letters, 226
Club movement, British, 225, 240
Clubs Industrial Organization, 302
Cold War, 85
Communism, 197-198

Conduct, Personal, influenced by religion, 24, 26-30, 49-51, 52, 58, 61, 62, 103-111, 179-182, 367
Confirmation, 218
Conrad, Eric, 9, 16
Conrad, Sheila, 16
Converts, see Proselytes
Curwen, May, 181
Customs, Religious, see Religious customs
Dietary laws, see Kashrut
Doubts, Religious, 200-206; see also Faith
Drayton, Rosina, 9
Eden, Garden of, see Garden of Eden
Edgar, Leslie, 12, 223
Education, 89, 291
Education of Lily Montagu, see Montagu, Lily, Education of
Education, Religious, 163, 169
Elijah (Biblical prophet), 276
Eliot, George, 21-23, 35-37, 38, 41, 187, 378
Emancipation of the Jews, 140
Eternity, see Immortality
Evening School movement, 240
Evil, 107-108, 115, 347-348
Exodus (Event), 91
Faith, 58, 82, 93, 96-98, 101, 103, 105, 118, 189, 205, 227-228
Faith in humanity, 63-68
Family relations, 258-259, 260-263
Fear, 273-277
Feminism, 6-7, 13, 156, 158, 168, 171

Festivals, Jewish, see Holidays, Jewish
Franklin, Henrietta, 157, 286, 287, 297, 379
Friendship, 91, 255-257, 280-281
Garden of Eden, 47-51
Ghetto life, 139-140
Glover, Arnold (Mrs.), 303, 378
God,
   Fear of, 245-253
   "idea," 94, 114, 282-283, 313
   Lily Montagu's view of, 5, 246
   Man's relationship with, 111-119, 328-334
   of the Old Testament, 97-98, 116
   Unity of, 316-317, 330
God Revealed, 9
Gollancz, Israel, 322
Halachah, see Law, Jewish
Hart, Ethel d'Arcy, 380
Hats, 215
Hebrew, 215
Hebrew Union College (Cincinnati, Ohio), 361
Henry, A. Lindo, 299, 378
Hero, Lily Montagu as, see Montagu, Lily, as hero
Hitler, 64, 347; see also Nazism
Holidays, Jewish, 57-58, 124, 125, 209-211, 217, 289; see also Passover; New Year, Jewish; Purim
Holiness, 76, 82, 114ff.
Home, Jewish, 57, 84, 91, 94, 133, 162, 168-169, 174-175, 180, 263, 343-344, 367
Identity, Jewish, see Self-identity, Jewish
Imitation of God, 61, 72, 114, 252-253, 266
Immortality, 56, 68-69, 73-75, 87, 102, 133-134

Indifference, Religious, see Religious Indifference
Induction (as lay minister), Lily Montagu's, see Montagu, Lily, induction as lay minister
Institutional religion, 195-196, 328-334
Intermarriage, 5-6, 94-95, 137, 140-144, 211, 306
Isaacs, Dora, 281, 303, 390
Isaiah (Biblical prophet), 31, 51, 94, 116, 128, 347
Israel (State), 6; see also Zionism
Jacob, Lionel, 299, 378
Jeremiah (Biblical prophet), 51
Jessel, Albert, 286, 287
Jewish identity, see Self-identity, Jewish
Jewish Religious Union, 157, 158, 285-288, 292-296, 297-306, 313-314, 325-326, 338, 377, 383, 385-386, 391, 392-395; see also Union of Liberal and Progressive Synagogues
Jewish Religious Union West Central Section, see West Central Liberal Jewish Congregation
Joseph, Morris, 286
Joseph, N.S., 285, 287
Jowett, Benjamin, 115
Judaism, Lily Montagu's view of, 55-58, 60, 150-152, 193-195, 221
Kashrut, 218
King, Margaret, 282, 284 (note)
Kippah, see Hats
Lang, Peggy, 9
Law, Jewish, 216
Lay Ministry, see Ministry, Lay

INDEX 409

Lazarus, Olga, 269, 282, 303, 378, 382, 384, 391, 394
L.C.C., see London County Council
League of British Jews, 152, 154 (note)
League of Nations, 321
Leisure, 92, 177, 229-241
Letters, Club, see Club letters
Levine, Leila, 9
Levy, Jessie, 3, 10, 304, 358, 383, 386-387, 393, 394
Levy, Nellie G., 226, 269, 271, 272, 281, 303, 382, 385, 387, 390, 394, 396
Lewis, Constance, 278, 284 (note), 304, 377, 380, 381, 334, 385, 387, 388, 396
Lewis, H. R., 299, 378
Liberal Jewish Synagogue, 157, 302, 325
Liberal Judaism, 2-4, 56, 58, 86, 112, 187-190, 199, 207-218, 220, 222-224
Life, Simplification of, 234-235
Literature's effect upon Lily Montagu, 22-23, 31-40
London Club Union, 279
London County Council, 106-107, 111 (note), 146
Love, 73, 106, 258-260, 263-268
Maccabeans, 25
Marriage, 135-139, 142, 257, 274-275; see also Intermarriage
Marriage, Civil, 137, 367
Marriage Guidance Council, 135
Married Members' Guild, 280
Mattuck, Israel, 10, 147, 176, 183, 299, 301, 302, 308, 325, 335, 336, 337, 378, 383, 336, 393, 396

Maud Nathan Home, 389-390
Meditation, see Prayer
Messiah, 56, 70, 86-87
Messianic Age, 87, 221, 222
Mezuzah, 57, 84
Millais, John Everett, 44
Ministry, lay, 335-337; see also Montagu, Lily, induction as lay minister
Mission, Jewish, 69, 72-73, 87, 90, 93-95, 100, 120-128, 142ff., 153, 187-188, 330
Montagu Club, 363, 364 (note)
Montagu, Edwin, 95-96
Montagu, Ellen, 279, 297
Montagu, Henrietta, see Franklin, Henrietta
Montagu House, 283
Montagu, Lily,
    as hero, 11-13, 15-16
    as role model, 8-11, 13-14
    Education of, 21-22
    induction as lay minister, 1, 302, 326
    Lecture tours of, 326-327, 358-364
    sense of personal mission, 4, 187-188
    Spirituality of, 2-4, 8-12
Montagu, Louis, 371
Montagu, Marian, 228, 278-281, 304, 358, 371, 373, 377ff., 381ff., 388ff.
Montagu, Samuel, 2, 56, 279, 296-298, 371, 373-376
Montefiore, Claude, 2, 10, 55-56, 120 (note), 150, 286, 287, 296-299, 301, 337, 341, 378, 380, 381, 383, 386, 392-393
Montefiore family, 190
Moos, Marjorie, 9
Morality, see Conduct, Personal, influenced by religion

Morality, Sexual, see Sexual morality
Morland, George, 42
National Council of Girls Clubs and Mixed Clubs, 303
National Federation of Temple Sisterhoods, 359, 360, 363
National Organization of Girls Clubs, 303, 379
National Union of Women's Workers, 302
Nationality, 145-147
Nature, 23, 62, 73, 87, 92, 99, 133
Nazism, 7, 271, 346; see also Hitler
New Liberal Jewish Congregation, 304
New West End Synagogue, 297, 325
New Year, 243-245, 350
New Year, Jewish, 58, 82-88, 97, 102, 210, 350-351
Nothmann, Ruth, 9
Observance, Jewish, 4, 15, 21, 30, 57-58, 59-60, 62-63, 78, 112, 126, 163, 209-211, 217, 221, 296, 331
Optimism, 67, 68, 100, 115, 349
Organizations, Women's, see Women, Organizations of
Organized religion, see Institutional religion
Orthodox Judaism, 2, 188, 198, 202-203, 213
Parenthood, see Children
Passover, 58, 88-92, 210; see also Seder, Passover
Passover seder, 57, 91
Peace festival, 220-221, 288, 314-322, 356
Peat, Evelyn, 9
Personal religion, 328-334, 362

Personal religion, Judaism as, 93
Prayer, 23-24, 51-54, 65, 85-86, 89, 237, 319, 344
Prayer, National, Service of, see Service of National Prayer
Prophets, Biblical, 56, 57, 74, 97, 216
Proselytes, 143
Psalms, 57, 68-69, 74
Purim, 217, 220
Rabbinic literature, Lily Montagu's use of, 56-57, 74
Rabbinic ordination for women, see Women rabbis
Real religion, see True religion
Recreation, 240; see also Leisure
Religion, Institutional, see Institutional religion
Religion, True, see True religion
Religious customs, 329
Religious customs, Jewish, see Observance, Jewish
Religious indifference, 194-195, 311-312
Resurrection, see Immortality
Revelation, Progressive, 113
Riding to Synagogue, 216
Righteousness, 108-109, 117-119, 329-330, 349
Rosh Hashanah, see New Year, Jewish
Ruskin, John, 47
Sabbath, 58, 76-81, 125, 133, 189-190, 210, 214-215, 233, 248, 289, 368-369
Sabbath of Repentence, 96, 350-351
Seder, Passover, see Passover seder
Sexual morality, 135-136
Self-development, 89, 234

INDEX

Self-identity, Jewish, 2-3, 93-96
Self-realisation, 89-90, 92, 177
Service of National Prayer, 326
Shakespeare, William, 37
Shema, 3, 57, 61, 70, 82, 83, 84, 107, 200, 214, 232, 311, 315
Simon, Bruno, 9
Simon, Leon, 148-150
Simon, Oswald, 286
Singer, Simeon, 130, 287, 325, 380
Social responsibility, see Conduct, Personal, influenced by religion; Social service
Social service, 131, 237-240, 278, 366
Society of Jews and Christians, 393
Spielman, Isidore, 287, 295
Spirituality of Lily Montagu, see Montagu, Lily, Spirituality of
Stanley, Maud, 279
Stonestreet, Edyth, 381, 395, 396
Suggestions for Sabbath Eve Celebrations, 189
Symbols, Jewish, 15, 80, 126; see also Observance, Jewish
Synagogue, 130, 162
Synagogue, Riding to, see Riding to synagogue
Synagogue worship, see Worship, Synagogue
Tennyson, Alfred, Lord, 26-27, 32
Tours, Lecture, of Lily Montagu, see Montagu, Lily, Lecture tours of
Travel, see Riding to Synagogue
True religion, 21-24, 24-31, 41, 47, 55, 58
Union of American Hebrew Congregations, 359

Union of Liberal and Progressive Synagogues, 86, 131, 190, 219-220, 222-223; see also Jewish Religious Union
United Nations, 321, 357
Volunteer work, see Work, Voluntary
Waley, Florence, 326, 341-343, 380, 390
War, 7, 63-64, 159-160, 164, 173-174, 269, 275, 346
War caused by religion, 24-26
Watts, George Frederic, 44
West Central Club, 3, 10, 90, 142, 157, 225-226, 227-228, 268-273, 278-284, 285, 303, 325, 342, 379, 390-391
West Central Day Settlement, 384, 391-392
West Central Flower Company, 392
West Central Jewish Girls' Club, see West Central Club
West Central Liberal Jewish Congregation, 1, 10, 11, 23, 157, 226, 268, 302, 304, 325, 383, 394
West Central Section (of the J.R.U.), see West Central Liberal Jewish Congregation
West Central Settlement, see West Central Day Settlement
What Can a Mother Do?, 5
Whitefields Tabernacle, 270, 273 (note)
Women, 2, 150-151, 155-158, 177ff., 183, 228, 263, 265.
  Contribution to Jewish spirituality, 158-167, 172-173, 175, 182.
  in the synagogue, 168-170, 183-184, 218, 261-262

Women (cont'd)
   Organizations of, 165-166, 181
   rabbis, 157, 183-184
   workers, 229-241, 274-275, 278
Women's Industrial Council, 302
Wordsworth, William, 47
Work, 227, 229-241
Work, Voluntary, 229
Workers' Educational Association, 240
World Union for Progressive Judaism, 287-288, 301, 314-315, 325, 326, 355, 359, 362, 383, 386-387, 391, 395
World War II, 7, 268-273, 326, 344-349
Worship, 253-260
Worship, Synagogue, 57, 79, 81
Woyda, Bruno, 9
Yarmulke, see Hats
Zangwill, Israel, 139
Zionism, 6, 95-96, 145-154, 198, 313

STUDIES IN WOMEN AND RELIGION

1. Joyce L. Irwin, **Womanhood in Radical Protestantism: 1525-1675**
2. Elizabeth A. Clark, **Jerome, Chrysostom and Friends: Essays and Translations**
3. Maureen Muldoon, **Abortion: An Annotated Indexed Bibliography**
4. **Lucretia Mott: Her Complete Speeches and Sermons**, edited by Dana Greene
5. Lorine M. Getz, **Flannery O'Connor: Her Life, Library and Book Reviews**
6. Ben Kimpel, **Emily Dickinson as Philosopher**
7. Jean LaPorte, **The Role of Women in Early Christianity**
8. Gayle Kimball, **The Religious Ideas of Harriet Beecher Stowe: Her Gospel of Womenhood**
9. **John Chrysostom: On Virginity; Against Remarriage**, translated by Sally Rieger Shore
10. Dale A. Johnson, **Women in English Religion: 1700-1925**
11. Earl Kent Brown, **Women of Mr. Wesley's Methodism**
12. Ellen M. Umansky, **Lily Montagu and the Advancement of Liberal Judaism: From Vision to Vocation**
13. Ellen NicKenzie Lawson, **The Three Sarahs: Documents of Antebellum Black College Women**
14. Elizabeth A. Clark, **The Life of Melania the Younger: Introduction, Translation and Commentary**
15. **Lily Montagu: Sermons, Addresses, Letters and Prayers**, edited by Ellen M. Umansky